*Japanese Immigrant Clothing
in Hawaii, 1885–1941*

Japanese Immigrant Clothing in Hawaii 1885–1941

Barbara F. Kawakami

University of Hawai'i Press · Honolulu

© 1993 University of Hawaii Press
All rights reserved
Printed in the United States of America
Paperback edition 1995

95 96 97 98 99 00 5 4 3 2 1

Library of Congress Cataloging-in-Publication Data

Kawakami, Barbara F., 1921–
Japanese immigrant clothing in Hawaii, 1885–1941 / Barbara F.
Kawakami.
p.   cm.
Includes bibliographical references and index.
ISBN 0-8248-1351-0
1. Costume—Hawaii—History.   2. Japanese Americans—Hawaii—
Costume.   I. Title.
GT617.H3K39   1993
391'.0089'9560969—dc20   92-42593
CIP

ISBN 0-8248-1730-3 (pbk)

University of Hawai'i Press Books are printed on
acid-free paper and meet the guidelines for permanence and
durability of the Council on Library Resources

Designed by Kenneth Miyamoto

In
memory of
a dear friend,

Helen Fecenko

Contents

List of Crests

Preface

When I began this study, my objective was narrowly defined: to describe and to collect samples of the work clothing worn by *issei* (first-generation Japanese) men and women on Hawaii's sugarcane and pineapple plantations. It was clear that my main source of information would have to be the issei themselves, and so I began to interview all the ones I could find. As I conducted my interviews, the scope of my study became broader, for my interviews unearthed valuable information about other types of clothing and led to important insights into many other aspects of the immigrant experience on the plantations. In fact, I soon found that my research was taking me on an exciting journey from the Japanese villages to the Hawaiian plantations—a journey that has not only taught me a great deal about the clothing worn by the issei but also helped me to understand their struggle to survive and the relationship between their old traditions and the new plantation culture.

This journey has also given me a sense of continuity with my Japanese heritage, for my research led me on a spiritual journey back to Japan—my parents' native land and my birthplace. All of my siblings were born in Hawaii, but I was born in Japan: my mother was pregnant with me when my parents decided to return to Japan in 1921, the year after the big strike at the sugar plantations in Waipahu, Aiea, Ewa, Kahuku, Waialua, and Waimanalo. However, three months after I was born, we returned to Hawaii. My father felt strongly that Hawaii was a better place to raise and educate his children. I grew up and lived on the Oahu Sugar Plantation in Waipahu until my marriage at the age of twenty-two; I continued to live in Waipahu until my husband completed his service commitment to the United States Army.

My father died when my mother was only thirty-nine years old, and after his death my mother supported herself and eight children by taking in laundry. She was so busy working and raising her children that she had hardly any time for herself; her idea of relaxation was to join us at the end of the day on the veranda to watch us play. Most of the "free time" she had was spent patching our torn clothing or replacing lost buttons. But, for me, nothing was more fascinating than watching her nimble fingers sew a kimono out of fabric sent from her village home in Japan while she told us stories about her childhood. Those were precious moments; I remember how her face would brighten as she talked about picking mulberry leaves to feed the silkworms. She told us how, at a young age, she and her sisters learned to weave cotton cloth, and how her mother and older sister wove their own silk cloth—cloth that, when completed, was sent to Kyoto to be dyed and decorated with beautiful hand-drawn designs.

By the time I was twelve, I was collecting colorful scraps of fabric and using them to make dresses for American kewpie dolls and to make kimono—with fancy sashes—for Japanese bridal dolls. (Japanese bridal dolls with ornate bridal hairdos were sold at plantation stores for five cents each, which was slightly more than the cost of a kewpie doll.) Growing up when there were no radios or television sets in the plantation homes gave us *nisei* (second-generation Japanese) children a lot of time to use our imaginations to create playthings out of whatever we could find in our surroundings.

Like many other nisei children who grew up on the plantations, I had to end my formal education when I graduated from the eighth grade (in my case, in June 1936). Only three girls and six boys from my graduating class were fortunate enough to be able to continue on to high school. Of this group, only four boys went on to earn college degrees; one of these continued his schooling and became a doctor. For the rest of us, the choices were simple: we could go into service (usually as a housemaid) with a Caucasian family, work in the sugarcane or pineapple fields, apprentice ourselves to some skilled laborer to acquire a trade, or attend sewing school.

Like other plantation mothers, my mother felt that it was unnecessary for girls to obtain a higher education. And, like other issei mothers, she believed that all young girls should be trained in the household skills of sewing, cooking, and cleaning in preparation for marriage. Economic necessity dictated that everyone in the family who was able to work must do so, but my mother did not believe that young girls should work in the the fields among the male laborers; she was afraid that we girls might adopt the crude mannerisms of the male laborers and thus lose our femininity. So she was pleased when I decided to enroll in a local private sewing school.

Nisei girls who were sent to sewing schools during the prewar years were well trained in flat-pattern design, sewing, and men's tailoring. Many of us also learned to do intricate hand-smocking and to make corsages out of silk organza and leather. I put my early training at the plantation sewing school—and my later training at Kiester's Tailoring College in Honolulu—to good use, for, from June 1936, sewing was my profession for thirty-eight years. My husband and I raised a family of three children, and we made sure that we could afford a college education for all of them.

My career as a dressmaker reached its height in the mid-1940s when the servicemen in the United States Occupation Forces who were stationed in Japan and Okinawa returned with elegant silk kimono, hand-woven gold-brocaded *obi* (kimono sashes), and bolts of gorgeous silk cloth for their wives. Other servicemen brought exquisite silks from China, Thailand, and India. The period from the mid-1940s to the early 1950s was a fabulous fashion era, in any case, with the return of bustles and sophisticated draped gowns. And officers' wives kept me busy with their demands for new dresses for the many postwar social functions. The elegant obi and kimono fabrics presented me with new challenges in fashion design. Unfortunately, I never thought to photograph and document the many original fashions I created, some of which took weeks to complete; it was only after I had begun my research on the clothing worn by Japanese immigrants that I realized the importance of documentation and preservation.

While working as a homemaker and seamstress in the daytime, I attended adult education classes in the evenings to prepare for the naturalization examination to acquire citizenship. On May 26, 1955, I became an American citizen.

After my older son returned home with a college degree from the University of Oregon, I decided that I wanted to earn a high school diploma. I became a high school graduate in 1959 when I passed the ten-hour General Equivalency Diploma (GED) test at McKinley High School in Honolulu.

Perhaps the most important turning point in my life came when my younger son left for college. For a long time he had been urging me to pursue my dream of receiving higher education, and two weeks after he left for college on the mainland I enrolled at Leeward Community College—at the age of fifty-three. Once I entered the world of academia, there was no stopping me; there was so much to learn. I worked first toward a Bachelor of Science degree in Fashion

Design and Merchandising (a field of study that today is known as Textiles and Clothing). My friends thought my fashion background would work to my advantage, but it did not always do so; sometimes I had to unlearn what I had acquired from past experience and begin over again. After years of doing things free-hand and measuring by eye, it was difficult to adjust to new methods and techniques. But I survived, and I am grateful for the patience and understanding of my instructors.

It was during my senior year at the University of Hawaii at Manoa that I began my research on the clothing worn by Japanese immigrants to Hawaii. As I started investigating material for a term paper in Dr. Mary Ellen Des Jarlais' course on East Asian costumes, I became aware of the lack of information about the clothing worn by immigrants on the plantations. So I began to search for plantation artifacts—plantation clothes and old photographs. My first stop was Arakawas, a department store located below the sugar mill in Waipahu. From the early 1900s, Arakawas had developed a reputation for being a well-stocked supply store that catered to all of the ethnic groups in Hawaii. It still continues this tradition and has maintained strong ties with the old plantation families while forming new ones with the communities that have sprung up around the old sugar plantation. Renewing my friendship with Goro Arakawa, a classmate from grammar school, I told him about my interest in doing research on Japanese immigrant clothing. I learned that he shared my interest in the history of immigrant life and that he had collected and preserved many plantation artifacts. His enthusiasm further stimulated my own interest. He generously shared his knowledge with me, and he let me look through cartons and cartons of old photographs of plantation people—photographs that brought back many memories of my childhood.

Something happened to me as I looked through that seemingly endless collection of photographs. I was particularly impressed by the photographs of issei women working in the fields alongside the men, holding cane knives and bending over to cut the thick, tough-skinned sugarcane. All the Japanese women were wearing distinctive jackets made of kasuri tie-dyed fabric, gathered skirts with black sashes tied in back, kerchiefs snugly wrapped around their necks and faces, and straw boater hats.

Today, many of those issei men and women who toiled in the hot sun doing backbreaking work have passed away. The few who remain have moved into senior citizens' housing or are living with their children or grandchildren. In moving out of their old plantation homes, most have discarded their old possessions and their Japanese clothing in order to fit into smaller living quarters, but a few have carefully kept items from their past to remind them of times gone by. The issei men and women and older nisei men and women became the primary source for my research on plantation clothing. They gave me tremendous amounts of information, much of which has never, until now, been recorded. And they have been my inspiration throughout my work on this book.

When I began my research in the summer of 1979 I had no actual samples of work clothes and very little specific information about their use, construction, or origin. Most of the issei I interviewed in the early years of my research had either thrown away their well-worn garments or used them as rags. Frustrated in my search for samples of work clothing, I began to communicate with relatives who had returned to Japan, asking them if they had kept any of the clothes they wore while they were in Hawaii. Zenbei Saito, an uncle from Fukushima Prefecture who had come to Hawaii in 1904 and who had returned to Japan in 1913, was a great help to me. Uncle Zenbei was only fifteen years old when he left the islands, but he still remembered his early years on the plantation. He also knew something about the joys and problems of doing research: he had been interested in archaeology, and he had unearthed many Hawaiian stone implements in the Waipahu area and knew them by their Hawaiian names. He became interested in my research project and began to visit villagers who had returned from Hawaii, asking them if they had kept their old work clothes or if they had photographs from their plantation days. He was able to locate and send me copies of old photographs of issei women in their work clothes, photographs taken at the Kawailoa Plantation in 1906. To my amazement, he gathered enough information from former plantation workers to enable his daughter-in-law to fashion an exact copy of a woman's work outfit. He sent me these garments along with work accessories—arm protectors, leggings, and a pair of *tabi* (cotton socks with the big toe separated from the other toes)—made in the original style of the early 1900s.

These gifts from my uncle were a great help to me in my research. I took Uncle Zenbei's reproductions with me whenever I interviewed issei women, and when these women saw the reproductions their eyes would sparkle, they would smile, they would fondly touch the familiar garments, and they would share with me their stories and remembrances of sewing their first work outfits. Seeing the reproductions also elicited information about specific differences. Each woman would recall how she had cut and sewn her own garment, making slight changes to make the garment more comfortable and to express her individuality. The issei women also explained to me the distinctive style differences associated with their particular Japanese prefectures. And in the course of these interviews I learned that there were differences in the terms used to designate the various items of clothing.

I have been conducting my interviews since the summer of 1979. The fact that I grew up in a plantation community has enabled me to communicate easily with the issei and other people who have lived in a plantation setting. And, through my interviews, I have also been able to obtain some rare fabrics, bone buttons, and other plantation artifacts. In addition to collecting garments and accessories, I have collected many photographs of people wearing the clothing of that time. Some of these photographs I recovered in 1972 during my first visit back to my father's ancestral home in Kumamoto Prefecture, which is also my birthplace.

During my trip back to Japan in 1972, I learned from the village office records that my father's uncle was the recruiting official for immigrant workers for Hawaiian plantations in 1890, the year my father first immigrated to Hawaii. I also learned from research in village records that, before he came to Hawaii, my father had worked in the village office as a clerk. These discoveries about my family history helped me to uncover information about the clothing that the early Japanese immigrants brought with them to Hawaii.

Some of the issei who have shared their valuable memories and priceless knowledge with me have since died, but I am glad that some part of them will live on in this book. I hope that my book will serve as a valuable resource for all people who are interested in the story of the Japanese immigrants in Hawaii. And I hope that it may inspire others who are interested in studying the cultures of other immigrant groups in Hawaii and elsewhere.

Acknowledgments

In my research on the clothing worn by Japanese immigrants to Hawaii, I have benefited greatly from the advice and help of many, many people; without their assistance it would not have been possible to produce this book.

I owe a special debt of gratitiude to the issei and nisei men and women who have been my primary sources and support from the summer of 1979 to the present. I also want to thank members of other ethnic groups who provided valuable information and descriptions of clothing. It is impossible to name all of the people who helped me in this limited space. The names of the people whom I interviewed for this book are listed in the Sources section at the end of the book. To all those people and the many others who have helped me in the prolonged making of this book, I express my profound thanks. Most of the issei who contributed so much to my work are gone now. It makes me very sad that I cannot share the fruition of "our" work, but I hope their memories will be kept alive through this book.

My heartfelt gratitude goes to those who generously gave me articles of clothing worn by Japanese immigrants or rare photographs taken during the years covered by my study. I have acknowledged many of these contributions in the notes and in photo captions. I want to assure donors of articles or photographs that could not be mentioned or included in this book that their donations were no less appreciated; all these gifts were of tremendous value in my research.

Many people read the manuscript or portions of it at various stages in its production and gave me valuable suggestions and encouragement. I particularly wish to thank the following readers:

Dr. Mary Ellen Des Jarlais, Professor Emeritus, Department of Human Resources, University of Hawaii; Dr. Franklin Odo, Director of Ethnic Studies, University of Hawaii; Rikio Anzai, retired field supervisor, Oahu Sugar Company; Dr. Trudy Ettelson; Grace Dixon; Kenneth Toguchi; Ruth Tamura; Barbara Stephan, author and expert on Japanese textiles; Masako Nakagawa, retired principal of Wahiawa Gakuen (Japanese Language School), who has helped me in many ways to improve my research skills in Japanese for this book; Tomoyo Yanagihara, for her expertise on family crests and genealogy, and for her unwavering support and warm friendship.

I especially wish to thank Mikio Fujioka, instructor of East Asian Language at Leeward Community College, who lent me rare Japanese dictionaries that enabled me to find the origins of idioms used by the Japanese immigrants in Hawaii.

I owe a debt of gratitude to Blanche Klim, graphic artist, and Micheal Pecsok, media specialist, at Leeward Community College Media Center, for the excellent photographs of the original plantation clothing and accessories seen in this book; other credits are given in the photo captions.

I wish to thank the following for their professional advice and assistance: Warren Nishimoto, Michi Kodama-Nishimoto, and Cynthia Oshiro of the Ethnic Studies Oral History Project at the University of Hawaii, who gave me a good start in 1979; staff of the Hawaii State Archives Photo Collection; Bishop Museum Photo Collection; staff of the Hawaiian and Pacific Collection, Hamilton Library, and also the staff at Sinclair Library, University of Hawaii; staff of the Mission House; staff of the Waipahu Cultural Garden Park, especially Executive Director Calvin Kawamoto. Special thanks go to Bonnie Miyashiro at the Hawaii Okinawa Center and to Alfred Kina, textile artist.

I am grateful to those who helped in typing the manuscript from the roughest form to the final stages of transferring the material into the word processor, especially Freda Hellinger, who typed and edited the original manuscript (before I had ever heard of computers), and Teresa Bill, who spent many weekends with me getting the rest of the manuscript into my computer and taught me so much about word processing.

I wish to thank the late Dr. James Okahata for giving me the opportunity to exhibit my collection of Japanese immigrants' clothing at the Kanyaku Imin Centennial Celebration in 1985 at the Neal Blaisdell Center. Participating in this event enabled me to meet many people who gave me valuable information for my study.

I wish to express my deep appreciation to the staff of the University of Hawaii Press and particularly to Iris Wiley, executive editor, for her editorial guidance and encouragement over the past several years.

I am most indebted to my mentor and friend, Professor Dorothy Vella, now retired from the University of Hawaii, who helped me tremendously at various stages of my work over the past several years. Professor Vella did the final editing of the manuscript. I greatly appreciate her insights and fine editorial judgments, and the contribution of her valuable time and energy to this book.

My deep appreciation to Shigeyuki Yoshitake for helping me with proofreading, particularly on the Japanese words, and for his moral support from beginning to end, and to my daughter, Fay Toyama, for assisting me with the final proofreading.

I wish to express my deep gratitude to my brother-in-law, Shigeru Kawakami, for the financial contribution that made it possible to include many photographs in this book.

Finally, I want to thank members of my family, especially my husband, Douglas, for his moral support. He patiently listened to my endless discourse on the book, shared the domestic chores, and drove me to distant places for my interviews. My children—Steven, Fay, and Gary—assisted me in many ways and gave constructive criticism and moral support. Surely, no one could have had a more supportive and loving family; I thank you all for sharing this venture with me.

1

Japanese Immigration to Hawaii

Immigration of the Japanese to Hawaii began in 1868 during Japan's transition from the Tokugawa Shogunate (1603–1868) to the Meiji Oligarchy (1868–1911). The government was not officially involved. The sugar industry in the Hawaiian Islands sent recruiters to Japan in search of cheap labor, and people who lived in the Tokyo and Yokohama areas heard about the search and responded eagerly. At that time the sugar industry was offering a wage of four dollars a month plus food, lodging, and medical expenses, with boat passage to Hawaii and a return trip to Japan after the three-year contract expired, and this seemed to many to be a golden opportunity to earn good money and return home with new wealth and prestige.

The immigrants who came to Hawaii in 1868 were known as the *Gannen Mono*, or the "First-Year People," because they left Japan in the first year of the Meiji Era. There were 153 immigrant passengers aboard the British ship *Scioto*, including 5 women who ranged in age from nineteen to forty. It is reported that two of the women were pregnant at the time and a baby boy was born during the voyage but, since one man died during the voyage, the total number of passengers remained the same. This first group included people from diverse backgrounds: skilled workers, craftsmen, a few displaced *samurai* (warriors), a few farmers who had sold their land and drifted to Yokohama, and some vagabonds, coolies, and "rough-and-rowdy adventurers addicted to drinking and gambling."[1]

The *Hawaiian Gazette* of June 24, 1868, gives an account of the arrival of the *Gannen Mono* and the immigrants' first impressions of the waterfront and nearby areas. Honolulu, to the new immigrants, appeared to be a quiet fishing village. Everything seems to have fascinated them: they commented on the unusual rows of brick buildings, the fish market, the post office, the blacksmith shop, the quaint little Chinese shops, and even the oil lamps with their glass chimneys. They admired the lush tropical foliage, the taro patches, the rice paddies, and the ducks in the streams. The reporter also noted the reaction of the residents of Honolulu: their curiosity was aroused by the loud noise of the wooden clogs worn by the immigrants and by the overlapping folds of the Japanese robes, which flapped in the wind and exposed the wearers' undergarments.[2]

The importation of this first group of immigrants was looked upon as an experiment by the plantation owners. The newcomers worked from dawn to dusk in the plantation fields, an average of twelve hours a day in the tropical heat, and were often forced to endure brutal treatment. Labor conditions had not been stipulated in the contract, so the immigrants had no alternative but to obey their superiors. Consequently, forty-three of the people who came on the *Scioto* returned to Japan at the first available opportunity. And, because of their reports of the hard labor and the inadequate living conditions, further emigration from Japan was curtailed until 1885.

The second group of Japanese immigrants came during the period 1885–1894, known as the Government Contract Period.[3] During this period, a total of 28,691 Japanese—laborers and members of their families—came to Hawaii on three-year government contracts. The group consisted of 23,071 men, 5,487 women, and 133 children. During this period average wages ranged from $9.00 to $12.50 per month for men for ten hours of work a day; women were paid less than men for the same type of work.

Almost all of the immigrants who came during this period stayed in Hawaii, and many of the Japanese in Hawaii today are descended from this group. Most of these immigrants came from the southwestern region of Japan, namely, the prefectures of Hiroshima, Yamaguchi, Kumamoto, and Fukuoka, and most of them were small farmers or tenant farmers.

One of the major factors contributing to this large-scale immigration was the increase in population in the southwestern prefectures, which created severe economic hardship for the laboring class. There was intense competition among peasants trying to eke out a living from limited land areas. Great numbers of peasants were struggling under strong economic pressure from landowners; the annual yield from their land was not enough to provide a decent living for them and their families.

Japanese contract laborers waiting in Honolulu for the interisland steamer to take them to newly opened plantations on the island of Hawaii. Most of the men are dressed in kimono or in momohiki and shirts; a few wear happi over their other clothes. Headwear ranges from straw hats to tenugui; footwear from geta to straw sandals. The only woman in the group is dressed in a kasuri kimono tied with a narrow sash and has a tenugui over her head. 1888. Hawaii State Archives collection.

Geographic factors also made immigration to Hawaii attractive to the southwestern Japanese. Hawaii's subtropical climate was similar to the climate they were used to. And the fact that Hawaii was a group of islands surrounded by the sea was another attraction for these people who had spent most of their lives near the sea.

A third period of Japanese immigration began in April 1894, when the Japanese government turned immigration over to government-licensed private companies. During this period, which lasted until 1900 and is usually called the Private Contract Period, about fifty-seven thousand Japanese arrived in Hawaii. These immigrants often had a more difficult time than the immigrants who had come during the preceding period; the private companies frequently exploited their fellow countrymen through complicated financial arrangements that made it necessary for a laborer to spend his entire initial contract period working to pay off debts to the company. Average wages during this period ranged from $12.50 to $15.00 per month for ten hours of work a day for men, less for women.

Japanese family at Immigration Quarantine Station in Honolulu. The little boy is wearing hand-woven straw sandals. February 8, 1885. Bishop Museum collection.

Issei women at the Immigration Quarantine Station in Honolulu cooking a meal over an open fire. Women and children alike wear kimono. February 10, 1885. Bishop Museum collection.

The next eight years, 1900 to 1908, were years in which the importation of contract labor was prohibited by United States law. During these years, known as the Free Immigration Period, a great number of Japanese—about seventy-one thousand—immigrated to Hawaii. But many of them were subsequently attracted to the higher wages offered on the mainland United States, and so the outflow of Japanese immigrants was also great. Average wages on the plantations during this period ranged from fifteen to eighteen dollars per month for men, a few dollars less for women.

Resentment against cheap labor on the west coast of the United States led to the "Gentleman's Agreement" of 1907–1908, whereby Japan voluntarily placed severe restrictions on immigration to the United States. During the period from 1908 to 1924, usually called the Restricted Immigration Period, the only unmarried Japanese immigrants who were allowed to enter Hawaii were the immediate relatives of immigrants and returning former immigrants. (Married couples were still allowed entry.) Nevertheless, sixty-one thousand arrivals were recorded. First-generation Japanese refer to this period as the *Yobiyose Jidai*, or "Summoning by Relatives Period." The basic wage for a common laborer during this period was twenty dollars per month for ten hours of work a day.

During the Restricted Immigration Period there was a great increase in the number of Japanese women who came to Hawaii. Over twenty thousand picture brides, as they were called, were married to Japanese men in Hawaii in absentia through a *nakōdo* (marriage go-between) who negotiated the marriage by letters and by an exchange of photographs of the prospective bride and groom. Over half of all the Japanese women who immigrated to Hawaii came during the Restricted Immigration Period or the Free Immigration Period, and the years from 1900 to 1924 are often referred to as the Picture-Bride Period. The mass influx of picture brides marked the transition from a society of single male transients to one of permanent residents. In 1900, out of the total population of 24,326 Japanese immigrants in the United States, there were only 985 females (24 males for every female). By 1910, the female population had climbed to 9,087; by 1920, there were 22,193 women.

Before 1900, all of the Japanese immigrants to Hawaii had come from the four main islands of Japan. But in 1900, for the first time, the immigrants included Okinawans. The first group of Okinawan immigrants—twenty-six in number—arrived in Hawaii on January 8, 1900. Like the *naichi* (main-island Japanese), the Okinawans dreamed of amassing a fortune and helping to better the lot of their loved ones in the homeland. They came to Hawaii to escape poverty, corrupt tax-collection practices, and the consequences of peas-

Passport photographs of members of the Oyama family. All are wearing kasuri kimono. 1921. Barbara Kawakami collection.

ant uprisings in various parts of the prefecture in 1882, 1883, 1885, 1886, and 1888.

Okinawa had lost its political independence when it was incorporated into the Japanese prefecture system in 1879. While the former rulers and members of the upper class fared well under the conciliatory agreements, the commoners suffered. Although they were forced to pay high taxes, they were not given the full benefits of taxpaying citizens.[4] Many of the peasants had to sell their land and become tenants. And others emigrated to foreign lands to search

Inspection at the immigration station in Honolulu. Dr. Tomizo Katsunuma (extreme right) and two other inspectors examine the kōri brought by the picture brides as grooms wait to claim their brides. Photograph taken between 1910 and 1915. Hawaii State Archives collection.

Village scene in Okinawa in the late nineteenth century, showing the clothing worn by various social classes. Drawing from *Okinawa Shiryō Shūsei: Shizen Rekishi Bunka Fūdo* [Compilation of Information about Okinawa: Nature, History, Culture, and Climate], 1975.

Taro Arakawa, who arrived in Honolulu in 1921. He is wearing a kasuri kimono and kasuri haori that were given to him by people in Kobe, Japan, after he survived a shipwreck near Kobe at the beginning of his voyage to Hawaii. Photograph taken in Japan in December 1920. Kay Arakawa collection.

for a better life. Between 1900 and 1924, approximately twenty-five thousand men, women, and children came to Hawaii from Okinawa.[5]

On June 30, 1924, the United States Congress passed the Immigration Act of 1924 (called the Japanese Exclusion Act by many Japanese). This act prohibited the entry of all aliens who were ineligible for citizenship and thus virtually ended Japanese immigration to the United States. Under this law, only "non-quota immigrants"—for example, government officials, ministers of religion, professors, students, merchants, travelers—were admitted but only for brief visits. And, of course even these visits came to an end with the outbreak of war between the United States and Japan in 1941.

2
Wedding Attire

Some of the more than 210,000 Japanese who arrived in Hawaii between 1885 and 1924 were men who came with their families. Others were men who left their wives and children with relatives in Japan. But by far the largest number of immigrants were single men who had aspirations of acquiring enough wealth within the three-year contract period to return to their villages in Japan and live in comfort for the rest of their lives. Some of them did make this dream come true. But the great majority never went home again. As time went on and they were faced with unexpected adversities, they realized that, for better or for worse, their future was going to be in this new land. As they gradually made new friends and improved their standard of living, they began to develop a sense of pride in the land, a feeling of belonging, and a desire to put down roots in Hawaii.

The men who came with their families established a comfortable home environment much sooner than the others. The men who had been married before coming to Hawaii sent for their families during the 1908–1924 *Yobiyose Jidai* (Summoning by Relatives Period). A limited number of bachelors were fortunate enough to be able to secure wives from among the small number of marriageable young women who had accompanied their parents to Hawaii at the turn of the century. And there were some bachelors who were successful enough to be able to return to their native villages to select wives for themselves. But the great majority of the bachelors had picture-bride marriages. When these men felt that they were ready to settle down, they wrote home and asked their parents to find suitable wives for them or they asked a friend in Hawaii or Japan to act as a *nakōdo* (go-between). This was the beginning of a long series of picture-bride marriages arranged by nakōdo through exchanges of photographs across four thousand miles of the Pacific Ocean from the early 1900s to 1924.[1] No official record of the number of picture brides was kept either at the Hawaii State Archives or at the Japanese Consulate, but it is believed that over half of all the Japanese women who immigrated to Hawaii came in this way during this period.

Historically, picture-bride marriages were a continuation of the arranged marriages that had their origin among the warrior class during the late Tokugawa Period (1603–1868) in Japan and later became accepted even among the peasants in rural communities. The exchange of photographs was a natural extension of the system, an obvious way of introducing a couple to each other when a face-to-face meeting was impossible. Such exchanges are believed to have been resorted to in Japan even before the beginning of Japanese immigration to Hawaii when prospective matches lived in remote villages. When starting the procedure of matchmaking, it was often simplest for the nakōdo to bring a photograph to show what the prospective match looked like. It was a way of saving embarrassment, too; if one party was rejected, the matter could be quietly resolved without anyone's losing face.[2] Of course, in the Japan-Hawaii matches the exchange of photographs served an additional purpose: the photograph the groom had received enabled him to identify his bride at the immigration station.

The nakōdo, who could be a man or woman (or, occasionally, a couple), played a significant role in arranging marriages between the issei laborers who worked on the plantations in Hawaii and prospective brides who came from the grooms' villages in Japan. Because of the importance of the task and the difficulties that might be involved in arranging such marriages, the nakōdo had to be carefully selected; he or she had to have integrity and above-average intelligence and, of course, be highly respected in the community. If the nakōdo was a relative or friend of the family back in Japan—as was the case in most of the issei plantation marriages—the nakōdo's work might be relatively easy; the families might already know each other's backgrounds. But if that was not the case, then the nakōdo was expected to conduct a thorough investigation of the intended couple's socioeconomic status, educational background, and family bloodline. A conscientious and sincere nakōdo would try to find an ideal match—one in which the man and woman were of equal educational background and socioeconomic status or, more often, in which the man had slightly more education or higher status so that the woman would respect her husband and be willing to obey him.

This type of investigation was conducted for most of the picture-bride marriages negotiated between the plantation bachelors in Hawaii and women in villages back home. Until World War II the practice was, in fact, often followed in Hawaii even for nisei marriages. For example, my older sister was married in 1936 through matchmaking, and the nakōdo came from the same prefecture as my mother and the groom's family. Both families asked family friends to conduct a thorough search of the other family's background, especially to check for insanity and leprosy. I remember how relieved my mother was when she heard that her prospective son-in-law had a healthy bloodline and that the water from his village was pure (according to the beliefs of the time, pure water in the village streams was a sign that the family bloodline was healthy).

When trying to find a suitable bride for an issei man, the nakōdo usually did not look outside of the prospective groom's home village —and certainly not outside of the prospective groom's home prefecture. The ties between people who came from the same village became very close indeed in Hawaii, where the issei were sharing the hardships of poverty and the loneliness of living away from their families. People who came from the same village were affectionately termed *tokoromon* (a colloquial shortening of the proper term *tokoromono*, meaning people from the same place). The relationship became especially important in times of crisis, when a tokoromon could be relied upon to provide comfort and help. Issei men and women gathered from near and far, even from other islands, to attend a tokoromon's funeral. And marriages between the families of tokoromon further strengthened the bonds. Until World War II, the majority of even nisei marriages were arranged between tokoromon; to marry someone from a prefecture other than one's own was considered almost improper.

No matter how cautious a nakōdo might be, there were sometimes disappointments when the prospective brides and grooms finally met in Hawaii. For one thing, it was not uncommon for bachelors to send photographs of younger and better-looking men instead of photographs of themselves; some men sent pictures of younger brothers. One beautiful picture bride whom everybody admired during the voyage found that her groom was about twenty years older than the man in the picture that had been sent to her parents through the nakōdo. (She later ran away from her husband.)[3] Sometimes, of course, it was the anxious groom who received the shock: a bachelor who had looked forward to meeting the attractive girl in the photograph the nakōdo had sent him might see a homely woman step forward upon announcement of his last name at the immigration station.

There were other kinds of disappointment, too. For example, one issei woman found herself an unclaimed picture bride at the immigration station. She waited for two weeks for her husband to come for her, but he never came; she cried every day as she watched other brides who had come with her leave with their husbands. She did not have any money to pay her passage back home to Japan, but that fact was of minor importance to her; what really mattered was the humiliation of being rejected. (She never forgot the kindness of Dr. Tomizo Katsunuma, the immigration inspector, who sympathized with her, took her home, and gave her shelter. Later he played the role of nakōdo and found her a husband who, she says, proved to be an ideal match.)[4]

Not all of the picture-bride matches were successful. Some mismatches occurred when the nakōdo was too eager to make money. The nakōdo usually received a gratuity from both families; this gratuity usually ranged from five dollars to fifty dollars, but it might be as high as one hundred dollars—or even more—if the family was wealthy and well known in the community. And some nakōdo who engaged in matchmaking as their sole source of income were more interested in bringing together as many couples as they could in a short period of time than they were in doing a careful job of investigating. The most successful unions were marriages arranged by friends or relatives who were closely associated with both families.

Another type of arranged marriage negotiated by the nakōdo for the plantation laborers was that of marriage with a *kari fūfu* (temporary, or borrowed, spouse). To come as a "temporary spouse" was one way to gain entry into the United States or its territories during the Restricted Immigration Period (1908–1924), when married couples were allowed to enter but unmarried persons were barred unless they were immediate relatives of immigrants or were themselves former residents of the United States. After the temporarily married couple entered Hawaii, each applied for a divorce and waited a year, the required waiting period to be free to remarry. Undoubtedly some of the women who came as kari fūfu are included in the estimate of approximately twenty thousand picture brides who were married by proxy or in absentia to Japanese laborers in Hawaii. There are no official records of their numbers, and, because of the delicate nature of the matter, it is difficult to arrive at even a reasonable approximation. One issei woman I interviewed said, almost in a whisper: "You ask me if I came as a picture bride. Not really. I came to Hawaii as a kari fūfu. So, actually, this is my second marriage. But I hardly knew the man I came to Hawaii with. I do not even remember his name. We parted as soon as we got here."[5]

Takayo Iwamoto, who was sixteen years old when she came with a family friend as a kari fūfu, or "temporary spouse," to gain entry to Hawaii. Later a family friend arranged her marriage to Nobuichi Ishimoto *(right)*, who worked for the Oahu Sugar Company. Wedding photograph taken on February 22, 1908. Jerry Ishimoto collection.

Okinawan picture brides dressed in their best kimono and with hair done in kampū style. 1918. Kana Higa collection.

Tsuru and Jiro Omine. Tsuru is wearing a hand-woven cotton kimono that she brought from Okinawa; bold stripes were very popular there at the time. Wedding photograph, November 1923. Tsuru Omine collection.

There were some cases in which the borrowed spouses fell in love with each other during the ten-day voyage across the Pacific and decided to stay married. When that happened, the anxious groom waiting in Hawaii simply lost out and had to send for another bride through the help of the nakōdo who had arranged the marriage.

The clothing worn by the bride and groom in the weddings of issei immigrants who came to Hawaii from 1885 to 1924 varied considerably, depending on the geographical area from which they came, the socioeconomic status of the principals, the traditional practices of their families, and the time and place of the wedding.

The biggest difference was between the clothing worn by the naichi and that worn by the Okinawans for formal weddings: at least in the early years of Japanese immigration, the main-island Japanese wore the black five-crested kimono known as *montsuki*; the Okinawans did not. It was not traditional for Okinawans to get married in montsuki; in fact, most of the early Okinawan immigrants had not seen a montsuki until they came to Hawaii. (However, after they arrived in Hawaii, they adopted the montsuki enthusiastically;

most of the Okinawans bought montsuki as soon as they could after they were settled here.) Instead of the montsuki, the customary dress for special occasions for Okinawans was a colorful dressy kimono that was worn without a sash in the *ushinchi* style—that is, tucked firmly, but with ample looseness, into the waistcord of long cotton underpants worn under the kimono; this gave a graceful blouson effect.

There were other differences in the styling of the kimono worn by the Okinawans and those worn by naichi. The Okinawan kimono sleeves were open the entire length of the sleeve to allow ventilation (to suit the hot and humid climate of Okinawa), whereas the sleeves worn by the naichi were closed except for seven inches at the wrist that the hands went through. Also, in most of the Okinawan kimono a diamond-shaped gusset was inserted in the underarm for comfort, while the kimono worn by naichi were made with an opening under the arm. The Okinawan kimono was shorter, too: the Okinawans exposed their ankles; the naichi covered theirs. Finally,

Wedding photograph of Masu and Kameshichi Arakaki, taken with Kameshichi's brother and the brother's children. The groom is standing. Masu was one of the few Okinawan brides who had a wedding photograph taken wearing a montsuki; she purchased it in Honolulu after she arrived. August 1921. Masu Arakaki collection.

the Okinawans wrapped their kimono right over left, while the naichi wrapped theirs left over right.

There were also differences in the types of fabrics used by the naichi and the Okinawans. Both used cottons, silks, and even some linens. Both used striped patterns. And both used *kasuri* (fabrics with a "splash pattern" produced by tying and dyeing the yarn before weaving), although the Okinawans tended to use much brighter colors than the naichi (in accounts of their sea voyages to Hawaii, the naichi brides often reported that they were fascinated by the bright red splash designs the Okinawans wove into their indigo kasuri). But the Okinawans had some fabrics that the naichi did not. One of these was *bashōfu*, a cloth made from banana plaintain fiber by a tedious process of stripping, pounding, boiling, combing, and spinning. The inner core of the plantain produced the highest-quality bashōfu, a fiber almost as soft as silk; it was used for dressy kimono. The fiber from the outer part of the bark was coarser; it was used for casual kimono. The fiber from the next layer of the bark was considered inferior; it was used for underkimono and smaller items. Bashōfu fabric was particularly popular in the summer months in Okinawa because it was cool, comfortable, and easy to care for.[6] Another fabric that the Okinawans produced was a fine hemp, or ramie, cloth *(jōfu)*. And certain areas of Okinawa specialized—and still do specialize—in certain fabrics. For example the village of Haebaru produces the exquisite silk fabric known as *Ryūkyū-gasuri*; the island of Kumejima produces splash-patterned hand-spun silk *tsumugi* (pongee) in deep brown with yellow; Miyako Island specializes in an indigo-dyed ramie cloth woven in an intricate splash-pattern design; Yaeyama Islanders are skilled in the technique of weaving white ramie cloth with small brown patterns made by the rub-dye method; and Yonaguni Islanders have preserved the tradition of weaving checked and striped ramie.[7]

But it was not the fabrics worn by the Okinawan brides or the manner in which they wore their kimono that most aroused the curiosity of the naichi brides; it was the bold tattooing on the backs of the Okinawan brides' hands.[8] The practice of tattooing in Okinawa is believed to date back to the period when the Satsuma clan took control of Okinawa; indigo marks were put on the backs of the hands of young maidens to discourage the Satsuma warriors from carrying the girls off. But as time went on, the tattoos came to be regarded as enhancements of beauty. They also became signs of status; at one time only women of the upper class were allowed to be tattooed. By the time the Okinawan brides came to Hawaii, in the

Kamado Kaneshiro, who arrived in Hawaii on July 5, 1907, with her husband, Jinwa, and settled in Kukuiha-ele on the Big Island of Hawaii. Her hands were tat-tooed in Okinawa before she was married. Note the dif-ference in the designs on the right and left hands. Kamado is holding her grandson, Wayne Kaneshiro. August 1944. Arthur T. Kaneshiro collection.

early 1900s, the tattoos had come to be used specifically to symbol-ize a woman's status as a married woman; they were more perma-nent symbols of marriage than Western wedding rings. Tattooing was eventually banned in Okinawa during the Meiji Period, but some mothers ignored the ban and continued to have their daugh-ters tattooed. The designs varied; usually they were fairly simple shapes such as stars, diamonds, or arrows. But Okinawan women who were expert dyers sometimes tattooed designs taken from the kasuri fabrics they wove. Sometimes it was possible to tell what region a woman came from by looking at the design on her hands.[9]

The Okinawan brides soon found that their tattoos were not regarded with admiration by the naichi. In the minds of the naichi, tattoos were associated with criminals, for in the main islands of Japan criminals were branded with similar marks.[10] And, therefore, the skin decoration that had been considered a thing of beauty back in Okinawa became a source of embarrassment and a reason for discrimination in Hawaii. Many of the Okinawan women tried to scrub the tattoos off their skin; some scrubbed so hard that their hands bled.

When I interviewed Kana Tsukayama, I noticed that her tattoos were lighter and more conservative than those I had seen during my childhood on the plantation. She thought they had faded with age. But she added another reason: while she was in the process of tattooing her own hands, as was customary in her village of Chatan, her older brother, who had been teaching in Taiwan, returned and stopped her; he said, "You'll look like the mountain people in Taiwan with the tattoo." She told me that, after she came to Hawaii, she felt fortunate that her brother had stopped her.[11]

Issei Weddings in Japan

The Japanese men who came to Hawaii as bachelors and were successful enough to be able to return to their native villages to claim brides were usually able to afford elaborate formal weddings.

The wedding of Torajiro and Take Sato, which took place in the groom's native village in Fukushima Prefecture, is a fine example of such a wedding. Mr. Sato had come to Hawaii in 1917 at the age of fifteen to work at the Ewa Sugar Plantation. His hard work paid off; by 1922 he had saved enough money to return to his native village to get married. His parents had asked their next-door neighbor, a tombstone-maker, to help select a bride for their son. He selected a girl named Take who lived in the next village. Her name was legally entered into the Sato *koseki* (family register) in the village office on October 26, 1922. The wedding reception was held on December 6, 1922, in the groom's village.

For his marriage ceremony and reception, Mr. Sato wore the traditional three pieces of formal wedding attire for men: a black five-crested montsuki, a black three-quarter-length *haori* (coat worn over a kimono), and a *hakama* (a divided, ankle-length skirt, with deep pleats at the waist, worn over a kimono). Both the montsuki and haori were made of black *habutae* (a glossy, lightweight silk) and featured Mr. Sato's family crest *(kamon)* in five positions: one on each side of the chest, one on the upper back center of each sleeve, and one on the center back seam about three inches below the collar line. The motif for Mr. Sato's family crest was a *maru ni ōgi* (a white fan enclosed in a white circle).

Underneath his black montsuki, Mr. Sato wore a long white underkimono with an attached white collarband that extended an inch beyond the black kimono collar. Beneath the underkimono he wore a short undershirt to protect his silk kimono from perspiration. Mr. Sato's underkimono and montsuki were carefully arranged, and then a stiff silk sash *(kaku-obi)* was wrapped around his waist and tied into a shellfish bow in the back.

On his feet Mr. Sato wore *tabi* (cotton socks with the big toe separated from the other toes), made of white calico, and *zōri* (slippers) made of fine bamboo sheaths. In his right hand he held a white folded fan inscribed with symbols of good luck.

Mr. Sato was particularly proud of his hakama of striped *Sendai Hira* silk (a stiff, flat-weave silk in which the warp is a fine glossy silk and the woof is a moistened, untwisted raw silk), which had been made by the skilled weavers of the Sendai Plains, Miyagi Prefecture, in northeastern Japan. Very few young men in the village owned such a hakama, but Mr. Sato's father, a fencing master, owned several hakama and lent his son the best he had. The Sendai Hira hakama is still considered one of the finest articles of men's formal wear throughout Japan.

For Take, Mr. Sato's bride-to-be, preparation for the wedding began early in the morning. A bridal dresser started with the bride's long hair, which she pulled, combed, and molded into the complicated bridal coiffure by the use of camellia oil and cosmetic paste. She then created a fancy knot in the back part of the bride's hairdo, placing a dark blue paper on the inner side of the knot to help shape the elegant hairstyle. A tortoise-shell comb and ornamental hairpins completed the hairdo. This specific type of bridal coiffure, known as a *takashimada*, was worn only by single women of marriageable age and only for a first marriage; it was taboo for married women. To fashion the bridal coiffure required skill and special training; and the process was time-consuming; however, the finished product was considered the ultimate in Japanese feminine beauty.[12]

After the bridal coiffure was completed, the bride's face was made up: her skin was covered with a thick white powder paste; her eyebrows were shaped with a pencil; and her mouth was drawn into a bright red cupid's bow, smaller than its natural size, to create a demure look.

Next came the wedding clothing. First, Take put on a pair of white tabi. Then she donned a *koshimaki* (a wrap-around under-skirt), made of white silk crepe, and a *hada juban* (short cotton undershirt with sleeves) to protect her outer clothing from perspira-tion stains. Over this went a long white silk crepe underkimono *(naga juban)*, with a silk crepe half-collar attached. This underki-mono, which was embroidered in plum and pine-tree designs with gold and silver threads, was fixed firmly in place by a narrow silk sash *(datemaki)* of Hakata weave. Finally, Take was ready to put on her montsuki.

Take wore the traditional black montsuki of fine silk crepe, with delicate hand-painted designs known as *suso moyō* on the lower front skirt of the kimono. The painting on Take's kimono depicted an autumn scene with pine trees against a blurred landscape and winding stream, done in gray tones. The trees were rendered in fine lines. Some of the branches and pine cones were embroidered with gold thread; a few branches were embroidered with brown silk thread. The painting was continued on the lining of the kimono front. Because, in the main islands of Japan, a kimono is always worn left over right, the design is usually more elaborate on the left side of the garment and more subdued on the right.

When Take's montsuki was in place, its hemline was adjusted to her height and the garment was tied in place with a narrow cord. The extra length of the kimono was tucked neatly below the waist-line and again was tied firmly with a narrow silk sash. At this point, the outer kimono collar and underkimono collar were aligned in parallel positions and the ornamental half-collar of the underki-mono was extended about an inch in the front. The back seam was straightened, and waist tucks smoothed over. Then a brocaded *maru obi* (sash of twenty-six-inch-wide fabric folded lengthwise) was wrapped around Take's waist and a bean-shaped pillow was tucked under the obi in the center of the back. Take's obi was patterned on both sides with pine tufts, bamboo leaves, plum blossoms, and chrysanthemums. The designs were woven into the fabric in gold and silver thread and colored silk thread. Dark green silk was used for the pine trees, shades of medium and light green for the bamboo, silver for the plum blossoms, and orange, maroon, and light gold for the chrysanthemums. Take's obi was tied into the drum bowknot *(ōgi-taiko)* used for such ceremonial occasions. To complete the obi-tying, a bustle sash of figured satin in Nile green and a white silk cord embroidered in gold and silver were passed through the drum in back and tied in front, and the extra length was neatly tucked under the corded belt.

There were many other issei brides who wore traditional costumes like Mrs. Sato's. But what made Mrs. Sato's wedding ensemble especially remarkable was the fact that she had sewn the montsuki, the long underkimono, and the brocaded obi herself. Few issei brides who came from rural areas were able to sew their own elaborate ceremonial costumes.

Mrs. Sato was also one of the few issei brides who wore an elegant silk *uchikake* (long outer robe, heavily padded at the hemline) over her montsuki. This uchikake had been woven, sewn, and embroidered by hand in Kyoto.

The final touches for Take's outfit were a white fan, which she held in her right hand, and a *watabōshi* (silk floss cap, traditionally regarded as a symbol of a bride's desire to curb any tendency toward jealousy).[13]

Mrs. Sato brought her wedding costume to Hawaii with her in 1922; when she showed it to friends here, she was the envy of all the issei women in the plantation community. She sent the uchikake back to her village home in Fukushima after World War II, since she was sure that she would never wear such a luxurious garment again. She also sent back all of her dressy silk kimono except her wedding kimono, which she carefully folded and stored in a bleached rice bag.[14]

Another formal wedding held in Fukushima Prefecture, equally elaborate but with a Western flavor, was that of Masanari and Tei Saito. It took place in July 1913. Mr. Saito was an entrepreneur in the pineapple business who made a triumphant return to his village. The bride-to-be's father was a scholar, and he and his wife were so impressed with the young man who had amassed a fortune in Hawaii that they arranged the wedding with the groom's parents and the nakōdo without their daughter's knowledge. Tei was better educated than most of the women who came to Hawaii at that time; she had graduated from a girls' high school in Fukushima City.

For her wedding, Tei wore traditional attire. Mr. Saito made quite an impression on the village people in Fukushima with his dark wool, Western-style three-piece suit, white shirt with long sleeves, cuff links, and the wing collar that was in fashion in the United States during the early twentieth century (described as a "debonair collar" by Mrs. Saito), worn with a bow tie. Western clothes were still a novelty to Japanese villagers in 1913; few had ever seen such distinguished-looking attire.

The wedding clothing and the large wedding reception caused a stir in the village. The Saitos were also exceptional because they sailed to the Hawaiian Islands in first-class accommodations; the other young couples or picture brides traveled third-class or steerage. But when Mr. Saito took his new bride to their home in an isolated camp near the mountains, her exceptional status soon disappeared. Mrs. Saito thought her new home in Hawaii looked like a "chicken coop." And, since her husband ran a boardinghouse for the bachelors who worked under him in the pineapple fields, she immediately had to learn how to cook and do laundry—chores she had never done when she was single.[15]

Ushii Nakasone had quite a different type of wedding in her home village of Misato in Nakagumi Province in Okinawa. She had planned to go to Hawaii as a picture bride and be married there, but she had to change her plans very suddenly.

Ushii had dreamed about going to Hawaii ever since she was a young girl. Some of her friends had gone there, and they had written letters telling exciting stories and had sent back intriguing pictures. When Ushii reached the age of eighteen, the parents of Matsukichi Nakasone, a boy from her home village who had gone to Hawaii to work on a plantation, came to her home to discuss marriage between Ushii and their son. Ushii had seen him briefly once, when he had left Okinawa for Hawaii, but she had been too young then to have any romantic notions about him. Now, however, when she saw his picture, she thought he was very handsome and agreed to marry him. Ushii's mother was concerned because the prospective groom was eleven years older than Ushii. But Ushii had fallen in love with the picture she had seen; her mind was made up; she agreed to go to Hawaii and began to make preparations for her journey.

Then, unexpectedly, her husband-to-be's mother caught the Spanish flu and died, so he rushed home. And one day Ushii's mother came to her and said, "Today is your wedding day." For the occasion Ushii simply put on a kimono that was a little dressier than one she would wear around the house or in the fields, combed her hair in *kampū* style (an Okinawan hairstyle that features a topknot), and added a fancy hairpin to secure the topknot in place.

Ushii's husband left for Hawaii soon after. Ushii stayed in Okinawa for three months to help her father-in-law; she was finally able to begin her journey to Hawaii in November 1914.[16]

Some of the issei women married plantation workers in ceremonies that were conducted in Japan even though the grooms remained in Hawaii. An example of such a wedding is that of Shunso and Sagami Shinozawa, which took place in Hiroshima Prefecture in 1918. Sagami's parents, who owned a great deal of land, had chosen a man of high social status in the village to be her husband, but, when she objected to their choice and begged a family friend to find

Ushii and Matsukichi Nakasone and their five children. Ushii is wearing the one dressy kimono she brought with her from Okinawa. 1927. Ushii Nakasone collection.

her a suitable husband in Hawaii instead, they withdrew their candidate and helped to carry out her wishes. Mrs. Shinozawa had an elaborate formal wedding. She did not choose to wear the traditional black montsuki; instead, she wore a *shiromuku* (pure-white silk bridal kimono) complete with a white silk brocaded obi and white accessories. She told me that she chose white because it symbolized the purity of the bride and the sincerity of her intention to fit into her husband's family; furthermore, since white also symbolizes death, it meant that, once the bride entered her husband's household, she could never return to her natal home. Mrs. Shinozawa embroidered her father's family crest, the "hanging wisteria" motif, on her white kimono.

The wedding ceremony and reception were held at the home of the bride's parents. The family hired a professional bridal dresser for the entire day. The dresser combed Sagami's long hair into the traditional takashimada and dressed Sagami in a colorful visiting kimono for the first stage of her journey to her husband's home in the next village. The procession stopped midway in Miyoshi City, and there Sagami's hairdo was recombed into a *marumage* (a rounded coiffure that was reserved for married women and symbolized her new status) and Sagami was dressed in her formal white kimono. It was dusk by the time she arrived at her husband's home; the groom's family and relatives awaited her in the pathway with lighted lanterns. Before Sagami entered the house, her hairdresser put the traditional watabōshi on her head.

Mrs. Shinozawa recalls that she changed kimono three times at the reception: first, she changed into a black montsuki; second, into a sky-blue silk kimono with gorgeous hand-painted designs; third, into a maroon-colored silk kimono. She wore the same long underkimono under all three of the kimono; it had two half-collars sewn onto it to make it appear that there were two layers of underkimono.

Although the groom was in Hawaii, the marriage ritual was performed in the presence of both families. The essence of the marriage ceremony is the *sansankudo* (the exchange of nuptial cups), and Sagami might have chosen to have a proxy play the role of her groom in this exchange. But, instead, she went through the motions of exchanging the nuptial cups of sake herself, facing the groom's photograph, which was placed in an elevated position to show respect. Sake cups were also exchanged by the parents of the bride and groom to symbolize their unity.

Mrs. Shinozawa's parents provided her with a generous dowry. Her willow-vine *kōri* (wicker trunk) contained a dozen fine kimono and accessories.

Despite her social and educational background, Mrs. Shinozawa ended up working in the sugarcane fields like other issei women to support her family when her husband fell ill. She says she often wished that she had married the man her parents had originally chosen for her. When her husband died, she thought about returning to Japan to receive help from her parents. But she was too embarrassed to do so. Instead, she made up her mind that she would accept the challenge of living and working in Hawaii and she took up a hoe and worked in the sugarcane fields. At first, she was ridiculed by her women co-workers for being too slow, but after three years of blistered hands, she became one of the first issei female overseers (in Hawaiian, *wahine luna*) at the Oahu Sugar Company. She hardly ever wore any of the fine kimono she had brought from Japan—except for the black montsuki, which she wore for weddings and funerals. After World War II, when she felt that her relatives in Hiroshima Prefecture must be in desperate need of clothing, she sent most of her kimono home.[17]

Ushi Tamashiro was another issei bride who was married in a ceremony that was conducted in Japan—in this case, in Okinawa—although the groom was in Hawaii. Ushi had been born in a farming

Ushi Tamashiro's picture-bride exchange photograph. The striped silk kimono and kasuri haori were lent to her by the photographer in Okinawa. 1923. Ushi Tamashiro collection.

village in Naha, Kokuba, Okinawa, on September 20, 1902. Her grandparents were all farmers who owned their land. The family worked together raising sugarcane, sweet potatoes, burdock roots, dasheen, and other vegetables that they sold at the market in Naha.

When Ushi was still very young, her father emigrated to Hawaii as a contract laborer. He died there three years later. Ushi, who worked in the fields, wove straw hats, and performed domestic chores, could see what a grim life she would have if she married a farmer's son in the village. She began to dream of going to Hawaii as a picture bride, visualizing a life of luxury.

Ushi's mother had a male cousin who had also emigrated to Hawaii and had a good friend, Jintaro Tamashiro, who was looking for a wife. This cousin and Ushi's father had been like brothers. So, when Ushi was almost twenty years old, her mother and this cousin arranged to have pictures of Ushi and the cousin's friend exchanged without Ushi's knowledge. When Ushi's mother and grandparents saw the friend's picture, they liked what they saw and went ahead with plans for the marriage.

The family decided to hold the marriage celebration in the Okinawan village before Ushi left. Since the groom could not be present, the family decided not to have a formal wedding celebration; however, Ushi's relatives and close friends celebrated the occasion with a small party. Ushi told me:

> I wore a casual kimono with a sash, and a simple hairdo. Even if my husband was not present, I made the pretense of entering his home as his bride. On the way to the groom's home, my girlfriends formed a circle around me "to shield my face" and escorted me to the groom's home. (According to ancient custom, the bride should not be seen until she appears at her wedding reception.) The girls wore casual kimono—kimono made of kasuri cloth, of bashōfu, or of striped tsumugi. These were hand-woven and sewn at home, either by the girls or by their mothers. No one in those days saw or wore black montsuki in the Okinawan villages. At the groom's home, there was much feasting and drinking to celebrate our marriage even without the groom.

Shortly afterward, Ushi boarded for the trip to Hawaii; she arrived in Honolulu on February 18, 1923.[18]

Issei Weddings in Hawaii

Some of the issei marriages that took place in Hawaii were traditional; some, nontraditional. Some were elaborate; some were simple. Some men sent the bride's family a monetary betrothal gift

Wedding photograph of Torazo and Komano Sugai. When this photograph was sent to the bride's parents in Niigata Prefecture, Japan, they were shocked to see their daughter dressed in an ordinary kimono for such an important occasion. They immediately sent her a montsuki and a silk obi, but by the time they arrived, the bride was busy working in the sugarcane fields and saw no need for them; she sent them back. 1915. Komano Sugai collection.

Early issei plantation wedding on Kauai. The bride is dressed in a formal black kimono and has a pompadour hairdo topped by a large bow. The groom is on her left. The rice bags with congratulatory notes written on them were given as wedding gifts. About 1920. Mabel Hashisaka collection.

large enough to enable the bride to have a set of formal bridal wear. Usually, however, the issei groom made barely enough money to pay for his bride's passage to Hawaii, and, in such cases, the bride's parents sometimes provided the wedding apparel for their daughter.

Certainly the issei women who came to Hawaii to be married brought with them an exciting collection of kimono that ranged from elegant silk bridal costumes and accessories to practical cottons. Most of the cotton textiles had been hand-woven by the women themselves or by members of their families. Many of the women also brought silk and cotton kimono for their husbands; usually these had been supplied by the groom's family. Unfortunately, hardly any of the clothing brought during the very early years of immigration, the years from 1885 to 1890, has been preserved and there are very few photographs of this clothing available

Formal wedding portrait of issei couple in Kapaa, Kauai. The bride is wearing an elegant mu'u mu'u with lace ruffles on the yoke and sleeves. Photograph taken about 1912–1915. Mabel Hashisaka collection.

for study. A slightly larger—but still limited—number of garments and photographs are available from the late 1890s.

On the whole, the kimono itself has hardly changed in cut and construction since it became standardized in the late Tokugawa (1603–1868) and early Meiji (1868–1911) periods.[19] There are other decisions to be made in the selection of a kimono, however, and most Japanese—both women and men—have always considered it important to select colors, patterns, and fabrics that are appropriate for their age and their socioeconomic status as well as for the season in which the kimono will be worn.

Even before the first unofficial Japanese immigrants came to Hawaii in 1868, striped, checked, stencil-dyed, and tie-dyed fabrics were being woven in the countryside by farm women, and other weaves were introduced later in various prefectures of Japan. The women from Japanese peasant families who married issei plantation laborers did not, of course, realize how valuable their hand-woven, hand-dyed, hand-drawn cotton and silk kimono would become in later years. When I interviewed them, many were embarrassed to mention that they had been married in a kimono made of fabric that had been produced at home on the family's own hand loom.

We do not know whether the naichi women who came before 1900 brought montsuki. However, it seems clear that during the Picture-Bride Period (1908–1924) most of the naichi women brought either a plain black montsuki or one with a subtle hand-drawn design above the front hemline of the kimono. The montsuki with a design became very popular in Japan during the early Meiji and Taisho periods (1868–1911 and 1912–1925, respectively); since these periods included the years in which the picture brides arrived in Hawaii, it is not surprising that montsuki of this type were introduced into Hawaii by the naichi women. The plain black montsuki was a versatile garment—in this respect, it was like the Western basic black dress that can be dressed up with accessories. With a gold brocaded sash and suitable accessories, the black montsuki could be worn for festive formal occasions such as weddings; with a plain black sash, it could be worn for funerals. Moreover, because of its straight loose lines and adjustable length, the montsuki fit any figure and could even be worn during pregnancy. (I remember that, when my mother became a widow in 1928, she was five months pregnant with her ninth child and she wore a formal black montsuki with a white underkimono and black obi.) Today, the basic black montsuki with five crests is called *mofuku* (mourning wear). It is still worn in Japan for funerals and other formal occasions. But in Hawaii the issei women abandoned this custom shortly after the outbreak of World War II; they were afraid that it might be interpreted as being disloyal to the United States and, therefore, lead to their arrest.

Shizu Kaigo, who came as a picture bride in December 1916 from Yamaguchi Prefecture and settled on the island of Kauai, brought three sets of montsuki. As a young girl, she had specialized in kimono sewing, from casual cottons to silks; she had also sewn obi and men's hakama and haori. It was her sewing teacher who arranged the match with Tomoji Kaigo, the teacher's nephew, who was working on Lihue Plantation on the island of Kauai.

For her plantation wedding in Hawaii, Mrs. Kaigo wore all three of the montsuki she had brought with her—a white, a red, and a black—as a three-layered kimono. She first put on the white montsuki, which was hand-painted with plum blossoms, which bloom in February before any other flower appears. She then put on the red montsuki, which was hand-painted with bamboo, which is said to symbolize resilience and endurance because, even if it bends under the weight of the snow, it never breaks. Last she put on the black montsuki, which was hand-painted with pine trees, which represent strength because they stay green throughout the year.[20] These hand-painted designs were embroidered in gold and silver threads. All three garments were padded with cotton along the hemline. Such padding was unusual in Hawaii, but Mrs. Kaigo explained that the kimono is usually designed with the season of the homeland in mind; she came in December, and she followed the custom that would be followed in the winter season in Japan. The three layers of colors, and the cotton-padded hemline fell into a slight train in the back, which created a regal effect when the bride walked.

Underneath her formal kimono Mrs. Kaigo wore a *hiyoku* (an underkimono that is single and unlined but looks like a double- or triple-layered kimono because of the color contrast added at the sleeve opening and at the hemline). Few issei women possessed such an elegant undergarment, and Mrs. Kaigo had made it herself.

The groom wore a dark wool Western suit. In Japan, he probably would have worn the traditional black montsuki, hakama, and haori to match the bride's formal costume. However, in Hawaii, at plantation weddings, a navy or black wool suit was the standard attire for issei men.[21]

Of course the clothing worn by the picture brides at the marriage cermonies that were conducted in Hawaii depended to some extent on the setting of the ceremony. Before the picture brides were recognized as legal wives by the Territorial Government in 1917, all of them had to go through a group Christian ceremony with twenty or more couples at the immigration station before they could be granted the right to enter the Territory of Hawaii. But after 1917, when the picture brides were recognized as legal wives, they could be claimed by their husbands without going through such a ceremony. Thereafter the wedding ceremonies were performed in a more dignified setting—at a Shinto shrine, at the Japanese-owned hotel in Honolulu, at a minister's residence, or at a plantation home.

Haruno Tazawa arrived in Hawaii as a picture bride from Fukushima Prefecture on July 27, 1917. The nakōdo who had arranged her marriage was her older sister, who had preceded her to Hawaii seven years earlier as a picture bride herself.

Haruno was the only bride on her ship to bring two large kōri. In one, she carried her *futon* (cotton-filled bedding) and a *tanzen* (a cotton-padded kimono worn by people in northern Japan during the winter months). She brought with her three kimono, including a black montsuki. But she was married wearing the purple cotton kimono she had on when she arrived.

Haruno's husband-to-be was Chozo Tazawa, a foreman on the Ewa Sugar Plantation. When he stepped up to claim her at the immigration station, Haruno was not quite sure that he was the man whose photograph she had received. But he was dressed in a nice black suit and a white shirt with a wing collar, and, when he identified her from her photograph, she quietly followed him. He hired a *hakku* (hack) and took her to the Yamashiro Hotel, where they were married by a Buddhist priest.

They spent their wedding night at the hotel, and the next morning Chozo hired a taxi and took Haruno to Ewa Sugar Plantation. Her plantation home was quite a shock to her. She told me: "I had visions of beautiful Hawaii. My dreams were shattered, though, when I saw my new home located deep in the mountains. My new home reminded me of our horse barn back in the village."

The next day a huge reception was held for the newly wedded couple, and the entire community was invited. The men pitched a huge tent, while the women helped with the preparation of the wedding feast. Haruno was uncomfortable:

That was the first time I had ever laid eyes on a *gaijin* [non-Japanese person, Caucasian], and I was scared. I came face to face with the gaijin as I poured sake into cups to greet them. They had such big eyes and tall noses! Some of them shook my hand and said something like "nice girl." There were all kinds of people in Ewa Plantation Camp—Spanish, Hawaiian, Portuguese. . . . There were also Filipinos, Okinawans, and a few Koreans. Those faces seemed so strange. . . . I could not communicate with them, so it made things more difficult.

For the wedding reception, Haruno wore a simple black montsuki with her mother's family crest.

Haruno Tazawa's exchange photograph. Haruno wove and sewed the kimono and haori herself to wear for her trip to Hawaii. She wears white tabi and geta to complete the outfit. 1917. Haruno Tazawa collection.

Chozo Tazawa's exchange photograph. Chozo wears a kimono with a white obi and dressy kasuri haori. He wears black tabi and sandals. 1917. Haruno Tazawa collection.

She wore the same black montsuki for her husband's funeral in 1928.[22]

One of the picture brides I interviewed did not know she was one until she arrived in Hawaii. When Ayako Maruyama left her village in Kumamoto Prefecture she thought she was going to Hawaii to talk to her cousin Shitoku Kikugawa on a mission for his mother, her favorite aunt. Instead, she ended up being her cousin's picture bride.

A nakōdo had arranged for another woman to become Shitoku's

wife. In fact, this "bride" had already taken a formal portrait of herself. (This picture was sent to the groom in Hawaii and is still kept in the family photograph collection.) But, the day before she was scheduled to leave for Hawaii, this woman eloped with someone else. Six months later, when her marriage fell apart, she begged to be allowed to be Shitoku's wife after all and to join him in Hawaii. When Ayako overheard a conversation between her father and aunt about whether to take this woman back or not, she felt so much anger toward the fickle woman that she volunteered to go to Hawaii to prevent the other woman from taking advantage of Shitoku. This gave her father and aunt the idea that Ayako would make an ideal bride for Shitoku, and they sent her picture to him in Hawaii for approval without her knowledge. Ayako had never seen a photograph of Shitoku, but she knew his younger brother, who lived in a nearby village. She was happy to set forth to perform a "good deed" for her aunt.

Shitoku met Ayako at the immigration station when she arrived on August 6, 1918, and he took her by horse and buggy to the Yoshida Store in Haleiwa, where he had worked during the early years. There, to her surprise, Ayako found that Mrs. Yoshida had prepared a wedding feast for the young couple.

Ayako does not recall going through any marriage ceremony either in her native Japanese village or in Hawaii, but her in-laws must have recorded her name in the Kikugawa family register in the village office or she would not have been permitted to enter Hawaii. For the wedding reception at the Yoshida residence, Ayako wore a montsuki. She did not have her hair done in the bridal coiffure; instead, she wore a modified pompadour. The groom wore a dark Western suit for the festive occasion. He wore the same suit again for the formal wedding portrait taken at the photographer's in Haleiwa. But for this occasion Ayako also posed in a pretty Western outfit that Mrs. Yoshida lent her, one that Mrs. Yoshida herself had worn as a bride.[23]

Sadahiko and Tsugi Sonoda were one of the many issei couples who were married at the immigration station in Honolulu. He was twenty-five years old at the time; she was twenty. Sadahiko came from the Hootaku District, Miyuki Village, in Kumamoto Prefecture; he sailed on the *China-Gō* via Nagasaki and arrived in Honolulu on September 11, 1906. After working for a few months at Kahuku Plantation, Sadahiko transferred to the sugar plantation in Puunene, Maui, as a steam plow operator. His wife Tsugi, who was from the same village in Kumamoto, came via Kobe and arrived in Hawaii on April 21, 1912. They had their formal portrait taken soon

Wedding photograph of Shitoku and Ayako Kikugawa. Ayako is wearing a mon-tsuki and a gold-brocaded sash; both were gifts from her father. 1918. Ayako Kikugawa collection.

after in Puunene. Unfortunately, during the early years, Tsugi could not afford to buy material to sew herself clothing to wear in the sugarcane fields, so she had to take apart the beautiful hand-woven kimono she wore for the portrait and make it into work clothing.[24]

Another picture bride who was married at the immigration station was Ima Ohashi, who left Kobe on December 28, 1913, and arrived in Honolulu in early January 1914. Her marriage had been arranged by a relative in her home village in Yamaguchi Prefecture. She was sixteen years old, and her husband was eleven years older. At first she had thought her intended groom was a little too old for her, but her mother convinced her to accept the marriage arrangement, saying that, in going to Hawaii, Ima would have a better life and would not have to contend with in-law problems. Actually,

Ayako Kikugawa in borrowed Western outfit: blouse, skirt, cummerbund, hat, and shoes. She was one of the few issei brides who received a wedding ring from her groom. The photographer noticed the ring and had her turn her hand so the ring would be visible. 1918. Ayako Kikugawa collection.

Wedding photograph of Tsugi and Sadahiko Sonoda, taken on
May 1, 1912, one week after their marriage at the immigration
station in Honolulu. Tsugi Sonoda wove the fabric and sewed
the kimono herself. Alma Ogata collection.

Ima's in-laws were good people, and she visited them often during
her six-month waiting period. When she left for Hawaii, they gave
her a gorgeous montsuki, the color of wisteria flowers, with a delicate bamboo design on the hemline, and a gold-brocaded obi. They
also gave her some fine-quality cotton kimono and an elegant
kimono made of the striped silk known as *meisen*. In addition, they
sent with Ima a pongee kimono and a light blue sash to give to their
son. For an issei bride of 1913, it was unusual to bring such fine-
quality clothing.

When Ima arrived in Hawaii, she was wearing an everyday kimono; before meeting her husband, however, she changed into a dressy *omeshi* (pebble crepe) kimono with a lined sash. She was married wearing this kimono, even though she had the elegant montsuki that her mother-in-law had given her packed away in her kōri.[25]

The Okinawan picture brides did not arrive with montsuki in their kōri, since montsuki were not traditional bridal wear in Okinawa. (The only exception I have found in all of my interviewing is a woman from Okinawa who bought a montsuki at Kobe while waiting for her ship to leave for Hawaii.)[26] Most of the Okinawan picture brides were married in the Christian ceremony that was performed at the immigration station and were, therefore, married wearing the kimono they had on when they arrived. A good many of those kimono were of kasuri—usually indigo-dyed with brightly colored splash designs. Others were of bashōfu. Others were of striped or dotted cottons.

Very few Okinawan picture brides had second ceremonies or receptions after they arrived in Hawaii. Kama Asato, who came to Hawaii in 1920 from a small village in Okinawa, seems typical. She told me:

> We had no marriage ceremony, no party. He took me to Waiakea, on the Big Island, a desolate-looking place. My first house was not fit for a human being to live in. It was made of crude lumber. There was one woman from my village who was kind to me and invited me to her house for meals. There were three other women who came from nearby villages in Okinawa. When I was ready to go to work, one of them made all my work clothing and accessories for me.

Kama had not done any fieldwork at home in Okinawa; instead, as a youngster, she had woven hats to supplement the family income. But in Hawaii she worked along with her husband in the canefields —first on the Big Island and later on Oahu.[27]

Most of the issei wedding ceremonies that were performed in Hawaii took place immediately after the bride arrived. But some were held years later. The wedding reception for Mr. and Mrs. Nobuichi Higaki, which took place in the early 1900s, is a good example of a belated ceremony. Nobuichi Higaki's marriage was arranged by his father without his knowledge. When Nobuichi was sixteen years old, a sixteen-year-old girl from his village in Japan came to live with his family in Hawaii; their parents had arranged for them to get married. There was no marriage ceremony or any

Kama Asato's exchange photograph. Kama was sixteen years old when the picture was taken. She wears an intricately woven kasuri kimono with white underkimono. 1920. Kama Asato collection.

sort of reception. It was not until ten years later that a formal wedding reception was held. Mr. Higaki recalled the ceremony:

> I wore a black wool suit; my wife wore a black montsuki with hand-painted pine branches on the lower front skirt of her kimono. The Higaki family crest was drawn in five positions to show that she was now a Higaki. She wore a gold-brocaded obi, and her hair was done in the bouffant pompadour style. For the first time, we had our formal wedding portrait taken.[28]

Kama Asato and her grandmother, a farewell photograph taken in Okinawa shortly before Kama left for Hawaii as a picture bride. 1920. Kama Asato collection.

Not all of the issei women who were married to issei men in Hawaii were summoned as brides; some of the plantation marriages were between issei men and women who were both already working on the plantations. The wedding of Yasu Abe and Soshichi Sato is an example. Yasu was born in Shimizu Village, Fukushima Prefecture, in 1893. Her father died when she was four years old, so she never attended grade school in the village. Instead, she helped her mother raise silkworms. She was also trained from an early age to weave straw matting, which was sold to buyers who came from the next village. Then her older brother summoned her to come to Hawaii.

Yasu left Japan on the *Shinyō Maru* during an eventful time in Japan's history—the day it changed from the Meiji Era to the Taisho Era. There was much commotion and excitement in the port city of Yokohama. And the twelve-day voyage was a rough one; Yasu was greatly relieved when the ship finally anchored in Honolulu on December 21, 1912. She was detained at the immigration station for three days, spent one night at the Yamashiro Hotel, then took the train to Waipahu. From there, she was taken by horse and buggy to her first home, a whitewashed longhouse near the old Soto Mission Temple in Camp 1. A few days later she was sent to work in the sugarcane fields for Oahu Sugar Company as a field laborer, working ten hours a day for seventy-five cents. (Mrs. Sato is one of the issei plantation women who marched from Aala Park to Alapai Street in the 1920 strike.) Life in her Japanese village had been hard enough, but life on the plantation was even harder. She continued working until she got married in 1916, at the age of twenty-three—which was, in those days, considered an advanced age for marriage; most young girls were married by the time they were seventeen or eighteen years old.

Yasu's marriage was arranged by a nakōdo who came from her home village in Fukushima. He sold dry goods and Singer sewing machines, and, as he traveled through the plantation towns, he did a lot of matchmaking. The wedding ceremony was held at Yasu's home in one of the whitewashed plantation longhouses. She wore a formal black montsuki, with the Sato family crest, that her husband-to-be had given her as his betrothal gift. He purchased it at Nagao Gofukuten, a popular Japanese dry goods store where the Japanese immigrants could buy their dressy kimono. Yasu's montsuki had no design on the bottom, and her brocaded obi was not of the finest silk, because Mr. Sato was still struggling and sent half his monthly pay of fifteen dollars to his parents in Fukushima. Since her widowed mother could not afford a professional hairdresser, Yasu combed her hair into a pompadour hairstyle herself and arranged a wide white bow in the back.

Mr. Sato wore a black wool suit, a long-sleeved white shirt, and a necktie. The nakōdo officiated with the sansankudo. He also sang the *Sansa Shigure*, a ceremonial song sung at weddings in Yasu's village in Japan. The song moved Yasu to tears. Later Yasu reminisced:

> We did not have much of a feast, just simple food, but there was plenty of sake. We were so poor we could not afford to have a formal portrait taken. I still have the black montsuki, but I sent the

rest of the kimono back to Japan after World War II. I felt that the relatives back home could make better use of the kimono.[29]

The wedding of Kaichi Abe and Miki Takahashi is another example of a marriage between an issei man and woman who were both already working on the plantations. Although the wedding was held in Hawaii, the wedding reception was conducted in traditional Japanese style. It took place in 1923, a time when the issei who could afford to do so began reviving the old village marriage customs and turning receptions into community celebrations.

Kaichi Abe had come from Fukushima Prefecture when he was fifteen years old. He soon began working in a *konpan* (a group of people who formed a partnership to work a designated area of land). He worked very hard, and was able to send large sums of money to Japan to his older brother, who was taking care of the farm and their widowed mother back in their village.

Miki Takahashi was also from Fukushima Prefecture. She came to Hawaii as a girl of nineteen, summoned by her father, who worked at Waialua Agricultural Company on Oahu. She arrived in Honolulu on June 11, 1917, when people were celebrating Kamehameha Day. After a few days of rest, she began working in the rubber-tree fields in Kawailoa, where her family lived. Two or three years later, she moved to Ewa Sugar Plantation, where her older sister's husband was the leader of a konpan gang; Miki worked hard alongside the men. After the big strike in 1920, she moved to Waipahu Plantation, to live with an older brother and his family.

Miki's brother-in-law in Ewa told a friend of his, Kaichi Abe, who lived in a nearby camp, that he thought his wife's younger sister would make an ideal match for Kaichi, and he arranged an opportunity for Kaichi to get a good look at Miki without her knowledge. Kaichi told me:

> Although she was not an outstanding beauty, I liked her quiet and gentle ways. I felt that she would not be a domineering type of wife and felt safe enough to marry her. I feel that I made the right choice; we've been married sixty-one years and we've never had a fight![30]

The marriage was agreed upon, with Miki's older brother giving his consent in place of her father, who had returned to Japan by then. Miki did not see Kaichi, however, until the day the betrothal gift was brought to her home.

> Kaichi told me the details about the betrothal gift; I went to purchase the bride's montsuki and accessories at the Nagao Gofukuten in Honolulu and there saw my bride-to-be shopping for her trous-

Wedding photograph of Miki and Kaichi Abe. Miki is wearing the montsuki given to her by the groom, which has a delicate brush painting of autumn leaves and flowers at the hemline. Kaichi is wearing a custom-made suit of 100 percent wool. (He kept this suit in his sea trunk until 1989.) 1923. Kaichi Abe collection.

seau with her family. It was very embarrassing for both sides. At that time, a montsuki of fairly good quality cost about forty dollars. The store carried *mizuhiki* (fancy gift wrappers in colorful red, white, and gold coiled paper ties)—even wooden trays with legs, so everything could be presented properly. The betrothal gift consisted of a complete set of montsuki with my family crest, formal gold-brocaded obi, and accessories—and fresh sea bream, cuttlefish, dried laver, and sake, all symbolic of long life and happiness.

The Abes were married at the Kato Jinja shrine in Honolulu. The bride wore a Hawaiian mu'u mu'u, which was popular at that time, and the groom wore a dark wool suit.

The Abes' reception was held a few months after the marriage ceremony, in December 1923, at the groom's brother's home. More than eighty guests were invited, a large number in those days. A cook was hired from the boardinghouse to supervise the preparation of the feast. Among the foods served were a large sea bream, *sashimi* (thinly sliced raw fish), *nishime* (a dish of meat or poultry with vegetables seasoned with sugar and shoyu), a traditional assortment of delicacies known as *mori mono*, and plenty of sake. All this cost about $580.00, a sum that in those days took months to pay off. (The usual monetary wedding gift at that time was two or three dollars.)

The bride first wore a black montsuki given to her by her own family, which bore her father's family crest.

The nakōdo's wife served as the bride's attendant. The nakōdo made all the formal speeches and also sang the *Takasago*, a wedding song that was traditionally sung in Japanese villages.[31]

Issei Weddings in Both Japan and Hawaii

Technically, quite a few of the issei couples were married twice—once in Japan and once in Hawaii. Usually one or the other of the ceremonies was merely a formality: many of the couples for whom elaborate wedding ceremonies had already been conducted in Japan were married again in a brief Christian ceremony at the immigration station in Honolulu; some of the couples for whom more or less elaborate wedding ceremonies were conducted in Hawaii had, in the eyes of the Japanese at least, already been married in Japan simply by having the bride's name entered in the groom's family register. But some couples were married in more-than-token ceremonies in both Japan and Hawaii.

Tatsuno Ogawa was an issei bride who had two weddings—one in Japan and one in Hawaii. She was the oldest of ten children and had

Tatsuno Ogawa in kasuri kimono she wove and sewed herself. She learned the intricate art of weaving kasuri in her home village in Hiroshima Prefecture when she was thirteen years old. 1912. Tatsuno Ogawa collection.

begun working on the farm in her village back home in Hiroshima Prefecture when she was very young. She was married to Hiroji Ogawa in Japan in 1912 in a relatively simple sansankudo ritual. Hiroji left for Hawaii soon after their marriage to work in the pine-apple fields, but Tatsuno stayed behind to nurse her husband's ailing grandfather and to help her mother-in-law, who was a frail woman. Tatsuno lived with her in-laws for a year before she joined her husband in Hawaii. Because she came with a large group of picture brides from various prefectures, she was also categorized as a picture bride.

Hiroji Ogawa came to claim his bride at the immigration station on July 19, 1913. Since the groom's family had forgotten to register their marriage at the village office in Japan, he took her directly to the Daijingu Shrine in Honolulu to get married again. There was no time to change into a dressier kimono, so Tatsuno was remarried in the kasuri kimono she was wearing on arrival, one which she had woven and sewn herself. Tatsuno did not have a montsuki in her kōri; her parents could not afford to buy one for her, since they had nine younger children to support. (She finally purchased a black montsuki in Honolulu, after she had earned some money working in the pineapple fields.)[32]

Another issei bride who had wedding ceremonies in both Japan and Hawaii is Taga Toki. Taga came in 1917 from Yatsushiro, a remote village in Kumamoto Prefecture in southwestern Japan. Her marriage had been arranged by her older brother and by the prospective groom's uncle, Yahei Oodomo, who lived in a nearby village; the uncle assumed most of the responsibilities.

Taga's husband-to-be, Kamezo Toki, was living on the island of Kauai when the marriage was arranged. His parents had gone to Hawaii when he was very young, leaving him behind in Japan in the care of his grandparents. He had remained in Japan until he was about fifteen or sixteen years old; then his father sent for him.

Once the marriage was decided upon, Taga's name was entered into the Toki family register at the village office in Japan. But, in accordance with United States government regulations in effect during the Restricted Immigration Period, she had to wait six months before she could join her husband in Hawaii. If her in-laws had not been satisfied with her character or her performance as a bride, they could have removed her name from the Toki family register.

Taga's parents thought there should be some sort of interim marriage ceremony before Taga left for Hawaii. So they held one at the home of a family friend. For this ceremony, Taga wore a purple silk montsuki with an exquisite hand-drawn design on the lower front of the kimono, a misty mountain landscape done in shades of gray. Underneath her montsuki, Taga wore a long underkimono of brown silk crepe that was folded together with the outer garment to create the effect of a two-layered kimono. Underneath this, she wore another long underkimono of white silk crepe. The brown silk

Kamezo Toki's exchange photograph. 1918. Kamezo Toki collection.

underkimono and the gray tones in the painting denoted the time of year she left Japan, which was October. Her obi was made of a stiff, heavy brocade called *atsuita*. She combed her hair into a pompadour and tied a big bow in the back.

The bride performed the ritual of exchanging the nuptial cups in front of the groom's picture, placed on a higher level. About thirty or forty people attended the marriage ceremony—most of them relatives, neighbors, or close friends of the bride's parents. Female relatives were dressed in black montsuki or their best silk kimono. Most of the male relatives were dressed in the traditional men's formal attire: black habutae montsuki, hakama, and haori.

Taga was seasick and miserable throughout the voyage and sighed with relief as the *Shinyō Maru* docked in Honolulu on November 22, 1917. Kamezo, on Kauai, had been told by his father that morning: "Kamezo, go pick up your wife today." So he took the boat from Kauai to Honolulu, which took five hours. By then his bride was already at the immigration station. All the other grooms were anxiously waiting, "sort of in a daze," he said, because their long-awaited picture brides had finally come. No one said a word. While waiting, Kamezo reminded himself: "Well, no matter what she looks like, I can't do anything about it! I'll never complain one bit. It is too late to do anything." Kamezo had taken pains to look his best that day and had dressed carefully in his black wool suit, a white long-sleeved shirt, and a necktie. His shirt had been purchased at a Chinese store on King Street in Honolulu for thirty cents. The Chinese proprietor had even sold him a pair of cuff links. "The only thing I did not have," he said, "was a pair of shoes. But someone gave me an old pair of black leather shoes which were 'janku' (junk). They were a bit over-sized for me. As I walked, they went 'paka, paka, paka, paka'—how awful it was!"

Of all the grooms searching for their brides, Kamezo was the only one who knew exactly what to look for. A woman who had been on the same voyage with Taga and had already completed her examination came out early and whispered into his ear: "If you want to find your bride, look for the biggest feet underneath that curtain." Sure enough, when he lifted the curtain, and looked for the feet wearing the largest-sized tabi, he found his wife right away!

Even though Taga's name had been entered in her husband's family register, and she was accepted as his legal wife, they went to the Izumo Taisha (a Shinto shrine) in Honolulu to have their marriage blessed—in effect, to get married again in the new land.

Kamezo and Taga stayed for two nights at the Kyushuya (a hotel in Honolulu) and then boarded the *Kinau* for the island of Kauai.

Kamezo and Taga Toki in a formal portrait taken a few days after their wedding; a friend's daughter poses with the newlyweds. Taga is wearing a muʻu muʻu that her sister made for her. September 24, 1918. Kamezo Toki collection.

Taga was particularly impressed by the Hawaiians aboard. She told me:

> There was a Hawaiian lady who had on a lovely white holoku. I thought to myself, "she's chubby but looks very nice. The holoku hides her large hips and makes her appear graceful. When I heard the Hawaiians talking story, I thought they had beautiful rhythm, too, in their manner of speaking."[33]

When the young couple arrived on the island of Kauai, Kamezo's parents held a wedding reception for them. Taga had brought a purple montsuki to wear for her wedding reception, but she did not have time to change, so she wore the kimono made of silk serge that she had worn on the boat to Kauai.

On Taga's arrival on Kauai, her older sister, who had come as a picture bride a few years earlier, had presented her with a mu'u mu'u, one with a dainty floral print on a white background. It had rows of pin tucks and was trimmed with lace on the collar and edge of the elbow-length sleeves. A few days later, Kamezo took his bride to visit his mother's grave. (His mother had died some years before.) On the way he stopped at a photographer's studio to have a formal portrait taken. The bride, not knowing of his intention, was wearing the mu'u mu'u her sister had sewn for her. The portrait taken that day was the only wedding picture Taga had. And even this was not, strictly speaking, a wedding portrait, for a friend's child was included in the picture. Taga told me that she wished she had had a formal portrait taken in her purple montsuki. She was disappointed that her husband never saw her in her bridal kimono and that she had no wedding portrait taken in the traditional five-crested kimono to show her grandchildren. She wore that bridal kimono only once— for the interim marriage ceremony back in her village. But she kept it through the years, carefully folded in a silk wrapping cloth.

A few days after her arrival, Taga started working in the sugarcane fields with other picture brides. Kamezo's stepmother had Taga's kasuri work outfit and accessories all prepared for her. And, after that, Taga told me, it was nothing but work in the fields and having babies one after another.[34]

Weddings of Issei Groom and Nisei Bride in Hawaii

Not all of the issei men married issei women; some issei men married the nisei daughters of early immigrants. The marriage of Kichizo Sugimoto and Nobuko Matsuyama, which took place in Waipahu, Camp 1, in 1918, is a good example of such a union. Both families were from the same prefecture in Japan, and they had become acquainted in Hawaii.

Kichizo Sugimoto's father, Kumataro, after hearing many exciting rumors about plantation laborers who had amassed fortunes in Hawaii, emigrated to Hawaii in about 1902 from Kumamoto Prefecture. He left his wife and children behind with the intention of sending for them later. After waiting what seemed to her a reasonably long time, Kumataro's wife became concerned and sent their oldest son to urge his father to return to Japan. But the son ran into debt and was himself unable to return. So Kumataro's wife sent the second son, and he too failed to return. Finally she sent the third son, eighteen-year-old Kichizo. He arrived in Hawaii on November 21, 1916, intending to return right away. He found that his two older brothers had accumulated debts, and were unable to send their father home. He also found that, although his father had at times managed to accumulate enough money to go home, he had, each time, let someone borrow the money to pay gambling debts and it had never been repaid. Kichizo found his father working for a konpan group that was led by a Mr. Matsuyama, and Kichizo began working for Mr. Matsuyama too. He worked hard in the fields to save enough money to send his father home. Instead, when someone became impressed with the hard-working young man and suggested that he would make a good match for Mr. Matsuyama's oldest daughter, Nobuko, a marriage was arranged. Kichizo, an issei, and Nobuko, a nisei, were married in 1918.

The Sugimotos' formal wedding portrait shows that their plantation wedding was conducted in traditional Japanese style—although with a few Western touches. Both the bride and groom wore the groom's plum-motif on their montsuki. The groom's father, also in the photograph, is dressed in Western clothes: a bowler hat, a dark wool coat, a white long-sleeved shirt, a necktie, and homemade trousers with wide, turned-up cuffs.[35]

Another issei man who married a nisei woman was the Reverend Jitsuzo Morimoto, a former contract laborer who was one of the first of his generation to become a Christian minister. In a Christian ceremony performed at the River Street Methodist Church on August 7, 1911, he married Raku Saka, a child of Japanese immigrants who arrived in Hawaii on February 8, 1885, on the *City of Tokyo*.

Raku's father, Shoshichi Saka, had a successful brass- and copper-working shop in Yokohama. Coming to Hawaii as a contract laborer was not his idea: it was his adventurous wife, Chika, who wanted to take advantage of the opportunities in Hawaii, which she likened to "the sun rising in the sky" *(Hawaii wa asahi no noboru gotoshi).*

Wedding photograph of Nobuko and Kichizo Sugimoto. Kichizo's father is seated on the *right*. Nobuko is wearing a traditional black montsuki that has a striking hand-painted design of pine branches and plum blossoms at the hemline. With this she wears a two-layered underkimono, the first layer in white, the second in light blue; this produces a tri-color effect. Around her waist she wears a full-patterned gold-brocaded obi. Kichizo is wearing a black montsuki and a hakama wrapped around with a white sash. Kichizo's father, dressed in Western clothes, holds the wedding certificate in his hand. November 1916. Amy Sugimoto collection.

Wedding photograph of Toyoko Sugimoto, daughter of Nobuko and Kichizo Sugimoto, and Hideo Ito. They were married on February 14, 1937, at the Soto Mission Temple. Toyoko's wedding was more traditional and more elegant than her mother's had been. She changed her wedding attire three times during the wedding reception. 1937. Amy Sugimoto collection.

Moreover, she had discovered that there was no sake in Hawaii, and she wanted to curb her husband's fondness for the alcoholic drink.

The Saka family was sent to the Kekaha Sugar Company of Kauai. After their three-year contract was completed they moved to Sprecklesville, Maui. Raku was born in this plantation town on March 3, 1890, on Girls' Day. Four years later, her parents moved to Kula, where her father worked at the Haleakala Ranch Company.

In 1904 the family moved to Honolulu, and Raku's father set up a brass- and copper-working shop on Pauahi Street. Raku's older sister had been sent to the Susannah Wesley Home the year before, and Raku, then fourteen years old, decided to work part time and join her sister at the home. During her three years' stay, she studied English, sewing, cooking, and Western culture and etiquette. After that, she went to the Royal School and then to Kaahumanu School; she graduated from the eighth grade in 1907. It was through her association with the Susannah Wesley Home that Raku became an active member of the River Street Church, which had close ties with the home.

Raku was not aware that the Reverend Chuzo Nakamura of that church had previously approached her father about matching her with the Reverend Jitsuzo Morimoto, a young Methodist minister who was serving at a small church in Puukolii, Maui, a plantation town. She was told only after the marriage was agreed upon by the two men.

The people at the Susannah Wesley Home were happy and helped Raku prepare for her wedding. In 1911 it was very rare for Japanese girls to be married in a conventional white wedding dress; most parents dressed their daughters in traditional Japanese costume. But Raku had an elegant white silk wedding dress that was made for her by the mother of the superintendent of the home. It had a fitted bodice that was elaborately tucked; in contrast, the long skirt was plain, with slight flaring at the hem. Raku's hair was styled in the fashionable pompadour hairdo.

The bridegroom wore a dark morning coat and vest over a white shirt with wing collar. Raku told me that her husband must have borrowed the fashionable morning coat, for it was impossible for a poor minister to own such a luxury in those days.

Raku's wedding dress was only one of the many manifestations of friendship between Japanese immigrant families and the Christian missionary women who came from the eastern United States as "Bible women." From its beginning, the Susannah Wesley Home took in the children of poor Japanese immigrant families who had to work in the plantation fields. And there are many heartwarming

The Reverend Jitsuzo Morimoto and his bride, Raku. The bride's wedding gown was sewn for her by a missionary woman. The groom wears a white bow tie, which is unusual; most issei men wore black bow ties for formal occasions. 1911. Raku Morimoto collection.

stories of Japanese picture brides who found refuge at the home after running away from their husbands.[36]

A very different kind of wedding of an issei groom and a nisei bride—a traditional Japanese-style one— was the wedding of Masaki and Ayako Tabusa, who were married on April 3, 1932. Masaki's father had come to Hawaii in about 1906 and settled in Kukaiau Village in Hamakua on the Big Island. He had left his pregnant wife behind in his village in Yamaguchi Prefecture, and Masaki was born there on June 6, 1907. His mother joined his father in Hawaii a year later, but left Masaki in his maternal grandparents' care.

When Masaki was fourteen years old, he wrote his parents that he wanted to come to Hawaii. The arrangements were made, and soon afterward Masaki set off on the *Korea Maru*, wearing a Western-type suit that his grandfather had had made for him.

A year after Masaki arrived in Hawaii, his parents returned to Japan, leaving Masaki on his own. He managed to support himself— working first at Love's Bakery, then at Ogawa's Service Station. When, eventually, he met a nisei girl he wanted to marry, he approached the matter in the traditional Japanese way. He told me:

> To propose marriage, I asked two friends who had come from the same village in Japan to act as nakōdo. . . . otherwise, it would be insulting to the bride's family. All the betrothal gifts, signifying longevity and happiness, were individually wrapped in red and white ceremonial paper and tied with mizuhiki, red and gold paper cords.[37]

The wedding date was selected by the two nakōdo after consulting the ancient Chinese and Japanese astrological calendars to find a day that would be auspicious.

The traditional Japanese wedding ceremony was performed at the Izumo Taisha Shinto Shrine in the presence of the two nakōdo and the bride's parents. The bride wore a *hōmongi* (visiting kimono) with elaborate designs on the front skirt; she wore her hair plain. The groom wore dark wool trousers and a casual shirt.

The wedding reception was held a week later, at the Waipahu Japanese Social Club, and it was an important social event for the whole community. On this occasion Masaki wore a formal black suit with satin lapels, a white shirt with a wing collar, a black bow tie, and black leather shoes; he held white gloves in his right hand. The bride had begun her preparations very early that morning by having her bridal hairdo and make-up done by a Mrs. Ishizu (no one seems to remember her first name), who was the outstanding bridal consultant, kimono dresser, and hairdresser of the prewar period in

Ayako and Masaki Tabusa, married in traditional style in Waipahu in 1932. The three layers of the bride's kimono have been carefully arranged to show to best advantage the elaborate hand-painting on the front skirt, a painting that features peonies, pine trees, and other symbols of good luck, including a white crane with wings spread wide. A hakoseko has been inserted into the left side of her kimono collar a few inches above her sash. Masaki Tabusa collection.

Hawaii. (People could recognize her work just by looking at a wedding portrait.) Mrs. Ishizu, particularly noted for her skill at wrapping the traditional *tsunokakushi* (horn concealer), the white silk band, around the bridal hairdo and over the forehead, studied the facial contours of each bride to determine the position that would be most attractive. (The hairdressers preferred an oval-shaped face because this shape showed off the bridal coiffure to best advantage; they had to put more effort into the shaping of the bridal hairstyle for women with round- or square-shaped faces.) Ayako's mother, like most mothers of nisei girls during the prewar years, had insisted that Ayako let her hair grow long, and on the day of the reception Ayako finally realized why: Mrs. Ishizu was able to use Ayako's own hair to fashion the traditional bridal hairdo.

For the formal wedding portrait, Ayako wore her black montsuki with hand-painted designs on the front skirt. Her layers of kimono were wrapped around with a fully patterned brocaded *maru obi*, with a white silk cord in the center to hold it in place. She also wore a dapple-dyed bustle sash tucked into the upper part of the wide sash.

After Ayako had posed long hours for the formal portrait, Mrs. Ishizu dressed her in her all-white formal kimono for the reception. En route to Waipahu, the bridal party stopped in Aiea to have lighted lanterns placed around each car; the cars then continued in a spectacular procession to the Waipahu Japanese Social Club.

The bride entered the banquet hall dressed in her all-white formal bridal costume, the kimono hemline deliberately left long to form a graceful train as she walked to her place—slowly, in order to give the curious onlookers and guests enough time to have a good look at the beautiful bride. Mr. Tabusa told me that people even climbed up on window ledges and rooftops to catch a glimpse of the bride. And then the celebrating really began, with many congratulatory speeches, plenty of food, and much singing, including singing of the traditional wedding song, *Takasago*.[38]

Nisei Weddings in Hawaii

While the picture brides were still arriving from Japan, the children of the Gannen Mono and those of the first contract laborers were already reaching the age of marriage. In their marriages these nisei followed the old Japanese traditions. It was common practice for the marriages of nisei to be arranged by a nakōdo. Sometimes photographs were even exchanged to prevent the embarrassment of being rejected. And the weddings themselves were formal Japanese weddings like those held in the villages from which the issei parents had come. Most of the issei who got married in Hawaii during the early immigration period had not had formal weddings—for financial reasons or because of the unusual circumstances under which they were married—and they wanted their sons and daughters to have the traditional weddings they had not been able to have. The issei parents, especially mothers, sacrificed much to dress their daughters in traditional bridal clothing. Many used the *tanomoshi* (a mutual financing system into which many issei put half their pay) to finance the cost of dowries and to give their daughters formal five-crested black kimono and all the accessories. Others took in washing—sometimes after working ten hours in the fields—to make the extra money. A proper wedding gave issei parents a great deal of satisfaction; it linked their lives in the new land to their lives in the villages they had left behind in their youth. The proud issei parents seldom failed to have the young couples take formal portraits so they could send them to the grandparents in Japan, who had never seen their grandchildren.

One of the earliest nisei marriages was that of Asaichi Nekomoto, born February 12, 1892, in Paauilo, Hawaii, and Hayame Ebesu, born November 15, 1899, in Pepeekeo, Hawaii. It took place in Waianae, Oahu, on September 30, 1916. The parents of both the bride and groom had emigrated from Hiroshima before the turn of the century to become contract laborers on Hawaiian plantations.

After Hayame's family moved to Waianae, a quiet plantation town on Oahu, her father built her a little store at the Waianae Train Station to spare her such backbreaking plantation work as *hapai ko* (carrying bundles of sugarcane). It was at this store in Waianae that Hayame and Asaichi first met, and it was Hayame's uncle, Moritomo Yamasaki, who was responsible for Asaichi's visit to Waianae. One day, on a trip to the Odo Store on Holu (Hall) Street in Honolulu, Hayame's uncle told Mr. Odo that Waianae Plantation was in desperate need of a blacksmith. Just then a young blacksmith, Asaichi Nekomoto, came by, and Mr. Odo introduced him. Hayame's uncle was impressed by the young man and decided he was the right one for his niece. He invited Asaichi to come to Waianae. Soon after, Asaichi made a dramatic entry into the sleepy town on his motorcycle and headed straight for the little store in the railroad station to buy a rootbeer soda. While sipping the soda, he scrutinized the pretty girl who ran the store and immediately decided to apply for the blacksmith job. Not long after, the marriage was arranged by a nakōdo.

For the wedding, Hayame was elegantly dressed in a black silk

Mitsuo and Lillian Kikuyo Fujimoto, who were married on December 25, 1938. The bride received two white formal kimono, one from her parents and the other from the groom's family. The talented bridal consultant Mrs. Ishizu dressed the bride in one formal kimono and used the other as an uchikake, an outer robe. Mitsuo Fujimoto collection.

A nisei bride, her attendant, and the nakōdo crossing the Wailua River (on the island of Kauai) to go to the reception given by the groom's family. In Japan, where there are many inland seas and rivers, such boat trips are common. Photograph taken in the 1930s. Shizu Kaigo collection.

crepe montsuki, displaying an exquisite hand-painted design on the lower part of the skirt in front. A wide gold-brocaded obi was tied in a fancy fan-shaped bow in the back; many narrow cords and a silk sash were used to complete the intricate bridal obi knot. No formal hairdresser was available at Waianae Plantation—or any of the other plantations—during this early period; usually some issei woman who could create a reasonable imitation of the bridal hairdo took

Asaichi Nekomoto and Hayame Ebesu on a motorcycle during their courtship.
Waianae, Oahu, 1916. Dorothy Matsuo collection.

over the difficult task. In Hayame's case, however, her mother
solved the problem satisfactorily by borrowing a ready-made ornate
bridal wig and draping a tsunokakushi over the wig; no one knew
the difference.

In 1916 it was still a rarity for a Japanese girl on the plantation to
be dressed in full traditional bridal costume. But Hayame's parents
were an enterprising issei couple and had attained success in some
business ventures. The groom, too, was more strikingly dressed
than most grooms at the time: instead of the usual dark business
suit, Asaichi wore a Norfolk jacket with yoke and box pleats, a
jacket that was fashionable in the 1890s.

The group photograph taken at the Nekomotos' wedding in 1916
not only shows how this early nisei bride and groom were dressed
but also shows how others were dressed when they attended plantation weddings during those years. The guests were dressed in their
best clothes. But some were wearing less-than-proper attire, for in
the early years many of the issei in Hawaii could not afford to buy a
pair of shoes or a jacket. Often they borrowed such items to attend a
wedding or funeral. If two friends were attending the same affair, the

Asaichi and Hayame Nekomoto with friends and relatives in wedding photograph. The families of the bride and groom are wearing formal clothes for the occasion, but some of the guests do not have the proper attire. The woman standing behind the bride is dressed in the traditional formal black montsuki; the three women on the bride's *left*, however, are wearing dressy kimono, which may mean that they did not own any montsuki. One man standing behind the couple is dressed in a white long-sleeved shirt with wing collar. There are both bow ties and neckties seen in the photograph. On the *far right*, one issei man is wearing a jacket that was probably home-sewn or made by the village seamstress. On the *far left*, a man is wearing what appears to be a dark wool jacket over khaki pants, with a white shirt, narrow necktie, and wooden clogs. September 30, 1916. Dorothy Matsuo collection.

one who had closer ties to the hosts would try to dress properly because he might be called upon to fulfill some important role. Children frequently went to plantation weddings and funerals barefooted.[39]

One of the first of many outstanding traditional social events to be held in the plantation town of Waipahu was the wedding of Ryoto Yasui and Kimiyo Kanechika on August 13, 1923.

Ryoto's parents came from Hiroshima. They settled in the East (Higashi) Camp of the Oahu Sugar Plantation in lower Waipahu, when the entire area was nothing but rice paddies. Ryoto, the oldest of ten children, was born on May 6, 1898. He was sent to work at the sugar mill's electric power plant soon after he graduated from grammar school. Later he was promoted to a clerical position at the Oahu Sugar Company office, and he continued to work there until his retirement; he lived his entire life on the Oahu Sugar Plantation.

The Kanechika family lived at Pump 4 Camp of the Oahu Sugar Plantation in Waipahu. After Kimiyo Kanechika completed the fifth grade at the English grammar school in Waipahu, she was sent to her parents' village home in Yamaguchi Prefecture. There, she completed Japanese high school. In addition, she received training in the traditionally feminine skills of kimono sewing, etiquette, flower arrangement, and tea ceremony; issei mothers always tried to have their daughters "polished" with training of this kind so that the daughters could marry into upper-class families.

A mutual friend of the Yasuis and Kanechikas decided that Kimiyo would be an ideal wife for the Yasuis' oldest son and kept urging her father to consent to the marriage. Kimiyo's mother strongly opposed the match because Kimiyo had been brought up in a small family, with only two boys and two girls, in a carefree environment, and would be taking on too many responsibilities if she married the oldest of ten children. But the letters kept coming, and finally Kimiyo's mother agreed to send her daughter to Hawaii. Kimiyo arrived in Hawaii in late July of 1923. She married Ryoto Yasui on August 13, 1923, at Izumo Taisha Shrine.

Since it was a summer wedding, Kimiyo chose to wear a dark purple montsuki of silk gauze, which was light and airy. Because silk gauze is very sheer, she wore a long underkimono of white silk crepe. Under this she wore a colorful underkimono. Her montsuki was held in place by a wide gold-brocaded sash tied in the ornate fan-shaped bowknot. The brush painting on the lower front of the kimono suggested the season of the year, depicting a white sailboat drifting on water, with tall green rushes and dainty flowers along the banks. The sailboat, a few ripples on the water, and some of the flowers were highlighted in silver thread. The crest motif drawn on Kimiyo's montsuki was that of her mother's family. A family friend combed Kimiyo's bridal coiffure, adorned it with fancy combs and ornaments, and placed a silk headband over the hairdo. The groom's wedding attire was much simpler. He wore a black wool suit, a long-sleeved white shirt, and a dark necktie.

The whole community participated in the festivities. There were many congratulatory speeches and much singing of wedding songs, folk songs, and ballads; the feasting and drinking lasted for three days.[40]

One of the most exciting wedding stories of the 1920s was that of Robert Shigeo Muroda and Shizume Nakamura, who were married in 1924 in true plantation style. Shigeo was born on May 13, 1905, in Waianae, Oahu. Shizume was also born in Waianae, on September 24, 1906. They had grown up in the same neighborhood and knew each other by sight, and when the two were still very young their parents had decided that someday they should get married. When their parents felt that the two were old enough to settle down, they asked a close family friend to act as nakōdo.

Shigeo and Shizume were married on May 16, 1924, at the Izumo Taisha Shinto Shrine in Honolulu in a solemn ceremony, with the exchange of nuptial cups to seal their union. On that day, the groom wore a suit; the bride wore a fancy dress. The nakōdo and his wife served as witnesses.

The wedding reception was held a few weeks after the wedding at the groom's parents' home. A photograph from that event shows that both the groom and his father wore dark wool suits with the trouser legs tapered as was the vogue at the time. It also shows the nakōdo wearing a white linen suit. With this white suit he wore a long-sleeved white shirt, a black bow tie, and white shoes. By Western standards he looked quite dapper. In Japan it was customary for the nakōdo to be dressed all in black: formal montsuki, haori, and hakama. This traditional black ensemble was felt to give him an air of distinction that befitted his role. In the Muroda wedding, the white linen suit seems to impart the same kind of distinction and dignity. According to Robert Sato of Sato Clothiers in Honolulu, white linen suits during the 1920s cost about seventy-five dollars; only a few issei men could afford such luxury. (Ordinary dark wool suits could be made for about twenty dollars, and even that was a month's pay for a plantation laborer.)

Shizume was dressed in a traditional montsuki with a white silk crepe underkimono. An elaborate half-collar with rich hand-embroidery was exposed more than the usual inch. On the front skirt of Shizume's montsuki was a hand-painted design of pine trees, cranes, and flowers in muted shades of green, pink, lavender, and gold. When I interviewed her, Shizume told me that her kimono was not perfectly aligned, especially in the front of the skirt and in the overlapping of the collar, and her tsunokakushi was slightly off-center. But, she said, no one seemed to notice.

In the background of the Murodas' wedding picture can be seen more than thirty bags of rice and a few bags of barley, stacked high on a wooden platform and covered by a tarpaulin that was supported by poles. These were wedding gifts—an unusual number of generous gifts. The groom's mother was at one time the only midwife in the isolated Waianae area, and she had a great deal of prestige among the

Photograph taken at wedding reception for Robert Shigeo Muroda and his bride, Shizume. Mr. Makitaro Tamura is on the *left*; the nakōdo is on the *right*. The bags of rice and barley stacked in the background are wedding gifts to the new couple; the pieces of white rice paper have congratulatory messages on them. May 1924. Robert S. Muroda collection.

family's friends and neighbors, even people of other ethnic groups; therefore, many people in the community gave the Murodas bags of rice as wedding gifts. At the time a bag of rice cost about $7.50—an amount that most plantation families could not afford to give at a typical wedding, since an ordinary laborer earned about a dollar a day for ten hours of work. (The average monetary gift at weddings was about two or three dollars.) But the Murodas were special. Because so many people in the community wanted to give them bags of rice, the small neighborhood store ran short and temporarily substituted bags of barley. Each bag of rice had the name of the donor written in bold calligraphy on a long piece of paper that said "Congratulations!" at the top and had the donor's name inscribed at the bottom. Those who gave generous gifts were proud to have their names seen by everyone present. Prouder still were the parents of the bride and groom; these generous gifts were a reflection of the community's appreciation of the endless hours of service the groom's mother had given as midwife—sometimes without charging any fees at all to the struggling immigrant families. The young couple (and their in-laws) could not possibly consume all the rice they were given, so most of it was sent back to the store.

On the day of the wedding reception the bride left her home dressed in a white formal kimono and accessories. Since the bride and groom lived in the same neighborhood, the bridal procession simply walked down the dirt road from the bride's home to the groom's home. After the bride entered the groom's home, she changed into a brilliant red silk kimono, which symbolized happiness, good fortune, and rebirth into a new life. For the final phase of the ceremony, she changed into the traditional formal black montsuki, a gift from the groom's family, with the Muroda family crest.

The wedding celebration at the groom's parents' home lasted a week. The guests feasted on *kalua* pig (a whole pig roasted Hawaiian-style in an underground oven), fresh fish from the Waianae waters, *sushi* (rice seasoned with vinegar, salt, and sugar), squid, the traditional mori mono assortment of food dishes, and plenty of sake.[41]

On the third day after the reception, the Murodas observed the traditional Japanese village custom of *satogaeri* (having the new bride pay a ceremonial visit to her parents' home). On this occasion Shizume wore a colorful visiting kimono, which had elaborate floral designs on the front skirt. Her hair was recombed into the marumage, the married woman's coiffure.

The wedding of Torao Kobayashi and Takayo Kouchi, which took place on March 31, 1928, at the Honpa Hongwanji Mission of Honolulu, was an exception to the general trend: these two nisei did not have a traditional Japanese wedding; instead, they had a thoroughly Western-style one.

Both the bride and the groom taught at the Wahiawa Japanese Language School. Torao had been born in Honolulu on March 17, 1902, but in his youth he had been sent back to Tokyo to continue his education at the Foreign Language School there. Takayo had been born in Honomu, on the Big Island, on February 22, 1905. Her parents had come to Hawaii from Yamaguchi Prefecture at the turn of the century. Her father had worked his way up from a laborer to an assistant engineer at the Honomu Sugar Mill, and her parents had become affluent enough to send their daughter to Honolulu to attend the Normal School there and also to study at the Honpa Hongwanji Mission Japanese High School.

For the ceremony, the groom was dressed in a tuxedo-style formal black suit, with vest. The bride wore a short dress of white crepe de

Torao and Takayo Kobayashi, who were married March 31, 1928, in a fashionable Western-style wedding. The bride's gown, sewn by Shige Murata of Kiester's Tailoring College, was made of white crepe de chine with a bateau neckline and hand-beaded decoration. Takayo Kobayashi collection.

A nisei couple in traditional Japanese wedding attire. The groom wears a three-fourths-length haori over his black montsuki. 1935. Mabel Hashisaka collection.

Elaine Yayoe Suzuki, dressed in traditional Japanese bridal costume for her marriage to George Wasaku Suzuki on June 27, 1936, at the Daijingu Shinto Shrine in Honolulu. These views show the ornate bridal coiffure to full advantage. Kanaguri Photo Studio. Elaine Yayoe Suzuki collection.

The new bride, Elaine Yayoe Suzuki, about three days after the wedding reception. She has paid the traditional visit to her natal home and has had her hair recombed into the marumage (married woman's coiffure). Tanji Photo Studio, 1936. Elaine Yayoe Suzuki collection.

chine. A cathedral veil of silk tulle, attached to the bride's cloche-style headdress, fell into a long train. Short wedding dresses were very fashionable in the 1920s. Takayo's three bridesmaids wore short dresses of purple satin.[42]

There were other Western-style weddings in the 1920s, but, in general, the trend toward traditional Japanese weddings kept getting stronger and stronger during the decade. By the early 1930s, almost all of the nisei weddings held on the plantations were strictly traditional, and nisei weddings became more and more elaborate until World War II. Issei parents took pride in the lavish receptions they could provide for their children; there was even a feeling of competition among some of the parents, who tried to outdo each other in staging elaborate wedding receptions. Basically, however, the traditional Japanese wedding celebrations were a way for the immigrants to show their pride in their heritage, a way for them to link their lives with the lives of their ancestors. And, for the community as a whole, the elaborate wedding celebrations served still another purpose: they were important social events, festive occasions that provided much-needed breaks from the long hours of hard work in the sugarcane and pineapple fields.

3

Men's Work Clothing

Field Workers

In the early years of the Japanese immigration to Hawaii, the issei men started to work in the sugarcane and pineapple fields wearing their cotton kimono, *momohiki* (fitted pants), and shirts with long, narrow sleeves. Another group—the first Okinawans, the twenty-six who came in January 1900—arrived wearing Chinese coolie outfits, and they wore those into the fields. (These Okinawans had been sold Chinese-style trousers and jackets by the Morioka Immigration Company while they were waiting in Yokohama for their passage to Hawaii.[1] And there were a few other Okinawans—and a few naichi —who purchased coolie outfits for themselves in Yokohama or Kobe on their way to Hawaii.) Many of the issei men wore makeshift work clothes that they put together from various garments they had brought with them; photographs from the early years of 1885 to 1900 show a wide variety of hastily improvised work clothes.

But it did not take the issei men very long to see the practical advantages of the work clothing worn in the pineapple and sugarcane fields by the field workers of other ethnic groups. In a surprisingly short time, the work clothing of the issei men was almost indistinguishable from that worn by the men of other ethnic groups.

JACKETS

The usual men's work jacket was cut along straight lines, with long sleeves, cuffed with a two-and-one-half-inch-wide band that was closed with one or two buttons. The neckline was completed with a pointed, tailored collar. The jacket extended about four or five

Workers at the Oahu Sugar Company plantation in Waipahu. Gensei Maeshiro
(second from the right) was generally considered one of the best-dressed men in
the camp. The woman in the group is his wife. The couple came to Hawaii from
Okinawa in 1907. Iris (Maeshiro) Katsura collection.

inches below the natural waistline and was finished off with a band
about one and one-half inches wide. In the back bodice was a
pointed yoke, stitched on from the top side of the fabric with double
stitching. Some women even inserted extra layers of cotton between
the two layers at the shoulder to reinforce the area where heavy
loads of sugarcane were carried. Such padding helped to prolong the
life of the jacket.[2]

AHINA JACKETS. The fabric most commonly used for work jackets
was an American blue denim, known in Hawaii as *ahina*, which
means blue dye in Hawaiian.

The American ahina fabric came in three different weights and
strengths. Top-quality ahina—called grade one—was heavier and
more durable than the other two grades. It had a coarse, stiff texture
and a dull surface. Although it was strong, it was not as closely

Ahina jacket made by Kaku Kumasaka, *front* and *back* views.

Buttonholes on jacket finished by hand in blanket-stitching with white #10 thread. Blanche Klim. Barbara Kawakami collection.

woven as the other two grades (because of the extra thick staple yarn used). The third grade of ahina was the softest and had the roughest weave. All three were twill weaves.[3]

Another type of ahina that was used for work jackets was German ahina. The Japanese referred to Germany as *Doitsu* and therefore called this fabric, which was imported from Germany, *Doitsu ahina*. Unlike the coarse, stiff American denim, the German ahina was smooth and soft. It was also colorfast and durable and, because of its many fine qualities, was more expensive than the American ahina.[4]

SENSUJI, OR MANSUJI, JACKETS. The most expensive and highest quality fabric used for the issei men's jackets was a cotton fabric called *sensuji*, or *mansuji*, by the issei. *Suji* means lines, or stripes, in Japanese; *sensuji* means a thousand stripes, and *mansuji* means ten thousand stripes. The suji referred to in this case are the stripes running lengthwise in the fabric, against a gray background, and the terms sensuji and mansuji are obviously used to indicate that the fabric has a large number of such stripes.

This fabric is no longer made. And there are very few pieces of it still in existence; most of the plantation workers who owned jackets made of this fabric wore them for gardening after they retired, wore them out, and threw the scraps away. For some time after I began this study, I had to rely entirely on reports I obtained in interviews

Close-up of a piece of sensuji fabric donated by Tei Saito. Blanche Klim. Barbara Kawakami collection.

for information about sensuji, or mansuji, jackets. My most valuable source was Kameko (Kay) Arakawa, who, together with her husband and several other relatives, had operated a tailor shop in Waipahu on the old Depot Road from 1926 to 1946 and, before that, had worked with her father-in-law in the tailor shop located below the sugar mill in Waipahu.

According to Kay Arakawa, sensuji, or mansuji, was heavier and much stronger than ahina and resembled a lightweight canvas cloth. Because of its high quality, it was more expensive than other fabrics generally used for work clothing. The sensuji, or mansuji, jackets were worn primarily by the *konpan* men, as they were called by the plantation people. (*Konpan* was the Japanese pronunciation of the English word *company* and referred to a group of workers who formed a partnership to work a designated area of sugarcane or pineapple land under the direction of a group leader.) This fabric was also worn by other workers who did the heavy manual labor of cutting cane seedlings *(pulapula)* or carrying cane *(hapai ko)*. The men in the hapai ko gang had to carry heavy loads of cut cane on their shoulders to the train cane-cars. And cutting seed cane, the work done by the pulapula gangs (which sometimes included women) also involved constant exposure to the serrated edges of the sugarcane leaves. The men and women who did these jobs really needed jackets made of sensuji, or mansuji, fabric, which lasted longer than any other kind.

I did eventually get to see a piece of sensuji, or mansuji, material. It was given to me by Tei Saito, who had sewn many jackets of this material, for her husband and for other men who worked in the pineapple fields, and had saved three yards of it. But I had just about given up hope of ever finding one of the jackets made of this fabric. Then in June 1985 Arthur Kaneshiro, a *sansei* (third-generation Japanese), came to see the *Kanyaku Imin* (Centennial of Japanese Immigration) Exhibition at the Neal Blaisdell Center in Honolulu and took a special interest in the plantation clothing exhibit that I had arranged there. He noticed that I did not have a work jacket made of sensuji, or mansuji, fabric and informed me that he had one that had been worn by his grandfather, Ryogen Matayoshi, when he was working for the Hakalau Sugar Company in the early 1930s. The jacket had been sewn by Arthur's mother, Elaine Kaneshiro, sometime in the 1930s, when she was still in her teens. Many nisei girls were trained to sew from a very young age, but Elaine was exceptionally talented and met the sewing needs of her entire family. She even sewed work clothes and accessories for the bachelors on the plantations to supplement the family income.

Pupukea Pineapple Plantation konpan gang, led by Masanari Saito. December 12, 1919. Tei Saito collection.

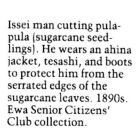

Issei man cutting pulapula (sugarcane seedlings). He wears an ahina jacket, tesashi, and boots to protect him from the serrated edges of the sugarcane leaves. 1890s. Ewa Senior Citizens' Club collection.

Arthur showed me the jacket. It was the style described above except that the waistband was two inches wide instead of the usual one and one-half inches. Mr. Matayoshi's striped work jacket was still in perfect condition; there were no tears, nor was there a single thread out of place. When I asked Arthur how he happened to have such a rare jacket, he told me that his grandfather had given it to him. It had become Arthur's favorite jacket, the one he always wore on family outings. However, after he saw my exhibit, he generously parted with it so that I could include it in my future exhibits.[5]

PALAKA JACKETS. The fabric known as *palaka* became popular for men's jackets in the 1920s. It is a heavy cotton cloth woven in a white plaid pattern with a dark blue background. The word palaka is actually a transliteration into Hawaiian of the English word "frock," the term used for the loose-fitting, long-sleeved work shirts worn by the British and American sailors who came to Hawaii. But gradually the word came to be used instead to mean the type of cloth from which these shirts were made. Apparently, when the Hawaiians asked about the fabric, they were given the name of the style of shirt rather than the name of the fabric. At any rate, the word *palaka* came to mean the dark blue and white woven material still used in today's palaka shirts.[6] The issei referred to the palaka fabric as *gobanji* (the Japanese term for a plaid, or check, design). They were particularly fond of the palaka because it reminded them of the plaid prints in the *yukata* (unlined kimono made of printed cotton) they had worn in the summer months in their villages back home.

The Arakawa store in Waipahu specialized in selling palaka fabrics to the plantation laborers. The Waipahu Plantation Store also kept a good supply of palaka and other fabrics for the plantation families.

During the 1920s and 1930s palaka was woven of 100 percent cotton and was very thick, very strong, and rough in texture. It was available only in navy or dark blue. Palaka sold for about 29 cents a yard in the early 1920s; in the late 1930s, it sold for about 75 cents a yard. Today, Arakawas carries palaka in a variety of colors, and the cloth is now a blend of polyester and cotton; its cost in 1990 ranged from $7.50 to $8.00 a yard. Both the original fabric and the polyester-cotton blend seen today are twill weaves. Today's palaka has a softer texture, and now men's shirts, women's mu'u mu'u, and children's clothes are fashioned from the palaka fabric.

Palaka was widely used by the issei men for field jackets, and these jackets were fashioned in the same way as the other work jackets except that they did not ordinarily have a yoke. Palaka was not as heavy as ahina, but it was durable and its price was reasonable.

Oahu Sugar Company plantation store in Waipahu. Since the Caucasian managers of the plantation stores found it difficult to master the names of the immigrant workers, they developed a system of credit based on the issuance of a numbered metal tag to each worker; this tag, which the Japanese workers called a *bango* ("number" in Japanese) gave the managers information about the ethnicity and status of each worker. Early 1920s. Carol Kobashigawa collection.

Three Ewa Sugar Plantation workers. Takashi Tsurumaki *(left)* wears a palaka jacket; Ichizo Sato *(center)* wears an ahina jacket; Gensho Miyashiro *(right)* wears a sensuji jacket. Dennis Irie, Wallace Sugai, Ewa Plantation Company Centennial Celebration.

Workers at the sugar mill on the Waianae Plantation. Photograph probably taken in 1895. This photograph was reproduced in *Historic Waianae: A Place of Kings*, by Bob Krauss, Edward McGrath, and Kenneth Brown (1973), pp. 38–39, but my

Apparently the early Japanese immigrants used palaka only for work jackets; they did not wear palaka shirts. One of the earliest records of palaka shirts is a photograph taken at the sugar mill at Waianae Plantation.[7] It was probably taken in 1895, which, according to an item in the Hawaiian Sugar Planters' Association file— from the United States Bureau of Immigration's *Reports on Immigration, 1866 to 1914*—was the first year that the Japanese contract laborers were assigned to Waianae Sugar Plantation.[8] In this photo-

reproduction is from a copy of the photograph given to me by Edward McGrath to use in memory of his father-in-law, Harry Yamada.

graph, the Portuguese and Hawaiian laborers are seen wearing palaka shirts. At least fourteen of the laborers in the photograph can be identified as Japanese (they are all seated in the foreground), but none of them are wearing palaka shirts.

TROUSERS

The trousers worn by the men who worked on the plantations were usually plain with four deep pockets, two inseam pockets on the sides and two back hip-pockets. The back hip-pockets, which were usually placed about two and a half inches below the waistband, were done in a double-welt style and were about five and a half to six inches deep and five and a half inches wide. The trouser inseam pockets were generally ten and a half inches in length and about six inches in width. For the pocket inseam lining, the issei women often used the thick material from rice bags, which was just as durable as the pocketing fabric sold at the plantation store. The women also learned to reinforce the lower part of the side pocket lining with double layers of cloth. These pockets were necessary for carrying personal belongings around while doing field work. A watch pocket was inserted under the waistband on the right side of the trouser front, with its opening in the waistband seam.[9]

From the early 1900s to the 1940s the fly closing of trousers was fastened with bone buttons and the buttonholes were finished with blanket-stitching. The bone buttons were imported by Theo H. Davies and were sold in all the plantation stores. (No one seems to know what kind of an animal the bones came from or what country they were imported from.) These buttons were very strong and outlasted the garments. Women always kept a jar of bone buttons handy. When a garment was completely worn out, the buttons would be carefully cut off and saved to use again on new garments.

A bone button was also used to fasten the end of the one-and-one-half-inch waistband. Hem finishing for the trousers varied from one-half inch to three-quarters inch. The belt carriers on the waist usually measured one and one-half to two inches depending on the width of the leather belt. Most men wore one-inch-wide belts made of black or brown leather; these belts were purchased at the plantation stores or through Japanese merchants.

In the early years the issei women sewed all of their husbands' field garments, even the trousers. They preferred to use the best-quality ahina for the trousers, but sometimes they could not afford the best and had to settle for lesser-quality fabric.

As the 1930s neared, some of the issei men began wearing ready-made ahina pants. These pants were sturdy and well-made, and sold at a reasonable price. And, of course, buying ready-made was a godsend to the busy wife, who often worked in the fields for ten hours a day.

HATS

Most of the issei men who worked on the plantations wore straw hats to protect them from sun, rain, and dust. They referred to these hats as *mugiwara bō* (hats woven out of barley straw, the straw hats the men had worn in their home villages). A variety of straw hats can be seen in photographs at the State Archives and the Bishop Museum taken from 1868 to about 1940. Many of the men took a fancy to unusual types of straw hats. One man told me that his two older brothers in Okinawa wove Panama hats to supplement the family income and even exported these hats to the mainland.[10]

The plantation stores sold various types of straw hats, from coolie hats to hats with wide, medium, and narrow brims. And some of the Hawaiian and Chinese women in the camps wove *lau hala* (pandanus leaf) hats and sold them to the issei men for seventy-five cents to a dollar. Both issei and nisei men said that the lau hala hats were so well made that they outlasted store-bought hats.[11]

Another type of hat worn by the issei men was called a *dongorosu.* It was called "dungarees" by the Portuguese and Spanish field workers because it was made from dungaree, the "duck" or lightweight canvas used in making the work trousers known as dungarees; the issei adopted the term, but, since the "s" sound is difficult for Japanese to pronounce, they ended the word with a "su" sound.[12] Sometimes cement bags, which were made of a heavy canvas, were used instead of dungaree to make dongorosu hats.

The dongorosu hat was also referred to as a *konpan papale* (*papale* is the Hawaiian word for hat) because it was worn mostly by the konpan men. It became something of a symbol for the konpan men who toiled in the isolated areas of the plantations. The crown of the dongorosu, or konpan papale, hat was made of five pieces that tapered together at the top; the brim was flat and faced downward. The brim had rows of stitching to reinforce it and to give added protection from the sun. The crown was riveted with an eyelet on the upper part to allow air to go through. These hats sold at the reasonable price of from eighty cents to one dollar. But, in order to economize, many of the issei women would buy a hat, take it apart to trace the pattern, and then sew other hats of this type themselves, making their own eyelets with blanket-stitching instead of a rivet.

The konpan men found the dongorosu hat more practical for them than the straw hat worn by the other plantation workers. They constantly had to walk through the tall, thick stalks of sugarcane, and the flexible brim of the dongorosu hat did not get caught in the tall cane leaves as easily as did the stiffer brim of the straw hat. Also, the dongorosu hat could be washed and boiled like other soiled work clothing.[13]

Mill and Warehouse Workers

Men who worked as plumbers, mill workers, warehousemen, and watchmen at the water pump station usually wore overalls made of heavy ahina. The issei men found the overalls strange at first, but they soon grew to like the loose, comfortable fit of the garment.

American-style overalls were first introduced in about 1905. The commercially produced overalls were reinforced at the pockets and straps, and they were both comfortable and durable. With them the men usually wore blue chambray shirts with long sleeves.

Plantation carpenters wore similar overalls, but theirs were made of heavy white twill or canvas. And theirs had pockets that were made especially long in order to carry hammers and other tools.

Lunas and Camp Police

No one commanded more respect and fear from the laborers than the plantation *luna*, or foreman, astride his horse. Issei men who were promoted to the position of luna wore the same type of trousers worn by Caucasian or Hawaiian lunas: special breeches made of fine khaki.[14] With these khaki breeches, the luna wore leather leggings, a long-sleeved khaki shirt, and a wide-brimmed felt hat.

The "camp police," as the issei called them, also wore khaki

Luna on horseback and luna in the field (with dark jacket) supervising issei laborers cutting sugarcane on Lihue Plantation, Kauai. Photograph taken about 1912–1915. Shizu Kaigo collection.

breeches, leather leggings, khaki shirts, and wide-brimmed hats, and they also rode horses. The mere sight of them made children run in fear, especially during cane-harvesting time when the children were trying to grab a little burnt sugarcane from the cane-cars. At such times the camp police always seemed to appear out of nowhere.

Office Workers

Most of the workers in the plantation offices in the prewar period were Caucasians, but a few issei and nisei men worked alongside the Caucasians. The issei who were given these white-collar jobs were usually men who had had above-average educations in Japan or were equipped with special skills or abilities. The nisei office workers were usually young men whose parents had been able to send them to high school in Honolulu.

The Japanese office workers usually wore tailor-made khaki

Photograph taken in front of the Oahu Sugar Company office, Waipahu Plantation, about 1907. The *fourth man from the left*, in the dark suit, is the plantation manager, E. K. Bull. The man on the *far left* is Torasaku Oyama, a clerk in the supply warehouse; he also served as an interpreter at times. The other men in the photograph are members of the office staff. Barbara Kawakami collection.

pants. One former office clerk told me that he wore dark wool pants or sometimes white linen pants, but that was considered quite dressy attire in a plantation town in prewar days. Most of the office workers wore white shirts, either long- or short-sleeved. Some wore neckties or bow ties.

4
Women's Work Clothing

The issei women, like the issei men, at first took whatever they had brought with them from their homeland and put together makeshift work outfits. Later they also adopted some of the types of clothing worn by other ethnic groups. But the women were more selective than the men in borrowing ideas about clothing; they were not as willing as the men to wear clothing that was indistinguishable from that of the other ethnic groups. They borrowed ideas, but they adapted those ideas to suit their own individual images of themselves.

There were many ideas to choose from in Hawaii. A large group photograph taken of the women of various ethnic backgrounds at the Kilauea Plantation on Kauai in 1888 shows Japanese women wearing the cotton kimono that they brought from Japan, a Chinese woman wearing a traditional Chinese fitted jacket with kimono sleeves and mandarin collar, and Spanish and Portuguese women wearing long gathered skirts, fitted bodices, and long sleeves.[1] Some Norwegian and German women had arrived earlier, and in 1900 Italian and Puerto Rican women came with their husbands, adding to the diversity of the ethnic groups working alongside each other or living in nearby camps on the various plantations.[2]

As the women from the different ethnic groups and cultures came into contact, a gradual exchange of ideas began. The issei women retained some of their traditional ideas and discarded others; they adopted useful ideas from other ethnic groups; often they blended the old and the new. Through this assimilation of new ideas into their traditional costume, the issei women created a unique fashion: the kasuri jacket, the dirndl skirt, the black cummerbund-like sash, and the straw hat.

A detail from a large photograph of women of various ethnic groups at Kilauea Plantation, Kauai, about 1888. The Japanese women are wearing their native kimono with aprons. Hawaii State Archives collection.

The Japanese people have long been noted for their ability to absorb from other cultures elements that they perceive as useful, adapting these elements to suit their specific needs. And the issei women in Hawaii, who soon learned to communicate with other ethnic groups in a language that was neither English nor Japanese but a distinctive plantation pidgin, a mixture of Hawaiian, Portuguese, Spanish, Filipino, English, Chinese, Korean, and Japanese, demonstrated this ability very clearly in the development of their work clothing.

It is impossible to say exactly when or where the issei women's design for their work clothing originated; the process of adaptation was a gradual one. But, according to the issei women who came early as picture brides, most of the new ideas were incorporated sometime during the late 1890s, when the mass assimilation of the various ethnic groups began. The women who came as picture brides during the early 1900s recall that the Japanese women who preceded them were already wearing the kasuri jacket, dirndl skirt, wide black sash, and straw hat.

The picture brides learned to sew from their issei neighbors who had preceded them to the plantation or from women of other ethnic groups who lived in nearby camps. There were many exchanges of

Group of field workers of various ethnic groups at Puunene Sugar Plantation, Maui. About 1915. Kaku Shishido collection.

garment patterns, which the issei women traced onto old newspapers and cardboard. Kaku Kumasaka, whom I interviewed, still had in her possession the Singer sewing machine that she purchased for $100 in 1922; she sewed all her family's clothes on this machine —even heavy work clothes. The only part of the sewing machine that no longer functions is the bobbin winder spindle; when replacements for this part were no longer available, she wound her thread by hand. She used the same sewing machine until the late 1980s.[3]

Many women had their first field garments made either by the plantation seamstress or by a neighbor, then took the garments apart and traced the outlines onto old newspapers. No one had knowledge of flat-pattern making or design; each woman learned through trial and error how to adjust the pattern to fit individual physical measurements. Some women were ingenious enough to add personal touches. Once the issei women learned to sew and acquired the skill of adjusting patterns, many of them began to do sewing for others to supplement their meager income of seventy-five cents for a ten-hour work day.[4]

Three young Okina-
wan brides who
worked at Kekaha
Sugar Plantation on
Kauai. The kasuri
woven in Okinawa
was particularly
colorful and of
fine quality. About
1919. Kenkichi Kane-
shiro collection.

Jackets

The first kind of clothing worn by issei women for field work was
the native kimono, as shown in the 1888 photograph from the
Kilauea Plantation on Kauai. The island of Kauai was one of the first
to be targeted for the production of sugar. Many of the issei I interviewed said that they had first settled on Kauai, where there were
eight plantations in operation by 1877: Koloa, Lihue, Kilauea, Hanalei, Grove Farm, Eleele, Kapaa, and Kawaihau.[5] The photo from
Kilauea shows issei women wearing cotton kimono with the wide
sleeves cut off and tapered into long, fitted sleeves. Before this, the
women probably had worn kimono with standard-length sleeves and
found them too cumbersome for field work. Women who worked in
the fields in their villages in Japan used a narrow cord called *tasuki*
to hold their kimono sleeves behind them while working, but in the

A copy of a kasuri outfit
sent by Zenbei Saito from
Fukushima Prefecture, Japan.
Modeled by Jill Fujioka Lee.
Dean Lee. Barbara Kawakami
collection.

Issei plantation worker on Maui packing harvested pineapples into crates. Her
jacket appears to be made of yukata fabric, her skirt of an American fabric. Slat
sunbonnets were particularly common on Maui. About 1915. Dole Pineapple
Company collection.

tropical heat of Hawaii the issei must have felt that it was wiser to cut off the sleeves to make the garment lighter and less cumbersome.

In the early 1900s nearly all of the issei women working on the plantations in Hawaii were making work jackets out of hand-woven kasuri fabric or hand-woven striped cotton brought from their native villages. However, as time passed and dry goods salesmen peddled their wares throughout the plantation camps, the Japanese women began to purchase whatever caught their fancy or whatever was available. Also, some received gifts of rolls of Japanese kasuri fabric or the less expensive cotton cloth used for *yukata* when they first arrived in Hawaii or when their babies were born. The peddlers usually carried an assortment of fabrics that were imported through Japanese wholesalers from various parts of Japan, so many issei women began wearing kimono fabrics that came from prefectures other than their own. Alice Kuroiwa Scharsch, a nisei who quit school when she was twelve years old to help support her widowed mother and siblings, working alongside the issei, gave me a work jacket made of an intricately woven *Kurume-gasuri* (kasuri with a distinctive design that originated in Kurume, Fukuoka Prefecture). Her mother-in-law had brought this hand-woven fabric already made into a kimono and had given it to Alice to make her work jacket.[6]

One of the first adaptations made by the issei women was to turn the kimono into a jacket similar to the Chinese women's fitted jacket with a narrow mandarin collar and long, tapered, set-in sleeves fastened with one bone button on the wristband. The jacket usually extended five or six inches below the waistline and was worn tucked under the skirtband.[7] The kasuri jackets I examined for this study measured from nineteen to twenty-two inches in length. Generally, the Japanese women were short, averaging from four feet, eight inches to four feet, ten inches in height; a woman of five feet was considered tall. Those who were five feet, two inches or taller seemed to tower over the other women; they probably required extra length for their jackets (and skirts).

In Hamakua, on the Big Island, the women put sport collars on their work jackets. But on all the other plantations in the islands, the women used the Chinese mandarin collar on their jackets. This mandarin collar did not meet in the center front, however. It was set in about one and one-half inches from the center front, and the buttons started about four inches from the top. This must have been more comfortable for working than the traditional mandarin collar.

The bodice seam was not always positioned in the center, nor

Original plantation work clothing worn by Kin Watanabe until she bore her first child in 1921. Modeled by Ushiko Miyasato.

Jacket opened to show lining of bleached rice bags used to extend the life of the garment. Photographs by Blanche Klim. Barbara Kawakami collection.

Work clothing worn by Kauai women, which is somewhat different from that worn on other islands. These two Kauai women are wearing thick ahina jackets and lightweight cotton aprons. Their hat style is also distinctive. The bags at their feet are bentō bags. About 1912. Kauai Historical Museum collection.

equally spaced from the center front as is done in Western clothing. The issei women had no formal training in Western sewing, and their primary concern was to economize by using every bit of the kasuri fabric, which was very narrow; seams were joined wherever it was convenient and practical to fit the individual's body measurements.

The sleeves did not have cuffs but were finished with a plain seam. There were two seams running lengthwise, one in back and the other in front; a gusset was inserted at the underarm. The yoke of the bodice was lined, and extra layers of old fabric were stitched in between to reinforce the upper shoulder, where a heavy load was often carried. Some women lined the bodice of the kasuri jacket with pieces of bleached rice bags. The front closure was usually overlapped about three-fourths of an inch. The buttonholes for the front opening were all hand-sewn with blanket-stitching done with #20 J & P Coats white thread.[8] The buttons were the same kind that were used on the men's trousers—strong, economical bone buttons.

There were various ways of utilizing the narrow kasuri fabric. Some issei women found it easier to divide the entire length of fabric into two parts, using one part for the jacket and the other for the skirt. Others bought the kasuri fabric that was sold in half-bolts and skillfully cut two jackets out of this half-bolt. In any case, the women were more concerned with using every bit of the fabric than with spacing the seams evenly. Thus the jackets were not always uniform in style and shape.[9]

Kon-gasuri, a cotton kasuri dyed with *ai* (vegetable indigo dye), was often used for women's work jackets. The Japanese people were very fond of kimono made of this fabric. It did not fade easily, and it was durable—in fact, many Japanese believed that the natural ai dye actually made the fabric stronger. Thus, farmers and outdoor workers in Japan preferred kimono dyed with ai to other types of work clothing. This preference explains why the issei women—most of whom came from farming villages—continued to use this dyed fabric whenever possible in Hawaii.

Another kasuri often used was the *tsumugi-gasuri*, which also originated with farmers. This kasuri was made from the cocoons that were left over after the best silks had been sold to the markets. The farmers would diligently collect the floss from the cocoons, spin it into thread by hand, and then weave the thread into kimono for the family. The tsumugi-gasuri kimono was unique in that the entire process of spinning the thread, weaving the cloth, and sewing was done by one person; therefore, the wearer often particularly

Young women from the Waipahu Plantation on their way to catch the train to Honolulu to participate in the 1920 strike parade. Yasu Sato recalled: "We marched in Honolulu through downtown. We held large banners telling people how little we got paid. Some of the haole ladies watching the parade cried, they felt so sorry for us." Ruth Nobuko Maki collection.

Kama Asato *(left)* and Kaku Kumasaka *(right)* were the last two issei women employed in the fields of Oahu Sugar Company. Kaku Kumasaka took an early retirement in 1964, after working for the company for nearly thirty-two years. Waipahu Cultural Garden Park collection.

treasured this kimono.[10] The women I interviewed were always nostalgic when they spoke of the tsumugi-gasuri. The thread produced for this fabric was strong, elastic, and glossy, and it was usually woven into bold and creative designs—stripes, checks, or splash designs. It is no wonder that the issei women prized these handspun silk kimono and, when the kimono were almost worn out, remodeled them into field clothing.

By the late 1930s, when only a small number of issei women were still working in the sugarcane and pineapple fields, some of these women began to wear the same kind of palaka jackets that their male counterparts wore (and the same kind of ahina pants). But other issei women continued to use kasuri for work jackets as long as it was available—almost until World War II.

Skirts

The skirts worn with the kasuri jackets were either simple gathered skirts, that is, dirndls, or pleated skirts of various kinds—single one-way pleats, box pleats, inverted pleats, or clusters of single pleats.

Originally, the issei women used the twelve-inch-wide kasuri fabric in four panels to fashion these skirts. But they soon found that such skirts did not provide enough fullness to be comfortable when working in the fields. They noticed that the Hawaiian, Portuguese, and Spanish women wore much fuller skirts that seemed to be more suitable for field work. The Hawaiian women had learned to sew their gathered skirts from the missionary women, and the Portuguese and Spanish women had traditionally worn long, gathered skirts in their native lands. The issei women soon realized that using a larger number of panels of kasuri was not the best solution, either. It was not only easier and faster but also far more economical to use thirty-six-inch-wide American cotton fabric, which cost ten cents a yard. Three lengths of the American fabric would make a short dirndl skirt; it would require a considerable number of panels of the narrow kasuri to produce the same amount of fullness. It was therefore actually wasteful to use the precious hand-woven kasuri for skirts.

Many of the issei women economized still further by using the most salvageable parts of their old, worn-out cotton yukata to make skirts. (The rest of the worn-out yukata was used to reinforce the shoulder or yoke of a jacket.)

The construction methods used by the issei women were quite simple. As they gradually learned to sew from the neighborhood Portuguese and Spanish women, those who used sewing machines learned to gather the waist part of the skirt by using a stronger thread for the bobbin than for the needle. Those who sewed by hand learned to use a short Japanese needle to draw the gathers. Some of the issei women also learned to make pleated skirts from the Portuguese and Spanish women. For the issei women who were accustomed to using a narrow fabric with limited possibilities of designing, the American fabrics offered new freedom in creating styles. The women found that it really did not matter whether the pleats were evenly spaced or of equal depth; they learned to feed in the appropriate amount of fabric, measuring with their eyes as they stitched along. The gathered or pleated skirt was finished off with a one-and-a-half-inch-wide waistband and fastened with a hand-finished buttonhole and a bone button. This new type of skirt obviously gave much more comfort and freedom than the traditional wrap-around kimono, which restricted movements.

Ewa Plantation women workers at the old St. Joseph's Church in Waipahu. Photograph taken December 1919. Haruno Tazawa collection.

At first the issei women made their skirts long, but they soon discovered that long skirts were hazardous for work in thick brush and dangerous terrain. So they began to cut their skirts shorter. By the early 1900s the issei women's skirts usually ended just below the knee or at mid-calf. The shorter skirt gave increased comfort and physical mobility; it also saved yardage.

When buying American fabric for their skirts, issei women favored conservative prints, usually in black and white, often the tiny floral or geometric prints that were always available at the plantation store. Some women preferred plaids, checks, and stripes that resembled the patterns in the hand-woven fabrics they had worn back in their home villages. Judging from the photographs, these fabrics blended well with the kasuri jackets.

Sashes

To complete her outfit, the issei woman wore a black cummerbund-like sash to hold her jacket and skirt in place. The sash could be made of any type of black cotton cloth, but was usually made of percale or sateen. It was about two and one-half yards long and eighteen inches wide. The seam edge was not usually sewn.[11]

This sash was the counterpart of the obi worn with the kimono and, like it, had a symbolic significance for the issei women. There had always been strong sentiments associated with the obi. In many parts of Japan, when a girl reached the age of three, relatives presented her with an obi to celebrate the happy occasion. The celebration known as *shichi go san* (literally, "the lucky numbers of seven, five, and three," a time in late October when children who have reached these ages are taken to a Shinto shrine to offer gratitude for their blessings) began with the idea of the obi worn as a mark of growth. Also, when a young woman became engaged, it was customary for the groom's family to send an obi to the bride's parents as part of the exchange of betrothals, and this custom was observed by the Japanese in Hawaii until World War II. One issei woman described her sentiments about the wearing of the obi in the fields as follows:

> The long black sash was used mainly for the purpose of holding the jacket and skirt firmly in place. We were so used to wearing an obi back in the village that the wide sash tightly wound around our waist gave us a feeling of assurance and comfort. . . . It also brought us closer to the village we left behind.[12]

In the interviews I conducted with issei women who worked on many different plantations—for example, Waipahu, Ewa, Waianae,

Three issei women in their
work outfits in Waipahu in
1916. Haru Ueno *(left)*, Haru
Sato *(middle)*, and Yasu Sato
(right) wear kasuri jackets
with dirndl skirts and aprons
of American fabric. Their
outfits are completed by black
cummerbund sashes, tesashi,
kyahan, straw hats, and tenugui. Note the "dollar pocket
watches" carefully tucked into
their sashes. Murakoshi Photo
Studio. Haru Ueno collection.

Kame Nakasone, completing
her work outfit with the black
sateen obi usually worn with
casual kimono in Japan. She
arrived in Hawaii on March
12, 1919, when she was thirteen, and she began working
at Kekaha Plantation on Kauai
a year later. 1920. Kame Nakasone collection.

Koloa, Lihue, Hakalau, Hilo, Olaa, and Paia—I found that there
were some variations in the obi to suit individual tastes, but these
variations were minor. A few women wore white sashes instead of
black. The length of the sash varied only from two yards, twelve
inches to about three yards. The width of the sash seldom varied at
all, since the women got the eighteen-inch width by splitting the
standard thirty-six-inch-wide percale in half. Some of the sashes
were neatly finished with a one-fourth-inch rolled hem, machine-
stiched in white thread.[13] The sashes wore surprisingly well; sometimes the edges came unstitched, but despite continuous use and
the harsh laundry methods used in the early plantation days (soiled
garments were boiled), the raw edges seldom raveled much.

Momohiki

In Japan, the issei women had never worn underpants; instead,
under their kimono, they wore wrap-around underskirts called
koshimaki. When they came to Hawaii, they, of course, continued
to wear koshimaki under their kimono. Some of the issei women on
the plantations made these underskirts out of *sarashi* (unbleached
muslin), bleached ricebags, calico, or cambric. They found the
bleached rice bags particularly comfortable to wear as underclothing
because the bleaching process had softened the texture of the material and it absorbed perspiration well.

When the issei women first began to wear skirts rather than
kimono for work in the fields, they naturally continued to wear
their koshimaki—now under their skirts instead of under their
kimono. But the koshimaki were fairly tight and took away some of
the freedom of movement that the skirts granted. And there was
another good reason why it was not wise to wear only a koshimaki
under a skirt: field work required a great deal of bending over, and
the women were often working with men in the fields; when the
wearer of a short skirt bent over, much too much might be revealed.
After being teased a few times, the issei women quickly learned to
substitute underpants for koshimaki.

Ankle-length breeches, or pantaloons, called *momohiki* with
pleats in front and back, had been worn in Japan to do farm work;
they were tied over the kimono to protect it and allow greater freedom of movement. In Hawaii the issei women revived this garment
but, instead of wearing it on the outside, wore it underneath the full
skirt to cover up the lower part of the body.

There were many variations of the momohiki. One of the first
had a waistband that was closed with a single bone button instead of

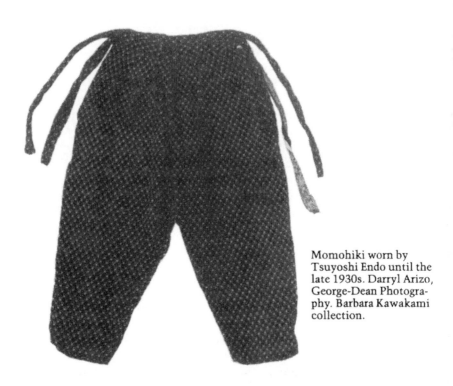

Momohiki worn by
Tsuyoshi Endo until the
late 1930s. Darryl Arizo,
George-Dean Photogra-
phy. Barbara Kawakami
collection.

Adaptation of traditional
momohiki; fastened with
buttons instead of ties.
Blanche Klim. Barbara
Kawakami collection.

ties. It also had a six-inch placket on the left side; to make it easier for the wearer to use the "outdoor facilities," this placket had no buttons or snaps or hooks.

Another type of momohiki, created by a woman who came from Fukushima Prefecture in 1922, was fashioned like the usual momohiki except that it was open on both sides and the sides were overlapped about an inch and a half and held in place by a long sash that extended from the waistband, completely encircled the waist, and tied in front. The women who created this style said that this type of momohiki was particularly comfortable during pregnancies. The overlapped side openings allowed for expansion and avoided the discomfort of a snug side seam.[14]

One of the most ingenious variations was made by a woman who came as a yobiyose from Yamaguchi Prefecture in 1916 at the age of sixteen. Her momohiki was similar to the others in front, with gathers across the waist; however, instead of closing the back with a center seam, this woman left the seam open, made the back panels wider, and overlapped the panels diagonally, securing them in place by means of long sashes that tied in front. Like the momohiki that overlapped on the sides, her momohiki was adjustable to any figure and a pregnant women could wear it comfortably through the final month. And the overlap in back made it much easier for women to use the "outdoor facilities."[15]

There were many other variations in the momohiki. For example, although most women wanted their momohiki to be ankle-length in order to provide the greatest possible protection from the sharp sugarcane leaves, some perferred to wear theirs knee-length. And some women lined the crotch area to extend the life of the garment.

Most of the issei women used Indian Head fabric in pastel colors for their underpants.[16] This fabric was very popular for clothing during the plantation era because it was colorfast and durable. Some women made their momohiki out of red-and-white-checked gingham, which added a welcome bit of brightness to their otherwise rather dark outfits. It took about one and a half yards of material to make a momohiki.[17]

Aprons

Many types of aprons were worn by Japanese women at home and at work in the fields. (The issei usually called them *apuron*, the Japanese pronunciation of the English word apron.) Aprons worn in the home were much like those worn by women of other ethnic groups in the plantation camps. They usually covered the whole front of the woman and had narrow straps going around the neckline. Most of the home aprons were gathered in front and finished off with a long narrow sash that was tied in the back. Some had dainty rows of tucks near the hemline, and others were decorated with ruffles and embroidery. The home aprons were made out of American dress fabrics, usually checked or striped gingham. Some women favored bold plaids that resembled the designs on their kimono.

The most important apron, however, was the full-length ahina, or denim, apron worn for protection from the sharp stalks of the sugarcane. Such aprons, which were commonly worn on all the plantations, were made of either American or German ahina. To make them, the women used the entire twenty-eight-inch width of the ahina; some women kept the selvage exposed, while others turned back the selvage and made an inch-wide hem to give the apron more firmness. The full denim aprons measured between thirty-two and

Haruno Tazawa's apron made of German, or "Doitsu," ahina. Modeled by Blanche Klim. Michael Pecsok. Barbara Kawakami collection.

thirty-six inches in length and extended below the knee, sometimes to mid-calf.

Some women used burlap bags instead of ahina for aprons, since these bags cost nothing; they were given out freely by the plantations. And some made aprons from cement bags, which were made of heavy canvas. The plantation laborers latched onto discarded cement bags whenever they were available, and they utilized them for many things.

Most of the women workers on the plantations wore a second apron, a small one, which they called *maekake* or *maedare*, over the dirndl skirt and under the full-length denim apron. Some women even wore an additional burlap bag over the hips; this provided extra protection from the sharp sugarcane stalks and also saved wear and tear on the denim apron.[18]

Hats

One of the most interesting components of the issei woman's work outfit was the straw hat. The boater hat, a stiff hat of braided straw, with a flat crown and brim, originated in France and was all the rage in the United States in the 1890s. It gradually caught on in Hawaii, and by the time the picture brides arrived in Hawaii in the early 1900s it was common to see issei women in kasuri jackets, dirndl skirts, black sashes, and boater hats working in the fields.

Underneath the boater hat—or, in some cases, over it—the women wore a triangular-shaped kerchief made of muslin or bleached rice bag. This kerchief measured sixty inches on the diagonal and thirty-nine inches on the other two sides. It was wrapped around the head with the pointed ends crisscrossing under the chin, then drawn to the back of the neck and tied in a small knot.[19] The kerchief covered the hair, the ears, and most of the face.

Some women bought men's straw hats from Arakawas or other Japanese stores. They always referred to these straw hats as *mugi-wara bō* (hats woven out of barley straw) because they reminded them of the barley-straw hats they had worn in their home villages.

An interesting modification of a store-bought straw hat is shown in a photograph of Shizume Nakamura (who later became Mrs. Robert Muroda) taken at the Waianae Plantation about 1923. When I first saw this photograph, I did not know who the girl in the photograph was; she was not identified. I was curious about the origin of her unusual hat, so I showed the photograph to various people who I thought might be able to provide an explanation. They came up with some interesting guesses. One woman said that the hat

Shizume Nakamura, a nisei, wearing a kasuri outfit with an unusual straw hat that was the fashion on Waianae Sugar Plantation. Photograph taken about 1923. Originally published in *Historic Waianae: A Place of Kings*, by Bob Krauss, Edward McGrath, and Kenneth Brown (1973), p. 117. My reproduction is from a copy of the photograph given to me by Edward McGrath to use in memory of his father-in-law, Harry Yamada.

Three pregnant issei women working on the sugar plantation at Paia, Maui. Early 1900s. Bishop Museum collection.

reminded her of a round Chinese placemat used for serving tea; she suggested that the wearer might have created this practical hat by simply putting a scarf through the center of such a placemat.[20] A nisei woman who had visited her mother's village in Kumamoto Prefecture as a young girl said that the peasants in that village had used a hat of that sort in the rice fields to scare birds away and that similar hats were worn by folk dancers during village festivals. She thought the girl in the picture might have brought this hat from her village and used it for a different, more practical purpose.[21] There the matter remained for some time. Eventually, however, I was able to establish the identity of the girl in the photograph, and, when I did, I was able to ask her about the hat. Shizume told me that she— and some of the other women at the Waianae Plantation—bought straw hats at the Japanese store in Waianae for fifty cents each, took them home and soaked them in water until they were pliable enough to bend into the shape they wanted, and attached a long scarf, pulling it through the crown of the hat, and kept it in place with a hatpin.

Another unusual type of straw hat is the slat sunbonnet shown in a photograph of three expectant picture brides who worked at the sugar plantation at Paia, Maui. The straw hats worn by these women were entirely different from the ones worn by the women workers on Oahu plantations, and their origin was a mystery to me until I interviewed Taniyo Tanimoto. She not only provided the details about how she had learned to make this type of straw bonnet but also gave me the last straw bonnet she had made in the 1930s. (It had been worn until the 1940s, and only the neck covering had had to be replaced before World War II.) She said that she had not been able to afford to buy a straw hat with the meager seventy-five cents she earned for ten hours of work a day, so she had made her own, an adaptation of a style worn by a Spanish neighbor. She obtained the material for the hat from the proprietor of a Chinese grocery store on King Street in Honolulu, where she went once a year to stock up on items that were difficult to obtain in isolated Paia. The kindly Chinese proprietor always gave her the straw matting that was used for wrapping tea exported from China. Since this matting was very crinkly, she sprinkled it with water and then dried it out; as it dried, the mat flattened out. She got four brims out of one matting. She quilted the underside of the wide brim with cotton cloth to make the brim stronger and provide more protection from the scorching sun. She made the back part of the crown slightly puffed to allow room for the bun on her hairdo. To the edge of the crown she attached a rectangular piece of cloth about eight inches long to pro-

Sunbonnet that Ayako
Kikugawa made in the
1920s. She wore it while
working in the pineapple
fields. Darryl Arizo,
George-Dean Photography.
Barbara Kawakami
collection.

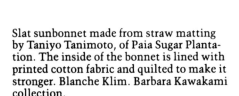

Slat sunbonnet made from straw matting
by Taniyo Tanimoto, of Paia Sugar Plantation. The inside of the bonnet is lined with
printed cotton fabric and quilted to make it
stronger. Blanche Klim. Barbara Kawakami
collection.

tect her neck from the heavy field dust. And she attached two narrow sashes, seventeen inches long and five-eighths of an inch wide,
starting parallel to the ears. These sashes tied underneath her chin,
and she secured the hat to the bun of her hairdo with a hat pin.[22]

A hat closely resembling this issei woman's bonnet was popular
during the early 1800s to the 1850s in France.[23] Margaret Schleif,

Issei women working in potato fields of Oahu Sugar Company in Waipahu. They are wearing straw hats that were often called *manjū* (tea cake) hats because they were shaped like Japanese tea cakes. Since the women are wearing palaka jackets, the photograph probably cannot have been taken before the mid-1930s. Goro Arakawa collection.

who was the curator and registrar of the Mission House Museum when I interviewed her in 1979, has suggested that this bonnet should be traced to the influence of early missionary women: the fashion had reached New England in the early part of the century and was brought to Hawaii by the missionary women.[24]

There were several variations of these slat sunbonnets—most notably the Shaker bonnets, sometimes referred to as poke bonnets; these were smaller, but also made of straw.

5

Work Accessories for Men and Women

Many accessories were necessary to make it possible to endure hard work in the sugarcane and pineapple fields in Hawaii. Field workers needed protection against the sharp edges of the sugarcane stalks and pineapple leaves. They also needed protection against the tropical sun and against the field dust that entered the nostrils, lungs, eyes, ears, and hair. And there were sometimes sudden rainstorms that caught the workers off guard in fields where no shelter was available. Most of all, issei men and women dreaded the sting of a centipede or scorpion. To protect themselves from all these things, the issei workers put to use many accessories that they had used on their farms in Japan. If they did not have the specific accessory with them, they searched around the plantation villages and nearby mountains and seashore for a substitute. They were skilled in handicrafts, and they quickly learned to improvise with whatever materials they could find around them. They also exchanged ideas with people from other ethnic groups who lived in nearby camps; each ethnic group had its own specialty or specialities. And sometimes, if the skills involved were difficult to master, the groups simply exchanged articles.

Kappa

One of the most indispensable accessories for issei plantation laborers was the *kappa*, a raincoat made of muslin that was treated to make it water-repellent. Especially during the fall and spring seasons, the field workers were often caught in heavy downpours and would be completely drenched if they had neglected to take their kappa. In Hilo, where it often rains, there was a saying "Even if you forget your *bentō* (lunch), don't forget your kappa!" The workers did not stop work when it rained; no matter how hard it rained, the work had to be done. The kappa, then, was an essential part of everyone's work clothing.

American-made rubber raincoats were available at stores for about five dollars, but that was too high a price for the immigrants to pay. Buying a rubber raincoat would mean sacrificing five days of pay, or fifty hours of backbreaking labor. A muslin kappa could be made for about half that cost. A Japanese wife understood that half of her husband's paycheck had to be sent to his parents in Japan, so she took pains to help save money. Usually, she was the one who sacrificed evening or weekend hours to make kappa. (There were a few women who could never master the techniques of Western sewing; either they asked their women friends to sew for them in exchange for something they could do better or they bought muslin kappa at Arakawas.) There was another good reason not to buy a rubber raincoat: it would become very heavy when it got wet and its weight would hamper the movement of the relatively small issei.

The kappa was worn by Japanese plantation field workers throughout the islands—on Hawaii, Oahu, Maui, Kauai, Molokai, and Lanai. People of other ethnic groups also used it. There were slight variations in the design and construction of the kappa, but the basic lines and method of construction were the same. The kappa was a full-length coat with a mandarin collar and wide kimono sleeves, and, whether made for men or women, it closed left over right on the front bodice.[1] It was made of heavy muslin. Generally, it was treated with *kakishibu* (persimmon tannin), then treated with a mixture of turpentine and linseed oil (although some issei left out the turpentine and used linseed oil alone). The kakishibu tightened the fabric and thus made it easier to rub on the linseed oil. The linseed oil, or the mixture of linseed oil and turpentine, completed the process of making the fabric water-repellent.

The kappa has a long history; its use in Japan dates all the way back to the Heian Period (794–1185). The first kappa were made of *washi* (paper produced from mulberry bark). The paper was treated with kakishibu, which gave the kappa a texture similar to that of deerskin. This paper kappa was fashioned into a long caftan with a wide kimono collar extending almost to the hemline. The front of the caftan overlapped left over right, like the modern kimono, and it was held together by a pair of long braided cords tied in front. The left front cord was positioned several inches higher than the right side cord.[2] Another type of paper kappa that was worn by peasants and laborers was similar to the *happi* (workman's livery coat) worn today: it was shorter than the standard kimono (reaching about mid-calf), and its sleeves were shorter as well. These kappa were treated with paulownia-seed oil.[3] Still another type of paper kappa that was used during the Edo Period (1603–1868) was fashioned like a Chinese jacket with short kimono sleeves.[4]

In the mid-sixteenth century, the Portuguese brought with them to Japan their rain capes (Portuguese word, *capa*; Japanese transliteration, *kappa*), which were made of wool. This Western fashion was adopted by the military elite in Japan, but the commoners still wore the handmade kappa treated with oil. During the Edo Period cotton cloth also began to be used in place of paper in making kappa.[5]

The issei, therefore, had prototypes in Japan for the raincoats that they wore when working in the sugarcane and pineapple fields in Hawaii. But I think it would not be an exaggeration to say that the kappa that became famous throughout the plantation towns in Hawaii was created through the genius of Zenpan Arakawa. Zenpan came to Hawaii in 1904, with the third large group of Okinawan contract laborers, to work for Oahu Sugar Company. While working in the sugarcane fields, he realized that the issei workers needed functional and sturdy work clothing and accessories that they could buy at a price they could afford. As he labored in the fields, Zenpan took orders for sewing and mending work that he did at night to earn extra money. Without previous training in sewing or tailoring, he taught himself to sew by taking apart old garments and studying the construction and sewing methods. Later, he enrolled in sewing classes to develop his skill in various phases of garment production. After the Japanese workers' strike in 1909 Zenpan left the plantation to open his own tailor shop in Waipahu, below the Oahu Sugar Company sugar mill. Zenpan supplied the plantation community with denim work jackets and trousers and with hats, aprons, kappa, and other accessories.

Because Zenpan offered a wide variety of sewn products and the demand for his kappa was great, he invested in seven Singer power sewing machines to speed up production. Zenpan Arakawa was one of the first issei to go into the mass production of garments; before 1927, almost all sewing was done on treadle sewing machines. Kay Arakawa, the wife of Zenpan's nephew Taro, remembers that Araka-was produced three to four hundred kappa per week. Theo H. Davies became the sole distributor for the Arakawa kappa, which was sold throughout the islands from 1927 to the outbreak of World War II.

Zenpan was assisted by his children, by his older brother Kama,

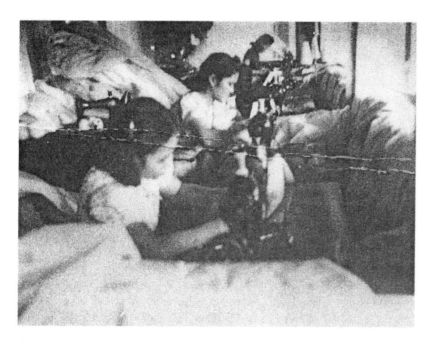

Original Arakawa Tailor Shop, founded by Zenpan Arakawa, who designed the first plantation kappa. He also pioneered the mass production of kappa and other work accessories by investing in Singer power sewing machines. 1932 or 1933. Kay Arakawa collection.

by Kama's oldest son, Taro, by Taro's wife, Kay, and by other relatives; all of them worked hard to make kappa production in Hawaii a success. Kay Arakawa worked at the Arakawa tailor shop for many years after her marriage to Taro in 1926. Taro supervised the application of the water-repelling formulas; Zenpan's sons Shigemi, Takemi, and Goro worked with Taro in this phase of the operation. Taro went to Okinawa to study the way kakishibu was used there to waterproof umbrellas. And, after much experimentation, he developed what seemed to be the perfect mixture to apply over the base coat of kakishibu—one that even made the kappa fire-retardant and safe for shipping. He mixed it himself and cooked it over low heat until it was the right consistency. Unfortunately, Taro was the only person who made the mixture, and, when he died, the secret died with him.[6]

Kay Arakawa was able to give me a detailed description of the way kappa were made at Arakawas. Until 1927, when he invested in a commercial pattern cutter, Zenpan did all the cutting manually.

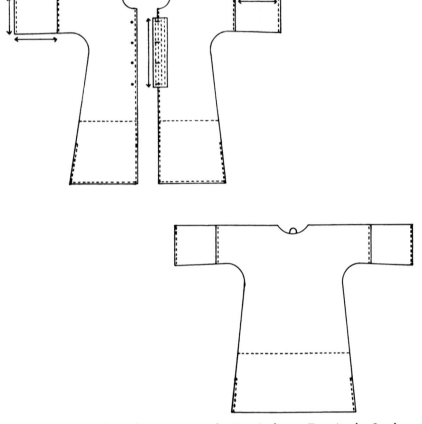

Design for the Arakawa kappa as given by Kay Arakawa. Drawing by Stephen Yuen from an original drawing by Barbara Kawakami.

Out of heavy top-quality muslin, he cut an A-line coat shape with wide, extended kimono sleeves. Since there was no shoulder seam, the fabric was folded in half lengthwise (down the center of the entire length of fabric) to determine the position of the collar. A moon-shaped cardboard pattern was placed at the marked shoulder line; there were patterns in different colors for the different neckline sizes (small, medium, and large). The neckline was lower in front than in back, as in any type of garment.

Because muslin came in thirty-six-inch-wide bolts and the bodice of the kappa took up the whole width, the kappa maker had to add a piece of fabric to get a sleeve that was long enough. This extended part of the kimono sleeve was cut in the same grain as the bodice. The joined seam of the sleeve and bodice was top-stitched for reinforcement. The next step was to sew the side seam and hemline of the coat. Before the collar and front overlap were attached to the bodice, the unfinished coat was sent to the warehouse to be treated with kakishibu and with the mixture of linseed oil, turpentine, and fire-retardant chemical.

The kappa had a mandarin collar that was one and a quarter inches wide and was machine-stitched in fine lines to make it stiff and strong. After treatment with the water-repellent solution, the collar was set aside until the final stages of garment assembly.

The overlap panel for the front opening was double-layered and was four or five inches wide. This was reinforced with fine machine-stitching. Buttonholes were made on the overlap panel before it was attached to the garment. This panel was also treated with the water-repellent solution and then set aside until the final stages of assembly.

The waterproofing process was a lengthy one. The kakishibu was applied first. Then the fabric was given a first coating of the mixture of linseed oil, turpentine, and fire-retardant chemical. The oil had to be rubbed on with a rag because it was too sticky to spread with a brush; only a soaked rag could spread linseed oil evenly on the muslin surface. The fabric with its first coating was left to dry for a few days in a huge open warehouse on Depot Road in Waipahu, facing the Chinese paddy fields. It was then given a second coating, which turned the color to a deep canary yellow, and was again allowed to dry for a few days. When completely dry, the pieces were taken back to the tailor shop to be put together.

The mandarin-shaped collar and a back neck loop were sewn in between the outer oil-treated bodice and a lightweight muslin lining. (The back neck loop was used to hang the kappa on one of the hooks found on the back porch or in the bathhouse of nearly every plantation home.) Attaching the lining to the bodice was the most difficult part of the entire process because of the differences between the two materials in thickness and texture; Kay Arakawa and Shizuko Tamashiro, one of Zenpan Arakawa's daughters, were in charge of this part of the assembly work.[7] Finally, the front panel piece was stitched on to the front left side of the kappa. And the kappa was completed by sewing on bone buttons.

Some issei women bought a kappa from the Arakawa Store and then did exactly what Zenpan had done to teach himself how to make various garments: they took the kappa apart, learned how it was put together, and made a pattern. Some who were even more frugal borrowed a kappa pattern a friend had made. And, in time, many of the women became quite proficient in kappa-making.

Many issei were accustomed to using kakishibu as a base coat in making garments water-repellent. The kakishibu was imported from Japan and cost seventy-five cents for a small bottle. But for some issei that was too expensive. Taniyo Tanimoto, for instance, who worked on Paia Sugar Plantation, said that she soon decided that the imported kakishibu was too expensive, because she had to work ten hours to earn seventy-five cents. So she experimented and found that she could get satisfactory results by substituting a solution used as a base coat by painters when they painted plantation houses.[8] And some issei laborers at Waianae Sugar Plantation who also found kakishibu too costly began experimenting with the bark of trees that was available in the mountains and valleys of the Waianae region and found an ideal substitute in the reddish-brown liquid that they obtained by boiling the bark of the *kukui* (candle nut tree, *Aleurites Moluccana*). When I asked Robert Muroda if the issei had learned this technique from the native Hawaiians, he said that he thought not; instead, "The issei remembered how the umbrella was treated for waterproofing back in their village in Japan. It was an innovative idea that grew out of necessity."[9]

The issei also developed some techniques for making the kappa last longer and for making them more comfortable. After the kappa had been worn in the fields for about three or four months, perspiration and the Hawaiian "red dirt" became embedded in the oil-treated muslin kappa. Instead of laundering the kappa like a regular garment, the Japanese then applied another coat of linseed oil, rubbing it on with a rag. The iron-rich red dirt embedded in the oil gave the fabric the appearance of tan suede and made it stiffer and more water-repellent, but it also made the kappa less comfortable to wear; when the fabric got wet, it became very slick.[10] Rikio Anzai, an old-timer who devoted his life to plantation work, remembers a technique used on new kappa: he says that kappa were always sticky when new and some people used to put ashes on the sticky parts to make the raincoats less sticky and more wearable. But, he added, little could be done about the fact that the kappa retained heat and was, therefore, always uncomfortable to wear.[11]

In Waianae, and undoubtedly in some other remote areas, the issei did not limit the kappa to its use as a raincoat. Waianae was still wilderness in the late 1890s; although it was one of the first places on Oahu to have an operating sugar mill (in 1878), it was isolated from other communities. During those early years, many women worked in the sugarcane fields even during their pregnancies; in fact, it was not uncommon to see issei women still working during their last month of pregnancy in order to earn the twenty-sixth-day pay of fifteen dollars with a bonus of one dollar. When these women started having labor pains while working in isolated fields, some were able to walk home but others had their babies right there in the fields.

No doctors or hospitals were available in Waianae, but, fortunately, a very capable self-taught midwife, Tome Muroda, served the entire area from Waianae to Nanakuli, and even as far as Ewa if someone needed help. She was often summoned to distant fields to deliver babies. Sometimes she walked several miles to get to the field; sometimes she rode on a horse or mule. The first problem was to find a safe place to deliver the baby. Then, with the help of field workers, Mrs. Muroda made a space the size of a large bucket in one of the furrows in the cane fields. She placed a kappa in the hole, oiled side down, to serve as a receptacle in which to wash the newborn baby. Mrs. Muroda's son has warm memories of the way people in those days helped each other in times of need. Fellow workers pitched in to start a fire with dry twigs, dry cane leaves, and whatever else was available; when the fire was going, they boiled water in a five-gallon can borrowed from the water boy. And, after the birth, mothers who had brought their babies to work would share their diapers—made from old cotton yukata or from bleached rice bags—with the new mother.

Mrs. Muroda was quite skilled in handling even complicated cases such as breech deliveries. And when babies were born not breathing, she knew how to start them breathing by pressing a certain nerve in the back of the neck; she had learned this technique from Dr. Kaneshige, a well-known judo instructor of the period.

Issei mothers returned to work as soon as their babies were strong enough to be strapped to their backs. They wanted to nurse their own babies and did not want to leave them with strangers. And, in any case, most of them could not have afforded to pay a babysitter the $1.50 or $2.00 a month that would have been required. When I interviewed Mr. Muroda, he said he could still see the tiny figures of these young mothers with their babies tied to their backs, a denim bag over one shoulder, another large bag filled with tent equipment and diapers over the other shoulder, and a hoe in one hand; they practically had to drag themselves across the fields.

Once she reached her work area, the young mother dug four holes to pitch a tent for her baby. She pounded the tops of the poles with a heavy rock to set the poles firmly in the ground, and then she used a kappa to form a tent to shield the baby from the hot sun. Often the lunas helped to pitch these tents. A kappa might also be used as additional ground cover over the straw matting in rocky terrain; it even kept the insects away.[12]

The kappa has been the most difficult garment for me to obtain. Even the Arakawas, who originated and mass-produced kappa in Hawaii, did not have one when I first approached them in 1979; Arakawas had ceased production of kappa during World War II and none of the earlier kappa had been saved. Many of the issei women who had sewn kappa at home and sold them to supply stores also stopped producing them during the war because of strict regulations applied to aliens. Some people did continue to sew kappa after the war, but by then raincoats produced from nylon and polyester materials had begun to appear on the market and, since these raincoats were lighter and more comfortable, they soon replaced the kappa.

It was not until 1985, the centennial year of Japanese immigration to Hawaii, that a kappa used during the plantation days appeared. It came from Robert Mukai, who saw my Japanese immigrant plantation clothing exhibit at the Neal Blaisdell Center and noticed that I did not have any kappa in my collection. Mr. Mukai had worked summers for the Honomu Sugar Company on the Big Island from the age of nine and, like most of the nisei boys in the area, had begun working full time after grade school. And his parents had run a supply store at the Honomu Plantation and had sold kappa to the plantation laborers. These kappa were sewn by Ine Nakamura (Robert Mukai's mother-in-law) and a Mrs. Ishimura of Olaa, Hawaii, and displayed fine workmanship. Mr. Mukai donated his own kappa to help further my research on plantation clothing.

I found another kappa later, quite by accident, at Camp 1, above the sugar mill, in Waipahu Plantation. While visiting an old friend, I saw the kappa hanging on a nail on the back porch, as if waiting for the man of the house to wear it to work the next morning. The kappa had belonged to Tomii Yahiro, who died in 1965, and it had hung there ever since. His wife, Kimiko Yahiro, had thought of discarding it many times, but she had sewn the kappa and treated it with kakishibu and linseed oil herself, and she had kept it because it reminded her of her husband.[13] She kindly gave it to me to help me in my study.

Ashigappa

A kind of plantation work clothing closely related to the kappa was the *ashigappa*. The word ashigappa literally means "kappa for the legs," or "leg covering." No one knows the origin of this uniquely

Kappa sewn by Ine Nakamura and sold at the Mukai Store in Honomu on the Big Island of Hawaii. It was worn by Robert Mukai until he retired from plantation work. Photograph by Patricia Kay. Waipahu Cultural Garden Park collection.

Front view of ashigappa. It is overlapped in the front and tied in the back.

Back view of ashigappa. The seat is cut out to make it comfortable for the wearer to bend over. Patricia Kay. Waipahu Cultural Garden Park collection.

shaped garment, which was often called *apuron pansu*, or "apron pants," because it seemed to be a combination of a long apron and pants. The back part was completely open, to make it easier for the wearer to bend over while working in the fields. The crisscross section in front ended with a long, narrow sash that was tied securely around the waist.

Pineapple field workers wore ashigappa made out of heavy canvas or duck—not waterproofed—as protection against cuts and bruises from the sharp, serrated edges of the pineapple leaves. Even school children who worked in the pineapple fields only during summer vacations were required to wear these pants. I had not known that workers in sugarcane fields ever wore ashigappa until I talked to Robert Mukai, who not only informed me that they did but also showed me the ashigappa he had worn in the sugarcane fields.[14] He told me that the ashigappa worn by the Japanese workers who worked in the sugarcane fields on the Big Island were cut in exactly the same way as those worn by pineapple field workers but were made of heavy muslin, the same quality used for their kappa, and were treated to make them water-repellent. Most of the issei treated the garments with linseed oil alone. However, some used kakishibu first, and some added turpentine to the linseed oil. Which method was used depended on individual preference, time constraints, patience, and expense.[15]

Long Kappa Worn by Lunas on Horseback

Another variation on the standard kappa was the extra-long kappa worn by the lunas. These kappa were first worn on sugar plantations on the Big Island. They were introduced on Oahu in 1928, when Ernest Malterre, Sr., and Ernest Malterre, Jr., transferred from the Onomea Sugar Plantation on the Big Island to the Oahu Sugar Company in Waipahu.[16] The issei men and nisei boys who worked under the Malterres admired the long kappa worn by their lunas when they rode on horseback; they felt that the long kappa gave the Malterres, who are of Portuguese, English, French, and Hawaiian descent, a majestic, authoritative image.[17] Ernest Malterre, Jr., explained that the long kappa was developed because the lunas who rode on horseback on the Big Island, which is known for its torrential rainfall, had a special need for a longer kappa than that worn by the field workers. When the lunas rode on horseback during a heavy downpour, they had to cover their legs and backs to keep their saddles and underclothing from getting wet. The luna's kappa had a long overlapped flap in the lower back seam that could be closed with three buttons. When the luna was astride a horse, this flap was left unbuttoned to allow the raincoat to spread to cover the entire body and the saddle. Ernest says that the long kappa provided good protection but posed something of a problem when he got off his horse and began walking in the muddy, rain-soaked ground; the long "train" dragged behind and soaked up mud.[18]

These long kappa had to be custom-made. When the Malterres moved from the Big Island to Waipahu, their kappa were made at the Arakawa Tailor Shop; Kay Arakawa remembers sewing the kappa for them.[19] At first I thought that this type of kappa was worn only by the Caucasian lunas. But later I learned from Robert Mukai that the Japanese lunas on the Big Island also wore the long kappa with the overlap in the back.[20]

Arm and Hand Protectors

Among the most useful accessories the Japanese immigrants brought with them from Japan were arm protectors, called *tesashi*

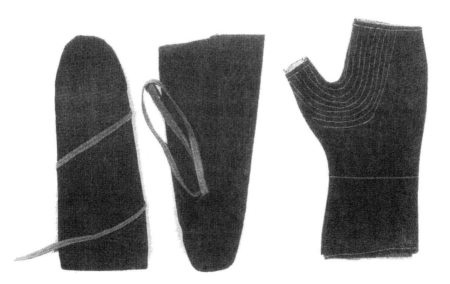

Left and center: Tesashi made of ahina sewn by Kin Watanabe. Given to author by Elaine Watanabe Yokota. Blanche Klim. Barbara Kawakami collection.

Right: Tekkō, used on the left hand only, for doing extra heavy work in the fields. Sewn by Kin Watanabe, given to author by Elaine Watanabe Yokota. Blanche Klim. Barbara Kawakami collection.

by those who came from Hiroshima and Yamaguchi Prefectures and nearby regions and called *teoi* by those who came from Fukushima and Niigata prefectures and nearby regions. The word tesashi literally means "to apply"; the word teoi, "to put over the hand." These arm protectors were worn on both arms. A type of hand protector that was worn on the left hand and used for extra heavy field work by both men and women was called a *tekkō*.

Methods of making the tesashi, or teoi, and the tekkō had in many cases been handed down in families for generations, so there were various styles. But basically, the tesashi, or teoi, was a protective covering that extended from the elbow to the knuckles, covering the back of the hand but not the palm, and held in place by a loop that hooked onto the middle finger; the tekkō was a mitten with the fingertip section cut off.

Back in their home villages in Japan, the issei had used heavy cotton fabric for these accessories. In Hawaii, they learned from other ethnic groups how to utilize ahina.

Kyahan

Kyahan (leggings) had also been used by the issei in Japan. The kyahan covered the leg from knee to ankle and were worn over the trousers or the momohiki. At first the kyahan were made of kasuri or plain cotton fabric or whatever else was available to the immigrants, but once the issei discovered the remarkable durability of ahina, they made their kyahan of heavy ahina, usually first-grade quality.

Some of the kyahan were finished off with narrow one-half-inch sashes on the corners, one of them thirteen inches and the other sixteen inches long, which wrapped around the leg and then laced over in crisscross fashion all the way to the ankle. This type was closed by a row of bone buttons. The ends of the sashes were tucked in between the loops. Thus, the kyahan provided protection from insects that might crawl inside clothing as well as from the sharp edges of the sugarcane stalks.[21]

Another type of kyahan was closed by means of a row of *kohaze* (copper fasteners that were sewn into the seam line; they were usually called "coin-shaped buttons" because their shape [an oval with one of the shorter ends cut off straight] was similar to that of a Japanese coin that was used during the Tokugawa Period). The kohaze fit into loops that were sewn on the underside of the kyahan; they were bent and hooked over the loops. Kohaze provided a snug closure, and they were completely invisible when closed. But this type

Issei woman carrying sugarcane. Burlap leggings, apron, and head covering indicate that she was unable to afford the typical work clothing. Papaikou Sugar Plantation, 1902. Hawaii State Archives collection.

of closure took more time and skill to sew and more time to fasten than the bone-button closure. This type of kyahan was finished off with a half-inch-wide sash, forty-two inches in length, that was wound crisscross around the leg and was tucked in at the top or wherever it ended.[22]

There were other variations in the ways in which the kyahan was made. And there was also at least one substitute: according to an issei woman from Hiroshima Prefecture who arrived in Hawaii in 1909 at the age of twenty-three and worked on a Maui plantation, the picture brides from Hiroshima Prefecture usually wore long black stockings instead of the kyahan. These long stockings were imported from Miyashima, in Hiroshima, and were sold for eighty cents a pair at the Japanese stores on the plantations. Some fortu-

A pair of kyahan made by Kin Watanabe and worn until 1921 for field work at Oahu Sugar Company plantation. The kyahan on the *left* shows the outer ahina; the kyahan on the *right* has been turned over to show the cotton lining and the kohaze. Given to author by Elaine Watanabe Yokota. Blanche Klim. Barbara Kawakami collection.

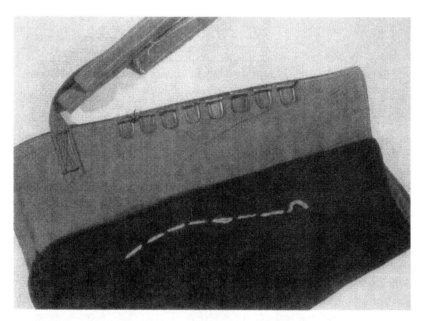

A kyahan made of heavy ahina sewn by Kin Watanabe. Note the white loops made of old "store strings" for the kohaze to go through. Given to author by Elaine Watanabe Yokota. Blanche Klim. Barbara Kawakami collection.

nate women even received a steady supply of the stockings from relatives in Hiroshima.[23]

Tenugui

The *tenugui* (a soft cotton towel about thirteen inches wide and thirty-two inches long) was an accessory that the Japanese immigrants could never have done without. It was used for bathing, for washing and wiping faces and hands, and also as a covering for the face and head for protection against the sun, wind, and rain. The simple tenugui was seen in every plantation home. And photographs of Japanese laborers taken in their field garments show the various ways in which the tenugui was used in the fields. Women wrapped tenugui around their faces and necks and over their straw hats to protect their skin from the sun and dust. Men also wore the tenugui as a head covering; they wound the tenugui around their heads, tying the ends into a knot at the forehead to keep perspiration from streaming down into their eyes when they were engaged in strenuous physical labor. (In Japan, young men and children who carry the portable shrines [*mikoshi*] used in festivals wear the cotton tenugui around their heads, tied in the front. When it is tied in this manner, it is called a *hachimaki* [headband, or sweatband], which symbolizes action or great physical exertion.)

Tenugui were given out by Buddhist temples during the *Obon* Festival (Festival for the Ancestors) and at various other functions in return for a small offering or donation. These tenugui were very colorful, printed with such designs as dancing figures, lanterns, Buddhist symbols, crests, or cherry blossoms. Some had floral border designs. And each temple had its name printed on the towel in bold black letters. Some issei who were fortunate enough to be able to return to Japan for a visit brought back colorful tenugui from their villages as gifts for their friends in appreciation for the farewell gifts they had received, which usually ranged from one to two dollars.[24]

The tenugui is still seen today at Obon Festivals in Hawaii. And it still has a multitude of uses. Some people now even use tenugui to make blouses or *happi*. Kay Tanoura, a hairdresser, used eight Obon towels to create a happi with long kimono sleeves that would protect the garments of her customers while their hair was being treated.[25] Matsue Yoneji of Kapaa, Kauai, used seven Obon towels to create a stylish happi with short sleeves to be worn as a leisure jacket at home.[26] And Mikiko Hirohata, a nisei with a multitude of talents, sews a *chanchanko*, a sleeveless kimono jacket for toddlers, from a single Obon towel; these jackets are always best sellers at the

Issei women from Fukushima Prefecture, Japan, in kasuri work clothing with tenugui wrapped around their hats. The women on the *left* and the *right* have bentō bags with them. Waialua Agriculture Company at Kawailoa Camp, Oahu, 1906. Photograph given to author by Zenbei Saito.

annual temple bazaars in her district.[27] Unfortunately, however, today's tenugui are not as sturdy or as colorfast as the ones made in the past.

Bentō Bags

All workers carried lunch bags, called *bentō* bags *(bentō bukuro)*, to the sugarcane and pineapple fields. The bentō bags were usually about twelve to thirteen inches wide and ranged from about sixteen to twenty inches in length. Attached to the bags was a strap that was about one and a quarter inches wide and about fifty to fifty-five inches long. Both ends of this strap were sewn into the side seam together, about five inches from the top, to form a long loop. After the double-decker lunch can and the tea container were placed in the bentō bag, the loop was wound around the top of the bag twice

Happi made from obon tenugui by Matsue Yoneji of Kauai. 1985, Douglas Kawakami. Barbara Kawakami collection.

A chanchanko made
from a single tenugui
by Mikiko Hirohata.
Douglas Kawakami.
Barbara Kawakami
collection.

and then the rest of the loop was slid through these windings from below, to close the bag securely; no knots were needed. The remaining loop served as a shoulder strap for carrying the bag.

There were some variations, of course. A bentō bag that was given to me by Alice Kuroiwa Schwartz, a type that was common on Kauai, had a strap that was forty-two inches long, and only one end of the strap was sewn into the side seam, at the lower corner. When the bentō was packed, about twenty inches of strap were left clear to form a loop from the bottom corner of the bag to the top of the bag, then the rest of the strap was wound around the top of the bag twice and tied with a square knot to close the bag securely. The loop from the bottom corner of the bag to the top served as a shoulder strap for carrying the bag.[28]

The fabric most commonly used for bentō bags was ahina, because it was durable and easy to care for; usually, bentō bags were made from ahina that was left over from making work pants and trousers. But some bentō bags were made from unbleached rice bags, with the bright red labels and Japanese characters still visible in bold black. Empty cement bags were also popular for making bentō bags because they were thick and strong and could be bought for about five cents each. The only disadvantage of cement bags was that they came only in white and, after a few weeks' use in the fields, the red dirt from the fields was hard to scrub out; after a few months of use, the cement bags were a light brown. Burlap bags were also used for bentō containers; they could be obtained free from the warehouse, and every penny counted in those days. Of all the fabrics used for the bentō bag, ahina and cement bags lasted the longest.

What was packed into the bentō bags had to be inexpensive and had to be able to keep without refrigeration. Many of the issei who came as single men during the early 1900s remember with nostalgia the bentō they took with them to the fields. Some fixed their own breakfasts and packed their own lunches. In the morning they might prepare *miso* soup, made by adding water to miso (a food paste made of soybeans, salt, and, usually, some fermented grain); they might add some *iriko* (small dried sardines) to the stock. They would have the soup for breakfast and pack the iriko, along with cooked rice and some pickled vegetables, for lunch. Sometimes they would add pumpkin or sweet potatoes to the soup and pack them for lunch—perhaps along with pickled radish. Some men had the women at the community kitchens fill their bentō box with vegetables that had been cooked with sugar and soy sauce; occasionally they were lucky enough to find salted salmon or dried codfish cooked in sugar and soy sauce in their lunches.

Lunch always consisted primarily of rice, but its blandness was made up for by adding pieces of vegetables such as radishes, cabbage, cucumbers, mustard greens, or scallions. Some issei men told me that during the early years their bentō consisted of only rice, pickled vegetables, and a large *ume* (pickled plum) placed in the center of the rice. Many of the issei recalled how good the ume tasted during the thirty-minute noon meal. One man told me that he thought the ume helped him to sustain his energy until the end of the work day.[29] Small sardines dried on a stick were also a tasty treat for a bentō.[30]

On days when the fish peddler came by with a lucky catch, the Japanese were able to buy some kinds of fish for fifty cents a bucket. This was a great treat for the entire family. And some of the fish were always salted and dried for future use in the bentō can.

Taga Toki, who was suddenly thrust into the position of making bentō for twenty bachelors when her husband was working on a tunnel project in Kokee, Kauai, in the 1920s, described her bentō-making experience as follows:

I got up at 3:00 A.M. . . . My second baby often woke up and cried, so I strapped him to my back to do the cooking. The rice was cooked in a large Chinese pot with a heavy lid, on an open fire outdoors, so it was very good. Every morning, I lined up the double-decker bentō cans—twenty of them—and filled them with rice, a piece of fish, and pickles. Then the workers filled their own tea bottles and packed their bentō cans in the ahina bags. Once I bought a lot of fish cheap, and I fried it the night before and put some in each of the lunch cans. One man complained that he did not have any fish in his lunch can; the fish was so tasty that someone had taken it. . . . So, at times like that, I was in a dilemma and did not know what to do! These incidents did occur occasionally even among the Japanese laborers when the food was especially good and a rare treat.[31]

One woman told me that a group of seven or eight women who took their thirty-minute break together made it a point to bring some kind of cooked beans for lunch every Monday. They could hardly wait for lunchtime so that they could peek into each other's bentō to see what kind of beans each one had brought. Indeed, there were many varieties of beans available: kidney beans, lima beans, the small reddish-brown azuki beans, string beans, soybeans, black beans, garbanzos (chickpeas), and even the Portuguese beans that grew abundantly along the ditches and roadsides of the plantations. But the main reason these issei women brought beans every Monday, the first day of the week, was that the word *mame*, which literally means bean in Japanese, has another meaning: it means diligent, hardworking, healthy, and fit. So, when the women brought beans on Mondays, they were saying "Let us work hard in good health all week!"[32]

Water and Tea Containers

The issei workers wanted tea to drink with their pickled vegetables or to pour over their rice at lunchtime (even though the tea would be cold by then). So they filled empty vinegar bottles or other glass bottles with tea and carried the bottles to the fields in their bentō bags. They had to be somewhat careful in doing this, for the bottles would break if the tea was too hot when it was poured and might break later if they were bumped too hard.

Issei water boys taking water to workers in the fields. Photograph taken in the 1890s. From William S. Bryan, ed., *Our Islands and Their People as Seen with Camera and Pencil* (1899), p. 466.

The issei workers also needed to take water with them, just in case they were sent to isolated fields where there were no water boys to bring them water. At first they used glass bottles for this purpose too. But eventually several types of water cans were invented by an innovative young man who came from Hiroshima Prefecture.

This ambitious young issei was Junzo Kurata, who came to Hawaii in 1899 to work for Oahu Sugar Company. After working a few years as a mechanic at the Oahu Sugar Company mill, he quit his job, opened a tinsmith shop in Waipahu below the sugar mill, and began to make water cans for field workers. He was the only tinsmith around and served all the plantation workers in the leeward area. Many issei and immigrants of other ethnic groups had their water cans made by Mr. Kurata until he died in the late 1930s. He acquired this skill on his own and was highly respected for the quality of the water cans he produced.

The largest water cans, which had a capacity of two and a half gallons each, were ordinarily bought by the plantation owners and were used to service the entire work gang. The water boy would

Issei laborers at the Ewa Plantation taking their thirty-minute lunch break. Note the handcrafted water can on the left. Photograph taken 1915–1920. Ewa Plantation Senior Citizens' Club.

string these large galvanized water cans on a long pole over his shoulders and walk through the sugarcane fields or pineapple fields to serve the thirsty laborers. The workers would dip their own cups into the water can. Sometimes, when the water boy was lazy, instead of walking some distance to the water truck to fill the cans, he would go to the irrigation ditch nearby to get the water. (The thirsty workers did not usually find out.) Some families who worked as a group—fathers, mothers, brothers, sisters, and other relatives— would also buy this size water can, which cost about $1.25. Some of these cans were essentially buckets, open at the top. Another type was shaped like a modern Clorox bottle with a cork on top.

The water container that individuals bought was made in the shape of a canteen. Mr. Kurata would wrap the canteen-shaped container with burlap cloth. The laborers would let the water can soak in the irrigation ditch while they worked in the hot sun, and when they took the cans out the evaporation from the wet burlap kept their drinking water cool.[33]

Goggles

One accessory that was indispensable for the men and women who worked in the sugarcane and pineapple fields was a pair of goggles; eyes had to be protected from the heavy dust and the strong winds and wind-borne fragments of sugarcane stalks and pineapple leaves. These goggles were made especially for plantation work and were sold at the plantation stores. Some of the issei called them *megane*, a Japanese term for eyeglasses, but most of the issei, when they asked for them at the plantation store, tried to say the English word goggles; since that was a difficult word for Japanese to pronounce, it came out sounding more like *gogurosu* (at least to people of other ethnic groups). The goggles used for field work were different from ordinary goggles in one important respect: instead of being made of glass or plastic, they were made of fine wire mesh.

Seedling Count Bag

An accessory worn only by the women who worked in the pulapula gang cutting sugarcane seedlings was a small bag, made from material taken from a thick rice bag, used to keep an accurate count of the number of seedlings cut. It was usually tied around the waist. For every ten seedlings cut, the women would pick a weed or leaf and place it in the bag.[34]

A pulapula bag. Sewn by Taniyo Tanimoto. Blanche Klim. Barbara Kawakami collection.

The Rice-bag Carry-all

Before World War II, the rice bag was commonly used as a carry-all. We had no suitcases; the only cases designed for transporting clothing were the kōri our parents had brought from Japan. So the versatile rice bag became a carry-all. For me, the humble rice-bag carry-all has a special association that dates back to 1932, when my oldest brother, then thirteen years old, was sent away to work in a konpan group the day after he graduated from eighth grade. Because he was the oldest son, he became the major breadwinner of the family. He was the youngest to join that group of adults contracted for irrigation work. Mother wrapped a couple of changes of work clothing and some casual clothes, including a yukata, in the rice bag. I still remember watching my oldest brother go off to work in an isolated camp with his few belongings wrapped in a bleached rice bag; it was a heartbreaking experience.

The "Dollar Pocket Watch"

The "dollar pocket watch" was an item that was never forgotten when the issei left for work in the morning. Some measure of com-

Complete issei woman's work outfit and accessories made by Haruno Tazawa in the 1930s. The slat bonnet was made by Taniyo Tanimoto. Modeled by
Blanche Klim. Michael Pecsok. Barbara Kawakami collection.

fort was gained from an occasional peek at the watch to see if it was getting close to lunchtime, when the workers had a few minutes respite to eat their lunches, or to see if the end of the work day was near.

The men kept their watches in a watch pocket that was sewn in under the waistband of their trousers; women kept theirs carefully tucked into their black sashes, with the chain left on the outside to give a decorative touch. The watch was something of a status symbol, since one dollar in the early 1900s seemed like a fortune.

6
Casual Wear

Casual Kimono

At home and around the plantation camps, Japanese men and women relaxed in their *yukata* (unlined kimono made of printed cotton). In Japan yukata were worn only in the summer months, but in Hawaii's tropical climate they were ideal for year-round wear. While the yukata were still new, they were worn for visiting friends and family. Later, they were worn at home. After the day's sweat and grime were washed away, both men and women relaxed in cool, comfortable yukata. During the prewar years, all the members of the family wore these cotton kimono after their baths.

Until World War II, issei mothers often wore yukata while doing household chores and running errands around the neighborhood. When a yukata became faded and reached the stage where it needed to be patched, the usable portion was remade into sleepwear or into a casual dress for the mother of the family or for a daughter.

Other types of kimono, such as those made of kasuri or of woven striped fabric, were also worn on informal occasions at home and around the camp. And sometimes a kimono that was originally worn only on dressy occasions would become a casual kimono: when a dressy kimono was no longer new and fresh-looking, it might be used for casual wear.

A good example of the "life cycle" of a cotton kimono is the history of one owned by Kimiko Yahiro. It was made of a cotton fabric covered with striking floral patterns in white on an indigo blue background, a fabric done in the style known as *Hakata shibori* (Hakata tie-dye), named after the city of Hakata, in Fukuoka Prefecture, where this particular type of design originated. The floral

136

Tsuyoshi Endo and Natsu Matsumoto, dressed in yukata, standing in front of the Oahu Sugar Company hospital at the Waipahu Plantation. Mrs. Endo was recuperating from a work injury at the time. 1922. Tsuyoshi Endo collection.

design was developed by tie-dyeing the fabric to create thousands of tiny white dots clustered to form the various elements of the design. This pattern of tiny dots is called the *kanoko* (fawn) pattern because it resembles the dappled coat of a fawn. The fabric was given to Kimiko Yahiro in 1907 by an aunt who had a dry goods store in Yasu Village, Fukuoka Prefecture. Kimiko remembers the way her aunt tied the white cloth before it was taken to the dye shop. She first drew the outline of the floral pattern on the fabric to guide her in doing the tie-dyeing. Then, to develop the dappled effect, she wrapped tiny bits of the cloth, at intervals of one-quarter of an inch, around tiny key-shaped nails and wound jute yarn tightly around each nail to keep color from seeping through in the dyeing process. It took weeks or even months of painstaking work before the intricately tied white fabric was ready to be sent to a dye shop in the village.

The dyed fabric was made into a dressy kimono that Kimiko Yahiro brought to Hawaii in her kōri in 1924. She wore it on social occasions, when visiting friends. She also wore it—and other casual kimono—in her first job as a domestic, for her employer required her to dress in a kimono and sash every evening when she served dinner. Caucasian families wanted Japanese domestics to dress in their traditional kimono—in part because the difference in dress signified the class difference between employer and servant. Kimiko's tie-dyed kimono outlasted her other kimono. When it began to show wear and tear, she took it apart and used the untorn section to make a casual dress. When it could no longer be worn as a dress, she made it into a nightgown. She preserved this nightgown for sentimental reasons, and, although the fabric is worn and patched, the beauty of the kanoko design is still evident.[1]

Although both men's and women's yukata were cut and constructed along the same lines, there were some distinct differences between them—primarily in the pattern and color of the fabric, the shape of the sleeves, and the types of sashes used.

Women's yukata were often produced in designs inspired by nature: for example, flowers, bamboo, and willow fronds. Fan and umbrella designs were also popular. Stylized designs of landscapes and waves were often used along the hemline. The designs on the men's yukata were usually more conservative—geometric prints, stripes, checks, and abstract patterns. Men's yukata were usually conservative in color, too; the colors most favored by men were indigo blue and navy blue. Women's yukata were usually more colorful than men's, although in this respect the difference depended primarily on the age of the woman: older women tended to wear rel-

Back view of nightgown made of Hakata shibori fabric that started its life cycle as a dressy kimono. The nightgown was given to the author by Kimiko Yahiro. Photograph by Sarah Tomei, Japanese American National Museum. Barbara Kawakami collection.

atively conservative colors such as blues and aquas, while younger women wore bright colors such as reds and pinks. Men's yukata sleeves were shorter and squared off at the bottom; women's yukata sleeves were longer and slightly rounded at the bottom.

With their yukata, women usually wore a narrow sash called a *datemaki*; it was usually wrapped around the waist and tied in a simple bow in the back. The narrow sash made of Hakata weave was particularly admired for its strength and quality; almost every picture bride who came to Hawaii during the 1908–1924 period had one or two of these packed in her kōri. The datemaki is ordinarily used beneath the dressy wide obi to hold the kimono in place. But, since

Issei women wore yukata while working as domestics for plantation
managers' families. This issei woman probably sewed the kimono for
her employers' children. Photograph taken in Kauai about 1910.
Mabel Hashisaka collection.

the issei women rarely had occasion to don their dressy kimono, it
was common for them to use the datemaki as a waistband for the
casual yukata. Another type of sash popularly worn by women for
casual wear was made of black sateen lined with American cotton
fabric printed with designs similar to those of Japanese prints. And

the simplest sash of all was a narrow cord made from leftover scraps; the frugal issei women never let anything go to waste. Men usually wore wider sashes. With their casual yukata (and other casual kimono), most men wore a *heko obi* (a sash about thirteen inches wide and three yards long, made of crepe or cotton) wrapped twice around the waist and tied in a soft bow in the back. Some men wore a dressier wide obi made of black crepe with a white tie-dyed kanoko design. And some men wore another type of dressy obi: a stiffer and narrower (about five inches wide) sash called a *kaku obi*, which was usually made of satin, brocade, or cotton. Although these dressier types of obi were meant to be worn with dressier kimono, issei men saw no need to save theirs for special occasions and instead used them for casual wear. This practice was quite evident during the issei pioneering days, when there was little cash available with which to purchase new clothes and it made better sense to use clothing that had been brought from Japan. Of course there were other possibilities: in the photograph taken in 1890 of an issei immigrant couple in Wainaku on the Big Island, the husband is wearing an *obi-jime*, a narrow cord usually worn by women over a dressy wide obi.

The colorful yukata is still worn during the Buddhist bon season, although its use is gradually declining. In the prewar period the Obon Festival, the traditional Japanese festival to remember the dead, was the most important and exciting event in plantation communities for both young and old. Obon Festivals are still held, usually from early July to late August, in various Japanese communities throughout the Hawaiian Islands.

Perhaps the high death rate among the Japanese immigrants led them to give particular importance to the Obon Festival. One Buddhist priest who studied the early records of his church found that during the early 1900s the median age of death among the issei men was about forty years. There were also many infant deaths, often not recorded. The Japanese immigrants, predominantly Buddhists, believed that the spirits of the dead returned to their former homes during the Obon period. For the issei, who were far away from their native land, Obon held a special meaning. During the Obon Festival in Hawaii, no matter how busy the issei mother was, or how poor she was, she stayed up late at night to sew bright yukata for her children. Some mothers dressed their daughters in their best silk kimono and tied their silk obi in a butterfly knot (today known as the plump sparrow bow).

For the Obon dances, both young and old wore yukata and formal wide obi. Issei and nisei men and women who were members of

Issei couple and a friend in casual cotton kimono. The woman has tapered her kimono sleeves. Her husband *(center)* appears to have used his wife's dressy obi-jime, instead of a man's sash, to hold his kimono in place. About 1890, Wainaku, on the island of Hawaii, by Charles Furneaux. Bishop Museum collection.

Buddhist church organizations or folk dancing clubs often wore matching yukata with decorative designs stenciled along the hemline and on the bottom of the sleeves. The tenugui, the cotton towel that was such an important accessory for issei men and women who were working in the pineapple and sugarcane fields, was also worn for Obon dancing. When the dancer was wearing a yukata, the tenugui was usually folded lengthwise into four equal parts (each about

Obon dance at Aiea Taiheiji (Soto Mission sect) in 1962. Kazuo Matsui collection.

three to four inches in width) and then draped around the kimono collar and tucked into the obi.

The Japanese Language School helped to teach the girls of immigrant families how to make kimono as part of its program for preserving and increasing appreciation of Japanese crafts. From the sixth or seventh grade, a special class instructed girls in various aspects of the Japanese culture. The resident minister's wife of our Soto Mission temple, for example, taught the young girls the basics of tea ceremony, Japanese etiquette, floral arrangement, Japanese embroidery (similar to the Western satin stitch), punch-picture embroidery with a large needle, kimono-sewing, *shibori*, and other handicrafts.

I remember that the minister's wife taught us girls, all eleven or twelve years old, how to make our own kimono out of bleached cotton cloth. And, after our kimono were completed, she taught us how to stitch-dye floral patterns: we drew our own designs, stitched the outline of the design, and then pulled the thread as tightly as possible to keep the dye from seeping through. We put our stitched-dyed motif on the front of the yukata along the hemline and also on the bottom of the long sleeves. We dyed the bottom portion of the

Young girls in front of the Soto Mission Japanese Language School in Waipahu
dressed in their kimono. About 1927. Ruth Nobuko Maki collection.

kimono blue and the upper two-thirds pink; we carried out the same
two-tone color scheme on the long sleeves. We wore our matching
kimono to the Obon Festival very proudly that year, 1935. And I put
my brief course in stitch-dyeing to good use years later when I used
the same technique in designing blouses, tablecloths, and other gift
items.

In Obon observance we learned to dress properly in kimono and
obi, and we learned to show respect for our ancestors and loved ones
who had passed away. It was delightful to see young and old dancing
in unison to the rhythmic beat of the drums. Atop the musicians'
tower, set up for the occasion on the temple grounds, about four or
five men and women dressed in bright yukata and straw hats sang
folk songs at the top of their lungs. Their songs, along with the
merry sounds of the flute and the inviting rhythms of the drums,
drew the spectators into the dance.

The issei contributed much to the spirit of the Obon Festival with
folk music and dancing brought from Fukushima, Niigata, Kago-
shima, Hiroshima, Okinawa, and Yamaguchi prefectures, and they
popularized the wearing of the colorful yukata and bright obi. The
Okinawan dancers wore the most colorful costumes and danced to
the liveliest music. Their costumes were distinctly different from
those of the naichi: the Okinawan costumes showed strong Chinese

influence in their vivid color and their design. Chinese influence was also evident in the stylized dance steps, the hand motions, and the rhythm and tempo of the dances performed by the Okinawans.

Now most of the talented naichi musicians and dancers who delighted the spectators have faded from the scene. And even the live music has been replaced by cassette tapes. But the Okinawan folk dancers, with their colorful costumes, still maintain their rich cultural heritage and enliven the joyous obon celebrations. Recently I had the privilege of meeting two talented nisei women who are keeping their Okinawan traditions alive. Both of them got their start in kimono-sewing at Japanese Language School. Ruth Higa Oshiro designs and sews outstanding costumes for her daughter, grandson, and herself to wear at classical Okinawan dance recitals;

Bashōfu kimono sewn by Ruth Oshiro. Darryl Arizo, George-Dean Photography. Barbara Kawakami collection.

she has even accepted the challenge of sewing stiff banana fiber cloth *(bashōfu)*, which is very difficult for the sewing needle to penetrate.[2] And Matsue Oshiro designs and sews all the elaborate costumes worn by her son, Keith Oshiro, a talented and highly respected performer of classical Okinawan dance.[3]

During World War II, traditional Japanese customs and observances were discontinued in Hawaii. But they were resumed after the war, and Obon festivals and dancing once again became annual events at Buddhist temples. After the war, instead of wearing yukata, many of the nisei and sansei dancers began wearing the short, lightweight coats known as *happi;* with these, they wore tightly fitted black pants. But happi and tightly fitted pants have not completely replaced yukata for Obon Festivals; yukata are still being worn today by many of the celebrants, both young and old.

Hawaiian-Style Casual Attire

Probably the first type of clothing adopted by the issei women from another ethnic group was the loose-fitting simple dress they called *kanakagi* (literally, "Hawaiian wear"; *kanaka* is the Hawaiian word for "Hawaiian," and *gi* is the Japanese word for "wear" or "clothing").

By the time the first official Japanese contract laborers came to Hawaii to work on the plantations, the Hawaiian women were already wearing the muʻu muʻu, the long, loose, flowing gown that the early missionary wives had taught them how to sew; the missionary wives had already revolutionized Hawaiian women's clothing.

When the first missionaries arrived in 1820, they were shocked to find the Hawaiian women wearing only paʻu (wrap-around skirts, sarongs). They quickly set to work to get the Hawaiian women to cover themselves up. And it was not too difficult, for the Hawaiian women were fascinated by the missionary women's clothes and readily adopted the Mother Hubbard-style gowns that the missionary wives designed for them, gowns that were flattering to the Hawaiian women's ample figures. The impact of the missionary wives on Hawaiian women's attire still continues today; muʻu muʻu are still worn by all ethnic groups living in Hawaii and are almost immediately adopted by tourists as well. They are well suited to the busy lifestyle people lead today, for, in addition to being graceful and comfortable, they are very easy to slip into; there is no need to wear a girdle or stockings with them.

As the issei women acquired a taste for the simple and comfortable Hawaiian dress, they began making some changes to fit their own special needs. What developed was an A-line sack dress with kimono sleeves and a simple V neckline or rounded neckline. Japanese women were accustomed to being completely wrapped in a kimono with long sleeves, a tightly overlapped kimono collar, and a hemline that covered the ankles. But they worked hard even when they were at home, and they needed more freedom of action than kimono or even long mu'u mu'u could permit. So they made some practical compromises: the skirt length of the kanakagi was slightly below the knee and the set-in sleeves extended just below the elbow. Eventually, this type of A-line dress replaced the yukata as casual wear. Sometimes a Peter Pan collar was added. Sometimes there was

Issei women in front of a grass hut in the late 1800s. The woman on the *right* is wearing a Hawaiian-style dress that at that time was called a holoku. The woman in the *middle* is wearing a Western blouse and skirt; the child wears a kasuri kimono. The woman who is breast-feeding her baby wears a kimono with tapered sleeves. Bishop Museum collection.

a slit (about seven inches long) in the front neckline that was finished with a binding of the same material as the dress and closed by means of snaps called *pit-chin* by the issei women. (Pit-chin may sound like a Chinese word, but the issei women gave the snaps that name because it approximates the sound of the snaps closing. When they went to the stores to purchase them, only an issei salesman could understand what they were asking for.)

Another name for the simple A-line dress that the issei women developed was *kappa dachi* (literally, "simple cut"; this *kappa* is not related to the word that means raincoat). The issei women were

Three issei women and their families near Honokaa, Hawaii, in the late 1800s. The woman on the *left* is wearing a mu'u mu'u that the issei women called a holoku. The woman in the *center* is wearing a long-sleeved blouse, long skirt, and apron of kasuri fabric. The woman on the *right* is wearing a jacket of kasuri and a long skirt of American plaid material. Photograph from William S. Bryan, ed., *Our Islands and Their People as Seen with Camera and Pencil* (1899), p. 526.

petite; their median height was four feet, eight inches. So usually only two and a quarter to two and a half yards of thirty-six-inch fabric were required to make a dress in kappa dachi style. One issei woman, Kaku Kumasaka, who was adept at cutting the kappa dachi dress freehand, described her method of cutting to me as follows:

> I first folded the thirty-six-inch material lengthwise into half (eighteen inches), then folded it crosswise, which formed four layers. I measured only with my eyes and trusted my instincts. I cut the outline of the dress freehand, shaping the side seams and kimono sleeves. On the folded side, at the top shoulder-line section, I cut out the back neckline first, using a cardboard guide, then unfolded the fabric lengthwise and cut out the front neckline into a V shape. The neckline was wide enough for my head to go through, so I didn't need to use any closing device. This was probably the easiest and fastest way to make a kappa dachi dress.[4]

Many of the issei women started off with this freehand method. They learned through trial and error and shared their acquired knowledge. Sometimes side pockets were sewn in between the side seams. They were made deep enough to hold such items as a coin purse, for often, when the vegetable peddler tooted his horn to announce his arrival, women who were busy in the washhouse or garden—which in some camps was quite a distance from the house —wanted to be able to run out to the roadside and buy from the peddler without having to go into the house first.

Most of the dresses the Japanese women made for casual at-home wear were made of inexpensive muslin, printed calico, or sturdy Indian Head cotton. The issei favored conservative prints that resembled some of the traditional Japanese designs—checks, plaids, or geometric patterns. And they favored conservative colors such as gray, navy blue, or light blue. The most frugal women made house dresses out of unbleached muslin, which was the least expensive material to buy, or bleached rice bags, which did not cost a penny. (Since large families consumed two or three bags of rice a month, rice bags accumulated in no time.) The eighty-pound or hundred-pound bags in which flour and certain kinds of livestock feed were packed were another free source of dress material. They had a variety of floral designs printed on them, and issei women would carefully select prints that were suitable for dresses. Mrs. Setsu Ishikawa, a much-beloved midwife, made her rounds in what many issei remember as her "midwife's uniform," a simple A-line dress made of bleached rice bags or printed flour bags.

Some of the Hawaiian-influenced garments that the Japanese

Chotaro and Yuki Kochi and their eldest daughter, Kimiko. Yuki wears a dressy mu'u mu'u that was sewn for her by a relative. Mr. and Mrs. Kochi arrived in Hawaii on July 29, 1909. He met an untimely death in a dynamite explosion while working with a road construction crew for Oahu Sugar Company. About 1923. Nobuo Kochi collection.

A sophisticated mu'u mu'u with leg-of-mutton sleeves worn by Tsugi Kinoshita, who arrived in Hawaii with her husband on May 31, 1898, from Kumamoto Prefecture, Japan. Photograph taken about 1925. From *Hawaii Zairyū Kumamoto Kenjin Yakureki Shashin Chō* [A Pictorial History of Japanese Immigrants to Hawaii from Kumamoto Prefecture] (1927), no page numbers.

women made for themselves were more elaborate than the A-line kappa dachi and stayed closer to the lines of the true Hawaiian mu'u mu'u. Sueno Koga, who was born in 1909 in an isolated camp called "Mango Valley," located several miles from Haleiwa town, told me that her mother learned to sew a garment that was similar to today's tutu mu'u. This garment had a straight yoke, a gathered bodice, long gathered sleeves, and a round neckline finished with narrow lace ruffles and had two shell buttons at the back opening. At first her mother made these garments in true Hawaiian style with a hemline that dragged on the floor, but she found that she could not tolerate the long skirt when she did her household chores, so she finally cut the length to just below her knees. That felt much better, and she decided to go one step further and cut the sleeves shorter, too, to give her more freedom; she cut them to end slightly below the elbow. Sueno remembered with a smile her mother's words: "Japanese women all time busy working, cannot wear long clothes!"[5]

Various styles of mu'u mu'u have developed in Hawaii over the years, and the term *holoku* is now usually reserved for the mu'u mu'u that has a train and is worn on formal occasions. But most of the Japanese women I interviewed for this study used the terms mu'u mu'u and holoku interchangeably. And there is a good reason for this, for the original holoku was not like those we have today. It had a plain yoke, a high neckline (with or without a collar), and long sleeves. Sometimes it was trimmed with ruffles at the hemline. It usually buttoned down the front. But, in the beginning, it did not have a train. When a woman with a full figure wore it, however, the skirt hiked up in front and made the back seem a little longer than the front, creating an illusion of a slight train. And the Hawaiian women loved this graceful effect, so they gradually extended the back of the skirt to form a true train.

One possible reason why the Hawaiian mu'u mu'u was so readily adopted by issei women was pointed out to me by Yasuyo Kuwahara, who came as a picture bride in 1921 to marry a plantation laborer at Waialua Sugar Plantation. A friend had made her a mu'u mu'u out of five yards of printed cotton material. It was made with a straight yoke, a high round collar with ruffles, and long sleeves. There were three panels in front, in which three lengths of fabric were used. Since it was so full in the front, she found it very practical and comfortable to wear at times when she was pregnant. And, in the days before the pill, those times came quite often. Japanese women were used to wearing kimono and obi during pregnancy because they did not have to worry about the fit of these garments. But the loose mu'u mu'u proved even better. No sashes were needed to hold the garment together, and the front did not spread open as they grew larger.[6]

7

Footwear

Geta

The *geta* (a wooden clog [basically, a wooden platform on two wooden stilts] that is held on the foot by a thong that passes between the first and second toes) was the most popular type of footwear among Japanese immigrants to Hawaii; geta were seen everywhere in plantation camps. In ancient days in Japan they had been made of hard and heavy wood.[1] They gained in popularity during the Edo Period (1603–1868), and it became common to make them out of paulownia or cedar, which are relatively porous and light in weight.[2]

A great number of Japanese immigrants are known to have brought these wooden clogs with them or worn them during their voyage to Hawaii. Residents were amused when these new arrivals strolled through the streets of Honolulu and politely left their wooden clogs outside when they entered a fancy establishment.

Before World War II older Japanese in rural areas wore geta every day. And all of us who grew up on the plantations owned at least one pair of these clogs. Men wore them with their yukata to visit their friends in nearby camps in the evenings because they were light and comfortable and because they kept their feet elevated and clean after the evening bath. Women wore them while doing laundry in the washhouse. The old-fashioned plantation washhouses had concrete floors, and they were always wet, so it was wise to wear wooden clogs to prevent slipping and to keep feet dry. (Japanese mothers believed that it was harmful for women to get their feet chilled—and particularly so for women who had just given birth or young girls who had just begun to menstruate.) Women also wore geta to go

Issei women wearing casual geta. Photograph from William S. Bryan, ed., *Our Islands and Their People as Seen with Camera and Pencil* (1899), p. 530.

shopping at the plantation store and to do various errands around the camp.

Some types of geta were worn on dressy occasions. During the prewar days, issei and nisei girls donned colorful yukata and wore dressy lacquered geta to dance at the Obon Festival. The stilts did not keep us from taking lively steps to the beat of the large drums. Some girls wore fancy geta we called *karanko geta* because of the "karan koron" sound they made when the wearer walked. (Today the usual term for these geta is *pokkuri*, which is also an attempt to reproduce the sound.) Sometimes little bells were attached to these geta so people would immediately know that someone was coming. In the karanko geta, either the platform was made thicker and the stilts were eliminated entirely or the front of the platform was made thicker, eliminating the front stilt, and the back stilt was made heavier to provide balance; it was a little difficult to walk gracefully

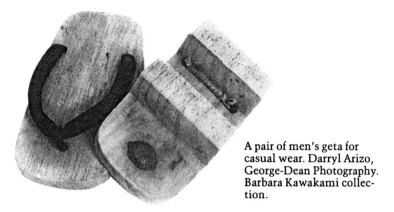

A pair of men's geta for casual wear. Darryl Arizo, George-Dean Photography. Barbara Kawakami collection.

in them. On New Year's, parents often gave girls new karanko geta to wear with their dressy silk kimono when they went around the neighborhood to wish everyone a happy new year.

The main difference between men's and women's geta was in the color of the thongs. Men's thongs were usually black or some other somber color that was considered masculine; women's were brightly colored.

Today, geta are hardly ever seen in stores; Western footwear has replaced them.

Zōri

The Japanese *zōri*, or sandal, consists of a flat sole that is held on the foot by a thong that passes between the first and second toes. Such sandals have been worn by the Japanese for many centuries. And they have been made of many different materials, including straw (of various kinds, for example, bulrush and rice stalks), bamboo sheaths, and cloth. (Most of the zōri sold in Hawaii today are made of rubber or leather or vinyl, but the use of these materials is relatively recent.)

WARAJI

Waraji (straw sandals) originated in Japan during the Tokugawa Period (1603–1868), when they were commonly worn by travelers and farmers.[3] In photographs taken before 1900, some Japanese immigrants can be seen wearing waraji brought from Japan. In Japanese villages, these sandals were usually made of rice straw. In the early 1900s, there were Chinese families still cultivating rice in

Hawaii and some of the issei remember gathering rice stalks that were discarded after harvesting, to make their own sandals. As the rice paddies gradually disappeared from the landscape, the issei experimented with various kinds of materials found in their new environment that could be used for making sandals. One of the most successful substitutes was the bulrush, which was found in abundance along the shoreline in brackish marshes where the plantation families often went to find crabs, clams, and oysters.[4] Bulrush was similar to the rush *(igusa)* used back in the villages in Japan for weaving floor mats.

Katsu Ochikubo from Yamaguchi Prefecture (mother of the late Bob Ochikubo, a well-known artist) and Ichi Kawakami from Kumamoto Prefecture were still weaving their own waraji sandals from Hawaiian bulrush even after World War II. There were no rice paddies in Waipahu by then, and they gathered bulrush from the marshes along the Hoaeae and Waikele shoreline. They washed the long, dark green, spongy stems of the bulrush and dried them in the shade for two weeks, and then dampened the stems again to make the fiber soft and more flexible. Katsu used her own big toe to form the framework on which to weave her sandals, but Ichi found the bent-over position tiresome and instead substituted a rectangular wooden frame (12" long, 5" wide) with a large nail at the tip. Both methods produced strong, sturdy sandals.[5]

Kenichi Tasaka, the oldest nisei I interviewed for my study (born in 1896, eleven years after his parents arrived from Hiroshima Prefecture with the first group of contract laborers), has revived the old craft of weaving waraji using the bulrush that thrives in the swamplands of lush Hanalei Valley on the island of Kauai. When he was young he had watched his father weave sandals and had helped gather the bulrush for his father. He had not been interested in learning how to make the sandals himself at that time, but after his father died and after his own retirement, he began to take an interest in this art. And then he regretted not having paid more attention to what his father had done. When he first tried to make the sandals, they did not come out right: one side was longer or wider than the other, or the two sandals did not match. It took more than two years of experimentation before he could weave a pair good enough to sell. Meanwhile, family, relatives, and grandchildren were happy recipients of the imperfect sandals, which they wore as house slippers.

Mr. Tasaka described the process of gathering and preparing the bulrush to me as follows:

I gather the bulrush about two miles away from my home. A friend of mine has a taro patch, and there's lots of bulrush growing in the marshes. After I cut them [the stems] near the roots, I put them on the table and sort them into large, extra large, medium, and small. I cut them into uniform lengths and put them in a burlap bag and pound them with a wooden mallet for about two to two and a half hours, to soften the fiber. I then tie the different sizes together in separate bunches and dry them in the shade. If you hang them outside, the bulrush will turn yellow, so I hang them in the shade; that keeps the rush green. In good weather, it takes two or three days for them to dry.

He described his method of weaving in these words:

First I need the measurement of the person's feet. . . . They're all different. . . . I need an outline pattern of the feet. To begin weaving, I take the long dried stems and then the regular size. The long stems are used for the center part of the sandal, so that I can control its shape. I make two double loops to form the framework for the sandal. I begin weaving from the front part of the sandal, which is the most difficult because you begin from nothing; you weave in and out . . . in horizontal fashion. . . . My father . . . utilized even the shorter fibers, joining them in the middle as he wove. That is too hard for me . . . I would rather use a longer . . . fiber. In the front (where the thong goes between the large toe and smaller toes), my father used to pull with his fingers, but I found an easier way: I use a plier to pull out the piece. It's really easy now. . . . Now I can weave these sandals in two and a half hours. I weave about one pair a day. Before, I sold crooked ones for three dollars, but as I got better, my friends encouraged me to charge five dollars for the long hours it took to make a pair. Then one lady friend began selling them at one of the resort shops on Kauai for eight dollars; then the price went up to ten dollars. Another artcraft shop offered twenty dollars.

Mr. Tasaka now also makes miniature straw sandals for Chistmas tree decorations and sometimes makes sandals out of multicolored yarns to go with colorful mu'u mu'u. He told me that he thought perhaps his desire to master this time-consuming handicraft arose because of loneliness after his father died. And perhaps his father, too, learned to cope with loneliness by keeping his village folk craft alive in isolated Hanalei Valley. There were not many Japanese there; the inhabitants were predominantly Hawaiian and Chinese.[6]

Another nisei who became quite adept at waraji-making is Hisako Yamasaki. She was taken to Japan by her parents when she was about three years old; she returned to Hawaii after World War II for a visit. She spent her childhood in the rice-farming village of Kameyama in Hiroshima Prefecture, where girls were taught from a young age to weave straw sandals, and she could weave several of them a day. One type of straw sandal she made was unusual because it had long cords that laced crisscross over the feet and tied firmly at the ankles. This type of sandal was used for traveling by foot in Japan during ancient times and was commonly used by farmers in Japan during the Meiji and Taisho Periods (1868–1925). It was often worn by Buddhist priests who traveled long distances by foot. It was the type worn by the Reverend Shiro Sokabe, a Christian minister who came to Hawaii in 1894 to begin his work in Honomu, Hawaii; his sandals were made of burlap fiber, which was very unusual.[7]

Mrs. Yamasaki also experimented with raffia (fiber from the

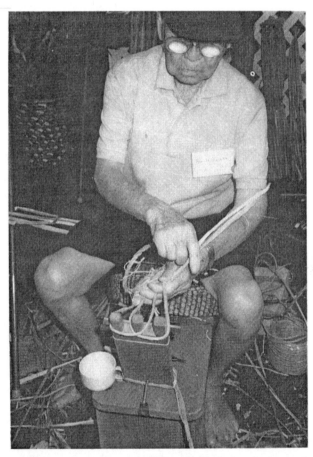

Kenichi Tasaka demonstrating his method of making waraji sandals out of bulrush. 1990, Douglas Kawakami. Barbara Kawakami collection.

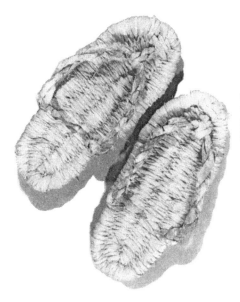

Waraji sandals made by Hisako
Yamasaki out of rice stalks.
Blanche Klim. Barbara Kawa-
kami collection.

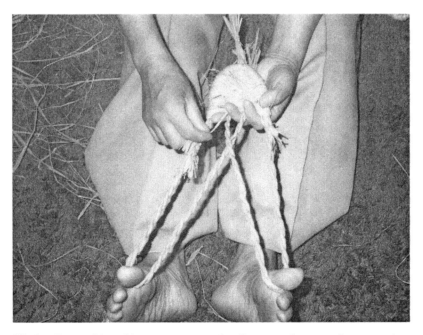

Hisako Yamasaki making waraji out of raffia. Douglas Kawakami. Barbara
Kawakami collection.

leaves of the African palm), which is commonly used for hula skirts in Hawaii. But she found that it was not as pliable as bulrush fiber or rice stalks and produced less comfortable footwear.[8]

One issei man found, however, that sugarcane stalks could be used effectively. A Portuguese woman described for me the way an issei neighbor of hers wove sandals from sugarcane stalks. He would remove all of the leafy parts from the sugarcane stalks, dip the stalks in water, then pound them with a wooden mallet until all the liquid was removed from the stems; he joined the ends of the long stems, which were sticky and paste-like after the pounding and "glued" nicely, to form a long strip; he dried the strip, then rolled it like a lasso to keep it from tangling. He had patterns made out of cardboard in several sizes. Because sugarcane stems are smaller than bulrush, the finished product was finer and smoother than the sandals made of bulrush. Like Mr. Tasaka of Hanalei, he enjoyed giving handmade slippers to friends and neighbors.[9]

OTHER TYPES OF ZŌRI

In Japan narrow strips of bamboo sheaths have often been used to make zōri. Bamboo-sheath sandals are more closely woven and smoother—and, therefore, more comfortable and more dressy— than straw sandals. Many of the issei women wore them with their dressy kimono for special occasions. And sometimes a bamboo-sheath sole might be combined with a cloth thong; for example, a bamboo-sheath sole might be combined with a black velveteen thong to make a zōri that would be appropriate to wear with a black montsuki to a funeral.

There were also zōri made entirely of cloth. Some of these zōri were created because of a need to economize; the thrifty issei women quickly learned that they could save money by making zōri out of narrow strips of fabric—either fabric that they salvaged from old clothes or fabric that was left over when they made new clothes. Katsu Ochikubo and Ichi Kawakami were experts in making the cloth zōri, which were made in the same manner as the bulrush sandals. In 1940, when Katsu Ochikubo's daughter, Patsy, began working in the newly established garment factory in Honolulu, she used to bring home strips of colorful Hawaiian fabrics and Katsu would weave them into colorful sandals. Such zōri were used for casual wear or worn for work around the house or garden. These could be washed often and proved to be practical.[10]

Sometimes cloth was used for zōri for aesthetic rather than economic reasons, and not all zōri were homemade. Some of the issei women and their daughters wore zōri that were imported from Japan and were made of exquisite brocaded cloth. For festive occasions such as New Year's Day, Girl's Day, and weddings, they carefully selected the colors of the thongs and soles to harmonize with the colors of their kimono and accessories.

Tabi

Tabi are heavy cotton socks that have a division between the big toe and the smaller toes and are closed at the ankle by *kohaze* (coin-shaped clasps). Traditionally in Japan both men and women have worn tabi; however, men usually wear black tabi, while women usually wear white. The early issei immigrants wore tabi that had soft soles like the ones they had worn back in their home villages. But these were not suitable for working on the rough terrain in the sugarcane or pineapple fields; the sharp rocks and pebbles cut through the soft soles, resulting in painful cuts that often became infected. So some issei women began to experiment and devise ways to strengthen the tabi.

The women found that if second-quality ahina was used, four or five layers of fabric were required; this posed a problem when they had to stitch the upper part of the tabi to the thick layers of sole. So, eventually, they learned to use only top-quality ahina to make the tabi.

Kaku Kumasaka told me that she used three thick layers of ahina and added a few extra layers of ordinary cotton fabric under the ball and heel of the foot, which enabled her to stitch around the sole to reinforce it. The stitching also acted as a cushion for the soles and made a thicker, longer-lasting tabi.[11]

Kay Arakawa was also instrumental in perfecting the plantation tabi. She learned the rudiments from Zenpan Arakawa and, through trial and error, learned how to position the front and back of the tabi for a comfortable fit. She also devised a special way of easing the front section to allow ample room for the toes. She ordinarily used three to four layers of top-grade ahina, with many rows of stitching to strengthen the sole; if she used less expensive ahina, she added more layers of cloth. Since power machines were already being used in the Arakawa tailor shop in 1926, it was possible to sew through several thick layers of ahina. The tabi designed by Kay Arakawa was unique in that the big toe was separated from the other toes by a partition that was skillfully sewn inside the tabi; from the outside, only the center seam was visible. The Arakawa tabi became very popular because of its comfort and durability.

The original immigrants' tabi were closed in the back at the ankle

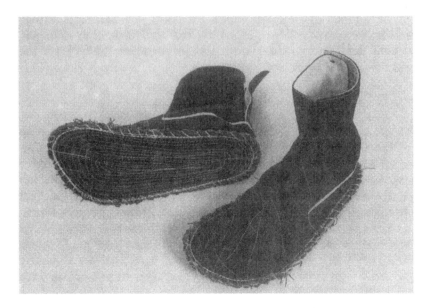

Tabi sewn by Sagami Shinozawa. Darryl Arizo, George-Dean Photography. Barbara Kawakami collection.

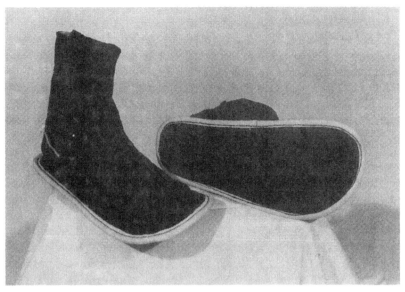

The well-known Arakawa tabi. Made and given to me by Kay Arakawa. Blanche Klim. Barbara Kawakami collection.

by kohaze. But a kohaze closure was more difficult to sew and more difficult to fasten than a bone-button closure, so issei women gradually switched to bone buttons and blanket-stitched buttonholes. And, of course, the kohaze closure was out of the question for mass-production techniques; the Arakawa tabi used bone buttons.

The original plantation tabi was simply stitched around the sole, leaving the raw edge exposed. Kay Arakawa, after unsuccessful experiments with bias tape for binding, devised an inch binding cut on a straight piece width-wise to bind the sole; the straight binding gave a firmness to the sole that helped to retain its shape. She also maneuvered the binding at the front section to give an upward tilt to the tabi, which made the tabi more comfortable because it allowed more movement for the toes.[12]

But not all the Japanese immigrants could afford to buy their tabi at the store; many wives spent long hours sewing them at home at night and on weekends. In 1979 Kaku Kumasaka still had in her possession the pattern for a tabi that was traced onto a *tanmono* wrapper (thick paper used as a decorative wrapper for bolts of narrow fabric from Japan); she had traced the pattern in 1922, the year she came to Hawaii as a picture bride.[13] Another picture bride who learned to sew tabi was Haruno Tazawa. When she came to Hawaii in 1917, a neighbor sewed an entire working outfit, including a pair of tabi, for her. After that, Haruno sewed tabi herself. She told me:

> I remember the first pair of tabi I had was soft-soled and used to cut my feet while I was working in the fields. They barely lasted a month, so I began using five to six layers of ahina on the sole; by the time I sewed the upper part to the sole, there were eight layers of cloth. I didn't have a sewing machine then, so I stitched the tabi by hand. I used a Japanese needle, and, for every stitch I took, I stuck the needle into wax; otherwise, the needle would not penetrate the layers of thickness. I used the Japanese metal thimble, the one with tiny holes, and that helped some. Until the late 1920s there was no electricity in Ewa and I did all my sewing under a big kerosene lamp suspended from the rafters.

Mrs. Tazawa realized that she needed to make stronger, more durable tabi, and she came up with the idea of affixing rubber to the soles of the tabi:

> Later, I learned to make a sturdier type of tabi with soles made from discarded conveyor belts or old automobile tires. That was impossible to stitch by hand, so I pounded U-shaped nails all around the edge of the sole. These tabi were good in rainy weather and lasted about three months.[14]

Tabi made by Haruno Tazawa using automobile tires for the soles. Blanche Klim. Barbara Kawakami collection.

Haruno Tazawa was not the only one who thought of putting rubber soles on tabi. Japanese immigrants in Hilo developed a similar technique, using rubber that they obtained from army surplus material from World War I.[15] And there was a precedent in Japan: *jika tabi* (outdoor tabi), or *sakana tabi* (fishermen's tabi), were worn in some farming villages in Japan, especially in the coastal areas from which many of the issei came. These tabi were made with a thick rubber sole and had a canvas top, usually black; they were closed with kohaze. Some of these tabi were imported from Japan; one person recalled paying about $2.50 for a pair in a Waipahu store in 1930.[16]

8

Children's Clothing

Very few of the issei could afford to buy ready-made clothes for their children. The issei women who, out of necessity, had learned to sew their husband's and their own work clothing had to learn a new kind of sewing when they began to have children. Most of them learned by borrowing patterns from their neighbors and tracing them onto old newspapers or cardboard. Some traced the outlines from a garment. Almost all of them used their ingenuity to change the basic pattern in various ways. For many, it was very difficult to learn to sew American clothes. And sometimes their creations were rather unusual. Many nisei children still remember being ridiculed by friends for wearing odd-looking clothes. And when one looks at some of the nisei children in class pictures from English School, it is hard not to smile at some of the "designs" created by issei mothers.

Many of the issei families had their children wear cotton or kasuri kimono at home after school, for the simple reason that these were easy to sew and maintain. Unlike Western clothes, which required individual fit, kimono were practical for a fast-growing family. They could be handed down from the older to the younger children without much concern about the exact fit or comfort of the garment. But for school the children had to have Western-style clothes.

Usually, little girls' dresses in the 1920s were a simple A-line, with a round or square neckline or a Peter Pan collar and either kimono sleeves or short set-in sleeves. Low waistlines were in fashion, and some girls wore styles identical to those worn by their older sisters. Florals, plaids, stripes, and checks were popular for school dresses as the girls advanced to upper grades.

Photograph taken about 1897 of students at the Ewa Japanese Language School, showing the great variety in the children's outfits. Bishop Museum collection.

Some girls whose fathers were lunas wore dresses that were trimmed with dainty lace and ribbons. But most of us wore very simple dresses. And none of us wore shoes.

Young boys from about two to ten years old were usually dressed in short pants that were referred to as "button-on pants" *(hetchi pansu)*, which were made of either khaki or navy cotton twill. The distinctive features of these pants were the hand-worked buttonholes at the waist, each positioned to match the position of a bone button attached to the shirt waistline. Usually there was one button in the center front, one in the center back, and one on each side (but six buttonholes had to be made because the side plackets of the pants overlapped). In Western garments, buttonholes are usually made with thread that is carefully matched to the color of the surrounding fabric. But the issei women, when making these khaki or navy pants, preferred a white #10 thread for the blanket-stitching used to reinforce the buttonholes. This white #10 thread was strong, thick, and quite conspicuous, especially against the dark-blue fabric.

These button-on pants were practical because of the loose fit around the waist. As the child grew taller, the buttons on the shirt

Hiromi and Susumu Kawamoto in kasuri kimono. Because of the loose fit of the kimono it could be handed down easily. Some boys were dressed in girls' kimono. 1921. Sakae Kawamoto collection.

Shoichi Sakaguchi family in a photograph taken about 1924. It was common practice to take kimono apart to fashion little girls' dresses; here the two younger girls are wearing dresses made of yuzen from a dressy kimono. 1924. From *Hawaii Zairyū Kumamoto Kenjin Yakureki Shashin Chō* [A Pictorial History of Japanese Immigrants to Hawaii from Kumamoto Prefecture] (1927).

could be adjusted. And, in families with many boys, they could be handed down from one child to the next. Many families handed down these versatile, easy-to-adjust outfits from the oldest to the youngest. The cloth was sturdy and long-lasting.

When boys were ten to twelve years old, they began to wear belted pants, either knee length or full length. By the time the boys were ready to graduate from grammar school, they were wearing full-length belted pants, still made of either khaki or navy twill cotton.

Boys' shirts were made with a sport collar. They were usually made of white broadcloth, fine percale, or Indian Head cotton. Some boys wore shirts of striped blue chambray instead. But in those days, when washing machines were still unheard of and all laundry was boiled out of doors in large cans over open fires, it was more practical for issei mothers to make white shirts for their boys; colors faded too quickly. These shirts were heavily starched and ironed with a charcoal-filled hot iron.

When I think of school clothes, my thoughts go back to September 1928, when my mother enrolled me in the first grade at August Ahrens School, an English School. (Kindergarten had not yet been established.) My parents spoke only their provincial dialect at home. It must have been difficult for them to enroll their children in an English school when they themselves did not understand or speak a word of the language. The children had different problems. Like other children in the neighborhood, my brothers and sisters and I spoke pidgin English with a mixture of my parents' Japanese dialect.

I was excited about starting school, and having my mother take me there was a great treat for me. The school was about a mile and a half away from Waipahu Plantation's Camp 1, where we lived, and we set off down the dirt road in plenty of time. Mother was dressed in her best cotton dress, stiffly starched and pressed; I was wearing a cotton dress she had made especially for this occasion. She wore Japanese sandals; I walked barefoot. (None of the children in camp owned a pair of shoes.) As we approached the red-stained schoolhouse, we saw many immigrant children of other ethnic groups with their mothers, all staring at each other; none could speak the language of the other. Mother tried desperately to find my classroom, poking her head inside door after door, trying to communicate in sign language. She finally gave up the search and left me in the second classroom with other immigrant children, all of us feeling insecure in these strange surroundings. Finally a woman entered the classroom. She was a big lady with pale skin and wiry gray hair and pale blue eyes. Those eyes seemed unreal to me; I had never seen a Caucasian woman before. I was seated on the bench in the front row when she came in. She bent over me and must have asked me, "What is your name?" But I thought she was going to devour me, so I shrieked, "Obake! Obake!" (Ghost! Ghost!) and ran out to the porch and held onto one of the posts with all my might. She ran after me, but the more she tried to comfort me the louder I cried.

It is not surprising that I had never seen a Caucasian before. For in those days plantation housing was ethnically segregated into Portuguese, Spanish, Puerto Rican, Chinese, Japanese, Filipino, and Korean camps. The Caucasian plantation manager lived in a spacious mansion at the top of the hill, and the other Caucasians—lunas, office workers, and supervisors—lived along the manager's road in comfortable homes. So, unless their parents worked as domestic help in Caucasian homes, the immigrants' children rarely, if ever, saw Caucasians.

I can still see the dress I wore that day, the one that Mother had stayed up late the night before to sew for me. It was lavender. The fabric was Indian Head cotton (because that was colorfast and would last a long time). The style was simple: a scoop neck, short kimono sleeves, and a small oval-shaped pocket on the right.

Other mothers worked just as hard as my mother did to provide suitable clothing for their children's first day of school; some took apart their own cotton kimono to fashion a new dress for a daughter. And, no matter how difficult the times, issei mothers always made at least one new outfit for each child for each new school year. I had two dresses that first year—both lavender, both Indian Head cotton. My brothers always had new outfits to begin the year. My mother even sewed them sailor hats, which were popular in those days. Children's wardrobes were usually supplemented by hand-me-downs from older children. Or, if a mother or older sister worked as a housemaid in a Caucasian household, the mistress might contribute some clothing that her children had outgrown.

Graduation from grammar school was another important day for plantation children. Most of them accepted the fact that any education beyond the eighth grade was impossible; even the few dollars it would cost for transportation and books was beyond their means. With the exception of a few children whose parents could afford to send them to high school, almost all began to do hard labor for low wages the day after graduation. Almost all of the boys went to work in the sugarcane and pineapple fields. Some of the girls also worked in the fields—at least until they got married. Other girls were sent to one of the many boarding houses for plantation bachelors to assist

Amy Umeko Sugimoto at her graduation from eighth grade in 1936. We grew up in Camp I, above the sugar mill, and walked to and from school every day until our eighth grade graduation. Amy continued her education in Japan for a few years to study the art of dollmaking. When she returned to Hawaii to a career in business, she was also recognized as an expert in dollmaking. Barbara Kawakami collection.

Graduates from a Waipahu Plantation sewing school with their instructor, Mrs. Yoneshiro *(center)*. Mrs. Yoneshiro charged five dollars a month for tuition. After instruction for six hours a day for ten months, the graduates became expert seamstresses. 1932. Carol Kobashigawa collection.

in cooking and laundry. Others began lifetime careers as domestic help. Some were sent to sewing schools on the plantation, where they not only learned a lucrative trade but were spared the ordeal of backbreaking labor. Parents who themselves had not had any formal education beyond the fourth or fifth grade at a village school in Japan were not aware of the benefits of a good education for their nisei children; they were happy to have another son or daughter contributing to the family income. Thus, graduation from grammar school was something to celebrate. Friends, neighbors, and relatives showered the graduate with huge flower bouquets, flower leis, silk leis, and paper leis in assorted colors.

There were strict dress codes to be followed for graduation day. Back in 1936, when I graduated from grammar school, a boy was supposed to wear a pair of dark-colored trousers (most wore navy cotton twill trousers), a white long-sleeved dress shirt, and a black bow tie. A girl was supposed to wear a white dress with a hemline eight inches off the floor. I particularly remember a fancy dress worn by a classmate: a white chiffon dress with a draped cowl neckline, flared sleeves, and a bias-cut skirt with tiered ruffles on the hemline. Chiffon was a luxury in those days for everyone. Because my classmate's father was a luna, her mother could afford to have a dressmaker design that fancy dress. Other classmates wore dresses made of organdy or cotton broadcloth. But the fabric most commonly used was dotted Swiss. My graduation dress was made of white dotted Swiss. It had two single pleats in the front skirt, two single pleats in the back skirt, a Peter Pan collar, puffed sleeves, and a fitted waistline with a narrow sash.

During all the years that plantation children attended school, they went barefoot. But at graduation, for the first time they wore shoes. Some had brand new ones purchased for the occasion; those who could not afford new ones borrowed shoes from their older brothers or sisters. As for me, I will never forget how I strutted across the stage to receive my eighth-grade diploma in my first pair of shoes. My mother had planned to buy my shoes at the plantation store because she could charge them there and also get them for a lower price than elsewhere. But the plantation store carried only laced shoes that looked too sporty to me; I didn't want them. Finally, Mother took me to the Naka Store down on Depot Road in Waipahu. They had a dressier-looking shoe with a button on the side. Mrs. Naka found me a pair that fitted perfectly. But my mother insisted that I take one size larger than I needed so that my younger sister would be able to wear the shoes a few years later. I had to oblige since I was getting the style that I wanted. On graduation day, as I walked across the stage to receive my diploma, I dragged my shoes across the stage as my feet bobbed up and down. It was a miserable feeling. But I wasn't the only one who felt that way; there were other students who also wore oversized shoes and had trouble walking on stage.

Most of the issei women bought their fabric from a peddler who came to isolated areas to sell his goods from a truck. Nobody owned cars in those days, and the only means of travel was by foot or by a train that ran infrequently. For people who worked ten hours a day, the dry goods peddlers were a godsend. They made their rounds once a month, and they were stocked with a little of everything from sewing notions, yardage, clothing, and slippers to medicine.

But not everyone purchased fabric from the peddler. Tei Saito, who came to Hawaii in 1912 to marry an issei who was an independent pineapple grower in Pupukea, bought dress fabric by the bolt from Theo H. Davies, where her husband also purchased his business equipment. Dress fabric in printed cotton cost three dollars a bolt and less than ten cents a yard at wholesale price. Her two older daughters wore identical dresses to school—the same print, the same style. Mrs. Saito told me: "They used to come home and complain to me, because the other students called them twins, but that was the way we economized on clothing. With nine children to clothe, every penny counted."[1]

Sometimes such "twins" weren't even related. Tatsuno Ogawa showed me a picture in which her daughter Ayako, then five years old, and a neighbor's daughter are wearing dresses of the same style made out of the same plaid fabric. At first glance one may not notice that the two dresses are identical in style because the neighbor's daughter's dress has distinctive white trim: a large collar, cuffs, a low set-in waistband, and pockets. Mrs. Ogawa explained that she had borrowed the pattern from her neighbor and they had bought the material together, but she could not afford to buy any trimming for her daughter's dress.[2]

As inexpensive as purchased yard goods were, there were some even more economical fabrics for girls' school dresses: bleached rice bags and printed flour bags. Bleached rice bags were an indispensable item in the Japanese plantation household; they were used for everything from diapers to dish towels to quilts to wrapping material to kimono underlining. During prewar days, issei mothers would soak their rice bags in hot soapsuds after every wash, rinse them thoroughly, then spread them on the grass and keep them in the hot sun until they were white. And the large bags in which flour and certain kinds of livestock feed were packed were another source

An issei mother's baby,
photographed in 1912. No
matter how poor an issei
mother might be, she tried
to dress up her baby.

Kiyojiro and Sada Hishinuma and their two children, in 1914. Mrs. Hishinuma
worked in the sugarcane fields with her husband for a while; she later became a
seamstress. Ruth Nobuko Maki collection.

The Inouye family with Tatsuno Ogawa's daughter Ayako *(right)*. The Inouyes' daughter and Ayako are wearing their "twin" dresses. Note the button-on pants on the Inouyes' son. 1922. Tatsuno Ogawa collection.

of fabric. Issei women would carefully select bags that had floral designs on them that would be appropriate for their children's school clothes.

Bleached rice bags were also used to make children's underwear. Issei families who could not afford to buy ready-made dresses or shirts and pants for their children certainly could not afford to buy ready-made underwear for them, and almost all of the plantation children wore underwear made by their mothers out of bleached rice bags.

Tatsuno Ogawa told me how she made her children's underwear:

The front part of the underwear was cut in one piece, but the back bodice and the pants were cut separately. The waistband on the pants in the back had three buttonholes to fit the buttons on the shirt waistline. The children could easily unbutton themselves when they went to the restroom. All my girls wore underwear made of rice bags. I never bought underwear for them.[3]

Another type of underwear commonly worn by girls in grade school on the plantations was a modified bloomer. It had a couple of pleats at the waist for ease, a four-inch placket on the left side, and a one-inch waistband fastened with a bone button. The bone button on the waistband was so strong that it usually outlasted the rest of the garment. The #10 thread with which it was attached was also strong, but after many washings, it did weaken, and eventually the button would pop off—always at an inopportune moment. I remember one such moment at the Japanese Language School, when some girls were playing a game called *make* horse (make is the Hawaiian word for dead). It was a rough game in which one group of girls jumped on another group of girls who pretended to be the horses. While playing this game, a bone button suddenly popped off the waist of one girl's underwear. It was a catastrophe.

In the very early years of the Japanese immigration to Hawaii, when the Japanese community consisted largely of single transient males, there were, of course, few children on the plantations. But as the picture brides arrived and the Japanese community became a community of permanent families, the number of children increased rapidly. The early issei plantation workers had so little money to spend that the only times a child of theirs could expect to get any new clothes were the day he or she started school, the first day of each subsequent school year, and the day of graduation from grammar school; there was no money available for fancy clothing for traditional Japanese festival days.

In the Japanese villages from which the immigrants had come, Girls' Day (*Hinamatsuri* [Doll Festival] or *Momo No Sekku* [Peach Blossom Festival]) and Boys' Day (*Tango No Sekku* [Feast of the Horse]) had traditionally been occasions for elaborate celebrations, and one important part of the celebration was the presentation of special clothing to a first-born girl or a first-born boy. But in Hawaii during the early immigration period, Girls' Day and Boys' Day were not celebrated at all; such expenditures were simply not possible. However, as time went on and the Japanese families accumulated a little extra money—and especially when the nisei became adults and started raising families of their own—the traditional Japanese Girls' Day and Boys' Day celebrations were revived in Hawaii. In the late 1920s and in the 1930s Japanese families even began to compete with each other in the elaborateness of their celebrations.

Girls' Day was celebrated on March 3, and for the first Girls' Day

Yoshinori Sugimoto's first Boys' Day, photographed in 1925 in Waipahu at Oahu Sugar Company's Camp 1. Because both the boy's father and grandfather were lunas, the paper carp received as gifts were particularly numerous and elaborate. Amy Sugimoto collection.

First-born son Kaoru Naito of Kauai, dressed in traditional montsuki for Boys' Day. Mrs. Shizu Kaigo sewed the montsuki and drew the family crest. He died in Europe while serving in the 100th Infantry Battalion during World War II. Shizu Kaigo collection.

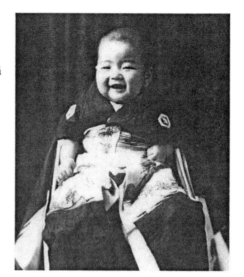

Matsu Oyama with her two daughters who were partic: pating as "Chigo" (a child in a Buddhist procession) t celebrate the opening of a new Buddhist temple in Wa: pahu in 1917. Elaine Yayoe *(left)* is three years olc Momoyo *(right)* is four. Mrs. Oyama is holding her firsi born son, Torao. Sakae Morita. Barbara Kawakami collec tion.

after the birth of the first girl in the family, the issei or nisei mother would sew or purchase a special silk montsuki for the first-born baby girl to wear. Elaborate designs—often of peach blossoms or other spring flowers—were hand-painted on the montsuki in gorgeous colors, and designs were also embroidered in red silk thread on a silk sash that was attached at the waist on each side of the kimono. The montsuki bore the mother's family crest in three places—on each side of the chest in front and in the center back below the kimono collar.

Boys' Day was celebrated on May 5, and the celebrations on this day were usually even more elaborate than the ones on Girls' Day because the oldest son was expected to continue the family name and the family traditions. On the first Boys' Day after the birth of the first son in the family some issei and nisei mothers dressed their first-born son in a Kintarō outfit (the diamond-shaped bib and headband associated with the legendary boy warrior Kintarō). Others dressed their first-born son in a montsuki on which were painted bold samurai figures, war helmets, falcons, and other symbols of courage. This montsuki, like the Girls' Day montsuki, bore the family crest in three places, but for the boy the crest was usually his father's crest.

9
Funeral Attire

In order to understand the dress and behavior of the Japanese immigrants at funerals in Hawaii, it is necessary to know something about the Buddhist laws of mourning. In the Buddhist tradition, a forty-nine-day period *(shijū kunichi)* from the day of death is set aside as the mourning period. During this period, the bereaved family refrains from eating meat or taking part in any public festivities. On every seventh day until the forty-ninth day, family, relatives, and close friends gather for a memorial service, either at a church or at a temple. On the forty-ninth day an even larger memorial service is held. And on this day the bereaved family usually prepares a feast and meat dishes are once again served. This feast is given primarily to thank the relatives and friends who have provided moral support and kindness during the difficult period. For us nisei children, it was a relief to taste meat dishes again after forty-nine days of eating only vegetable ones.

Other important memorial services are the *isshūki* (sometimes referred to as the second memorial service), which marks the first anniversary of death; the *sankaiki*, or third service, which marks the second anniversary; the *shichikaiki*, or seventh service, which marks the sixth anniversary; and the *jūsankaiki*, or thirteenth service, which marks the twelfth anniversary. There are also seventeenth, twenty-third (or twenty-fifth, depending on the sect), thirty-third, and fiftieth services. The system of numbering services and anniversaries can be confusing for the younger generations. And their confusion may be increased if the age of the deceased at the time of death is mentioned, for, in the traditional Japanese method of counting, a baby is considered a year old at birth and a year is

179

added to the chronological age at New Year's. If, for instance, a baby is born in late December, when the New Year comes he will be two years old according to the traditional method of counting age.

In the early years of the Japanese immigration to Hawaii, rules about mourning attire seem to have been more lax than rules about diet and participation in public festivals during the forty-nine-day mourning period. Many young widows on the plantations continued to dress in the same clothing they had worn before they were widowed, and, since their ordinary clothing was quite conservative, this behavior was apparently acceptable.

But it was extremely important for the family to provide a proper and decent funeral for the deceased—that is, a funeral that fulfilled traditional expectations; if the family did not do so, it would be shamed. The concepts of shame and guilt have always played a large role in Japanese culture and behavior, and, no matter how impoverished a plantation family might be, making a good impression on others in the community was of the utmost importance. To provide the deceased with an elaborate funeral, special measures had to be taken not just by the family but also by friends and community organizations. An "impressive" funeral meant not only that as many important people as possible came to pay their repects but also that there were numerous floral wreaths and that extra Buddhist priests participated in the service. At impressive funerals even the robes worn by the priests were different from those worn at most funerals: they were more elaborate, more colorful.

Traditionally, the Japanese have always considered funerals an important part of their lives, and all relatives, friends, and neighbors have been expected to participate in these rites. During the early immigration period the Japanese immigrants were predominantly of the Buddhist faith and Buddhist rites prevailed at funerals. The priests of the Hongwanji Jodo Shinshu and Sotoshu Mission of Hawaii, which had been established in Waipahu in 1902 and 1903 respectively, conducted many of the Japanese religious services in central Oahu. During this period, the issei men and women—lonely, beset with problems, and with no families in their new land whom they could ask for help—often sought the services of a religious sect that was not their own because their sect was not yet represented in Hawaii.

Although funerals were mostly religious affairs, they were also social occasions for the members of the family and the friends who came from near and far to attend the service and pay their last respects. The early plantation funerals—whether big or small, simple or extravagant—clearly demonstrated the cohesiveness of the

Japanese immigrant community. The importance of the deceased was measured not by how rich or poor he was but by how well liked he was and how charitable he had been to those who needed his help.

Before the funeral itself could take place, there were many important rites to be performed. When a person died, the first concern was to call the Buddhist priest to administer the bedside rites (*makura-gyō*; literally, "pillow prayer"). Close friends, relatives, and neighbors—especially those who had come from the same village in Japan—were notified. Everyone would hurry over to the family in whatever he or she was wearing; some would even arrive in their work clothes. (Such immediate gestures of respect and the sharing of grief are not as usual today as they were in the past.) During the bedside rites, everyone participated; they offered incense, clasped hands in prayer, and listened to the Buddhist scriptures *(sutra)* chanted by the priest. On these occasions, the priest would be dressed in a simple black kimono over a white underkimono, with a black sash, white tabi, and black-thonged zōri.

There were many complicated procedures that had to be followed in order to prepare the body of the deceased for the funeral; the expertise of an older person knowledgeable in these matters was required in order to make sure that all the procedures were performed properly. The aim of all of them was to provide the deceased with comfort, protection, and assurance of a safe journey to Paradise.

One of the basic Buddhist rites for the deceased was the purification rite, or *yūkan* (hot-water bathing). Traditionally, the yūkan was conducted at the home of the bereaved, and the bereaved family and relatives participated in it. (Today this ritual has been simplified and is carried out at the mortuary.) During the yūkan, every act would be done in a manner opposite from the manner in which it was done in everyday life. For example, instead of using the right hand to hold the water dipper, the pourer would hold the dipper in the left hand, with the dipper tilted backward and to the left. And the pourer would start pouring the water from the left side of the deceased's body.

After the yūkan was completed, the body had to be dressed properly. The garment most commonly used for the deceased by the early plantation families was the white kimono shroud. Adults, children, and infants of both sexes were dressed in these shrouds. Traditionally, a white, lightweight cotton fabric called *sarashi nuno*, which looked something like fine cheesecloth, was used to make the shroud. White was considered the proper color, since it symbolized purity and cleanliness, qualities of the life of the deceased that would, it was hoped, help the person reach Paradise. And the texture of the fabric—its sheerness and softness—was believed to provide comfort to the deceased through the long journey to the next world. Sarashi nuno came in twelve-inch widths and was available in many of the Japanese dry goods stores from the early 1900s until World War II.

Many nisei girls can still remember how the female relatives and neighbors of the bereaved family would gather at the home of the deceased to help in the sewing of the shroud. It was constructed like a kimono, and there were strict rules that had to be adhered to in sewing it. One such rule was that scissors could not be used except to snip the selvage a little. Bishop Gyokuei Matsuura explained to me that anything sharp was to be avoided during this period; using a sharp object was like "cutting the person's life."[1] (Japanese never offer roses at the altar or at the grave for fear that the thorns may hurt the deceased.) Tiny snips on the selvage were sufficient to allow the material to be torn apart to make the sleeves, collar, and length of the garment. Since kimono have always been constructed on a straight line, fit was never a problem.

Women took turns in sewing the garment together, taking a few stitches at a time. While one person worked on the right sleeve, another worked on the left sleeve. (The practice of having several women work together on a single garment was restricted to sewing funeral shrouds. When other garments were to be sewn, Japanese mothers taught their daughters never to allow two people to work on the same garment; having two people work on opposite sides of a garment was considered particularly unlucky.) No back-stitching or return stitches were allowed, and no knots were tied at the beginning or end of the seams. These precautions about back-stitching and knots were taken in order to make the path for the soul of the deceased as smooth as possible; there was no doubt in the minds of the issei that the manner in which the shroud was sewn affected the journey of the deceased.

The construction of the funeral shroud required skill, concentration, and patience as well as group effort. If the women were not careful, the long-running basting stitches without a knot or back-stitch could easily fall apart. The sewing ritual helped to alleviate the family's sorrow; the mourners would share their grief as they put the shroud together.[2]

When the kimono shroud was completed, the body of the deceased was carefully dressed with the right front overlapping the left front, which is known as the *hidarimae* manner. (Normally, a kimono is worn with the left front panel overlapping the right front panel.) In ancient times the Japanese had worn their kimono the hidarimae way. But this custom began to change in the seventh century, when Chinese court costumes were introduced. Because the Chinese wore their costumes overlapped in the opposite direction, there was a period of confusion: some Japanese held to the old way; some adopted the Chinese way. Finally, in the eighth century, Emperor Genshō (715-723) instituted a dress code that required the Japanese to wear their kimono with the left front over the right. After that, wearing a kimono hidarimae was avoided in Japan; it was considered an omen of misfortune or even death.[3] The issei immigrants to Hawaii of course brought these beliefs with them. Issei mothers would reprimand their children for inadvertently wearing their bedtime kimono overlapped the wrong way, and mothers would become especially upset if their daughters wore their kimono in the hidarimae manner on New Year's Day, since that might mean that the whole year would be unlucky. A plantation mother might say, "You wearing *make* man style?" (*Make* means dead in Hawaiian.) To this day, when issei women see people of other ethnic groups at Obon dances or teahouse parties wearing kimono the hidarimae way, they have the same reaction: they feel it is a bad omen. The younger-generation Japanese probably do not even notice.

In the new land, clothing regulations were bound to be relaxed somewhat—even for funeral shrouds. According to Henry Uyehara, whose father opened the Kukui Mortuary around 1912, funeral shrouds in Hawaii were not always sewn by a group of women. During the early plantation period, when there were many bachelors and there were also married men who had left their families back home in their villages in Japan, some issei men did not have any relatives or friends to attend to the sewing of the kimono shroud. In such cases, Eto Uyehara, wife of the mortuary owner, would often assume the responsibility of sewing the shroud to give comfort and dignity to the dead.[4]

Not all of the deceased were dressed in shrouds, however; some were buried wearing other clothing. And, in these cases, the family's wealth and status had an obvious influence on the elaborateness of the funeral clothing. If the deceased was a man of modest means, he would probably be dressed in his one and only black suit. If the deceased was a man who came from a prestigious background and had brought with him his black silk montsuki, hakama, and haori, his family would dress him in these fine garments to signify that he was the head of a household and therefore merited a dignified and formal departure on his journey to the next world. If the deceased was a married woman, she would probably be dressed in her formal black montsuki, the one she had been married in or had brought with her to Hawaii as part of her dowry. Or she might be dressed in her favorite kimono, obi, and accessories. If the deceased was a young girl, her mother would probably dress her in a silk kimono or even a pretty silk dress. Sometimes the young girl would be dressed in a white kimono shroud and then would have a silk kimono placed upon the shroud upside down, with the hemline toward her face and the collar at her feet. This practice, which follows the rule of doing things in the opposite manner for funerals, was especially common if the girl preceded her parents in death. If the deceased was a young boy, his mother would probably dress him in his Sunday best: khaki pants and white cotton shirt (or, if his parents were affluent, a dark suit).

An infant was usually dressed in a white kimono shroud unless there was some special article of clothing that was already closely associated with that infant. Not as much fuss was made over the death of an infant as over the death of an older person who had lived a long and full life and who was well known in the community. Newborn infants and young children were given simple funerals, with only the family, relatives, and intimate friends of the family participating.

Suye Kubo, who lived at Waialua Sugar Plantation in the early 1900s, bore twelve children and lost three of them while they were still young. One of these three, who was only sixty days old when he died, was one of twin boys born on November 21, 1919. She dressed him in a white kimono shroud made of unbleached muslin, the same way she had dressed her other children who had died. But, in his case, she did something else: she placed a doll in the coffin for the baby to hug. She did this because of an ancient superstition, a belief that placing a doll in the coffin will keep a twin from coming back to get his or her twin sibling.[5] It was also traditional to place a doll in the coffin with the deceased when a funeral had to be conducted on a day that was considered unlucky for funerals, a day called *tomobiki* (literally, "drawing another friend").[6]

Kaoru Matsunaga, who lost her four-month-old baby in 1927, told me that she sewed a kimono shroud for him, placed a toy in the coffin with him, and also placed six pennies in the coffin to assure a safe journey for him when he crossed the Sanzu River to reach Paradise. (Buddhists believe that the Sanzu River divides this world from Paradise and that coins are needed to pay for the ferry ride across the river.) When her husband died in 1973, Mrs. Matsunaga wanted to place the baby's remains near her husband's, so she had the baby's coffin exhumed. Nothing was left but the six pennies; everything else had turned to dust. So she had the dust gathered from the area where the six pennies were found, placed in an urn, and laid to rest beside the remains of the baby's father.[7]

At least until the late 1930s, the body of the deceased remained at his or her home before the funeral, and the family, relatives, neighbors, and close friends observed an all-night vigil there, called the *otsuya* (wake service). Everyone would come to this gathering wearing casual but conservative clothes. (Young girls were warned not to wear bright floral-print dresses.) During the wake service the mourners recited prayers for the salvation of the soul of the deceased, and the bereaved family expressed their sorrow over their loss.

Issei Men's Funeral Attire

In the early years of the immigration period, some burials were very simple indeed and were attended only by a few friends wearing their work clothes. Gijun Funakoshi told me about a burial he had attended when he was sixteen years old: the deceased was a bachelor, and his coffin, made by the plantation carpenter, was carried to the cemetery by four friends; the plantation luna had given them only thirty minutes off from work, so they, necessarily, performed this service for him dressed in their ahina work clothes smudged with red dirt.[8] If at all possible, however, the men in the Japanese community attended funerals dressed in proper funeral wear to show their respect for the deceased.

In Japan, men traditionally wore black montsuki with their family crests on them when they attended funerals. So, when the issei men first came to Hawaii, those who had brought their montsuki with them naturally wore those montsuki when they attended funerals. Soon, however, this Japanese attire gave way to dark Western suits. Photographs taken as early as the 1890s show that issei men had already adopted Western clothes for funerals: the issei men are wearing dark Western suits, white shirts, and black neckties, often bow ties.

In the traditional Japanese household, the man was expected to represent his family at all important life-cycle and community functions. And the issei men very early decided that in this new land it was necessary to wear a dark Western suit in order to be properly dressed on such occasions. When the issei men first saw the Western black suit, they thought it looked very dignified and formal—

Issei man's funeral attended by close friends and neighbors in Koloa, Kauai, in the 1920s. Photograph given to Mabel Hashisaka by the Reverend Motoyoshi of Koloa Hongwanji.

much like the black montsuki, hakama, and haori worn on formal occasions in Japan. Kaichi Abe, for example, who gave me an excellent description of the first funeral procession he witnessed in Hawaii, in 1913, the year of his arrival, seemed to be particularly impressed with the black suits worn by the men who marched alongside the coffin:

> In those days, no one had cars except the plantation manager and the assistant manager. Even the Buddhist priest walked a long distance to the home of the bereaved family, sometimes walking several miles to isolated areas of the plantation. He even went on horseback sometimes to reach his destination. The priest usually carried his ornate robe in a *furoshiki* (wrapping cloth) and changed into this formal robe when he reached his destination. In 1913 it was customary for those in the funeral procession to walk from the home of the bereaved to the cemetery. The simple redwood coffin that had been made by the plantation carpenters was draped in black cotton cloth and hammered with tack nails. The coffin was then placed in a dump car and was pulled by mules. Six bachelors,

The Hidekichi Ebisu family of Waianae, dressed in formal attire to observe Emperor Meiji's passing. 1912. Dorothy Matsuo collection.

all *tokoromon*, close friends who came from the same village in Japan as the deceased, walked alongside the dump car. The six men were all dressed up in black wool suits, white shirts with long sleeves, dark neckties, and black leather shoes. I was fifteen years old then, and I stood there in awe. The six men looked so magnificent in their black suits. I had never seen anything like that in the farming village of Fukushima Prefecture where I came from.[9]

Often, therefore, the first article of clothing an issei man would purchase with his meager savings was a dark suit to wear for funerals, weddings, the Emperor's Birthday celebration, Japanese Language School graduation ceremonies, and other important events. Most issei men chose a black wool suit or navy-blue serge suit that would be appropriate for both joyful and sad occasions. The investment was worthwhile, for the one outfit lasted the man's lifetime. The wardrobe of an issei man was very limited, and the same suit was worn for practically every occasion.

A man who could not afford even a single suit would borrow a suit from a relative or a friend when his attendance at a formal function was absolutely necessary. Or a man might be fortunate enough to inherit a suit from his father, or an uncle, or a friend who had fulfilled his contract requirements and was preparing to return home to a farming village where he would have no need for Western attire. Noriyu Koga, for example, who was only fourteen years old when he came to Hawaii in 1919 to work at Waialua Sugar Company, felt fortunate when he inherited a black suit from a friend of his father's who had returned to his home village after completing a three-year contract in Hawaii: "The adult suit was so big for my small frame, it must have looked funny, but I thought I was well dressed! . . . At least I had a black suit to wear for formal occasions until I could afford one."[10]

Issei men, not knowing much about the proper fit of a suit, would often wear suits that were too large for them. The average Japanese male was a good deal smaller than the Caucasian male for whom the ready-made garments were designed and constructed. And Japanese men were accustomed to wearing loose-fitting kimono, which are made in one standard size and fit everyone. So they thought nothing of wearing a loose-fitting dark suit that would be considered a bad fit by Western standards. In some photographs taken in the early 1900s, we see issei men wearing suits with sleeves that extend beyond their knuckles or with shoulders that are much too wide for them. Even the white dress shirts worn under their suits were too large. Sometimes, deep folds were made in the sleeves at the elbow, with the excess material tucked inside and hand-basted in place. Sometimes, arm bands were used to hold the excess sleeve length in place.

Ise Wakasa, who came from Hiroshima Prefecture in 1911, learned tailoring from a Chinese tailor in Hanapepe, Kauai, and helped her husband to operate a tailor shop on Kauai, told me that in the 1920s on Kauai a two-piece wool suit of standard quality cost thirty-five dollars, a sum that was difficult for the issei plantation laborers to save. Only a few could afford the finer-quality wool fabrics. To obtain enough money to buy even the thirty-five-dollar suit, the men usually formed a tanomoshi, and it took them six months to pay off the debt.[11]

During the early 1900s Japanese peddlers visited the plantation camps regularly around payday to take orders for made-to-order suits. The peddler was not only a salesman and a measurement-taker but—on his second visit—a fitter as well. "The peddler must have been an expert measurement-taker because most of the suits fit quite well," said Kaichi Abe, who remembered that he paid a peddler twenty dollars for his first black wool suit. He still has that suit in his sea chest. It is of fine-quality wool fabric and is in excellent

Ise Wakasa, who came to Hawaii in 1912 at the age of eighteen. She was apprenticed to K. C. Kai, a Chinese tailor in Hanapepe, Kauai. After her marriage to Wasaku Wakasa, she and her husband opened a tailoring shop on Kauai. Jenny O'Flaherty, 1989.

condition. When I asked him why the issei men wore wool suits in this tropical climate, he replied: "I did not feel too warm or uncomfortable in a wool suit at that time. Maybe Hawaii was not as warm as it is now."[12]

According to Robert Sato, of Sato Clothiers, there was, in any case, not much choice in fabrics for men's suits at that time: ready-made suits were made only in 100 percent wool—tropical-weight wool designed for spring and summer wear on the East Coast and heavier-weight wool designed for fall and winter wear on the East Coast. Mr. Sato says that the issei men usually chose the heavier-weight suit. It was a little cheaper, and some of the issei men were hopeful that someday they would return to Japan, where the heavier suit would come in handy in the harsh winters.

When Sato Clothiers began carrying ready-made wool suits in 1928, they sold for nineteen to twenty dollars, which was considerably less than a custom-made wool suit cost at that time. Men's suits made of synthetic wool fiber appeared in the late 1920s and early 1930s, and these were even more economical—and lighter in weight as well.[13]

Although most of the issei men wore black or navy-blue suits when they attended funerals, there were a few exceptions to that rule. The first dressy suit that Kaichi Abe owned was made of ahina, with the fabric used in a manner just the reverse of the usual manner: that is, the navy-blue side, which is usually considered the outer side of the fabric, was turned underneath and the lighter-colored side became the outer side. Mr. Abe wore this suit to funerals, to weddings, or when he took the Oahu Railway train to Honolulu to deposit his monthly pay at the Yokohama Specie Bank. It was made for him by the *mama-san* of the boarding house in which he lived. (Mama-san is a combination of the English word *mama* and the Japanese suffix *san*, a suffix that indicates affectionate familiarity.) She charged him $2.50 for the ahina jacket and $1.25 for the matching pair of ahina pants. Mr. Abe said that many bachelors who could not afford wool suits wore ahina inside-out suits instead. The denim suits were comfortable and could be washed at home. And when the fabric got faded and worn out, the denim suits could be used for field work.[14]

Ise Wakasa told me that denim inside-out suits were popular among the issei men on Kauai as well as on Oahu during the 1920s: she took many orders for them. The issei men on Kauai, she said, wore them for funerals and other dressy occasions until they could afford to buy wool suits.[15]

Furthermore, some men wore khaki trousers with a black or navy-blue jacket. A photograph taken in 1934 even shows an issei man wearing homemade overalls of khaki fabric to a funeral. With his overalls he is wearing a long-sleeved white shirt and a black bow tie; the black bow tie may have been his way of expressing respect for the deceased. Wearing khaki overalls to a funeral was quite unusual, even in those days; this man's neighbors explained his behavior by saying that he spent all his money on liquor and did not own a suit. There may have been others like him who did not believe in sacrificing their own pleasure for a suit that would be worn only occasionally, but most issei men felt that it was important to invest in one dark suit in order to show proper respect for the deceased.

With their dark suits the issei men wore white long-sleeved shirts made of fine percale or broadcloth. Most of these shirts had conventional soft collars. But some issei men who had special prestige in the community—for example, school principals, ministers, physicians, scholars, and lunas—wore stiff wing collars.

The issei man's funeral outfit was usually completed by a black

necktie and a pair of black leather shoes. Most issei men seem to
have preferred bow ties. Kaichi Abe had a simple explanation for
this preference: he said that issei men found it very difficult to tie
the *nekutai* (necktie). It was funny, he said, to watch them twist
their bodies and hands as they attempted to tie their own neckties.
Most of them got discouraged and switched to bow ties because
these could just be snapped into place.[16]

Issei Women's Funeral Attire

Before the Meiji Period, white was the traditional color for mourning attire for women in Japan. But by the time the Japanese immigrants came to Hawaii, the custom had changed: the preferred
funeral attire for both men and women was the black montsuki.
Therefore, most issei women did not need to look beyond their kōri
for their funeral clothing; they had carefully packed their traditional
five-crested black montsuki and the accessories that were appropriate for funerals.

The accessories that were worn with the black montsuki to funerals—such as the wide obi, bustle sash *(obi-age)*, and narrow finishing cord *(obi-jime)*—were all of black to show respect for the
deceased and the family. The black obi was usually made of dull bro-

Hatsu Urata in montsuki praying at her husband's grave. Her baby girl was born
a few months after her husband died in 1916. Mrs. Urata had this photograph
taken as a katami for her daughter. Photograph taken in Puunene Cemetery,
Maui, in 1917. Alexander & Baldwin Sugar Museum collection.

cade or sateen. Sometimes the black sateen obi was lined with broadcloth—perhaps in order to economize on fabric, perhaps because the broadcloth made it easier to keep the obi in place.

The montsuki that were traditionally worn to funerals were a solid black, with no design at the hemline. But montsuki with designs at the hemline might be worn to funerals if the designs were subtle and conservative. Nothing bright was acceptable. The most distinctive features of these black montsuki (which today, when worn as funeral attire, are usually called *mofuku*) were the family crests.

A few of the issei women wore navy-blue montsuki instead of black. In 1985, during the Japanese Immigrants' Centennial Celebration at Neal Blaisdell Center, I found that Yukie Okuno Kawano still had a navy-blue montsuki that her mother, Kimiyo Hamamura Okuno, had brought with her in 1898 from Hiroshima Prefecture. It was a five-crested formal kimono made of navy-blue crepe, without any hemline design. Yukie's mother died in 1915, when Yukie was

Issei couple seeing off to war a son who was part of the all-nisei 442nd Regiment. Because this is a formal occasion, the soldier's father wears a Western suit and his mother wears a dressy kimono and haori. As the war tensions increased, Japanese clothing and customs virtually disappeared from the Hawaiian scene. *The Hawaii Times.*

only fifteen months old, and at that time the navy-blue montsuki was carefully folded away with her other fine kimono and saved for Yukie. It was still in perfect condition in 1985.[17]

Even though issei men had adopted Western attire by the early 1900s, the women clung to their traditional kimono for special occasions until World War II. Since men had a wider range of social obligations to fulfill within the community and therefore had more contact with people of other ethnic groups, they felt the need to adjust to Western attire much more quickly than the women did. Traditionally, in Japan, women rarely took part in community social affairs. Even weddings and funerals were attended primarily by men; women participated only if the event involved their own families or close neighbors. And issei women continued these traditions in Hawaii. For the funerals they attended, the black montsuki was, therefore, the appropriate attire—until the outbreak of World War II, when all Japanese customs were frowned upon in the United States.

After the outbreak of World War II, issei women gradually accepted the Western way of dress and the black montsuki gave way to the black dress. In the beginning, issei women felt that the black dress was not as formal as the traditional montsuki, but they soon began to appreciate its advantages: the time saved in getting dressed, the greater comfort in Hawaii's tropical climate. And, in any case, as nisei boys lost their lives overseas, more issei mothers began attending funerals, and, since most of the Buddhist priests were interned in concentration camps and Buddhist temples were closed, the funeral services for Japanese boys were held at Christian churches, where Western dress prevailed.

Children's Funeral Attire

Young nisei children attended funerals only when members of their immediate families or their grandparents or other close relatives died. And very few of their parents could afford the luxury of having special mourning clothes made or bought for the children.

When a child had to attend a funeral, his or her mother or a close friend would take a quick survey of the child's limited wardrobe. A conservative kimono or a white dress was considered the most appropriate garment for a child to wear to a funeral. But if no such garment was available, the mother or friend would try to select the garment that was least faded or least worn out, the garment that would cause the least embarrassment to the mother. In a large family, most of the children's clothes were hand-me-downs. But nearly

all children had one outfit that was considered their "Sunday best":
a boy had a pair of khaki pants and a broadcloth shirt; a girl, one
dressy dress or a silk kimono sent from Japan by her grandparents.
Sometimes, however, a desperate mother might have to dress a
young boy in a sister's clothes or dress a young girl in a brother's
clothes; there are photographs that record such occasions.

Sometimes mothers allowed their older daughters to wear to
funerals the colorful *hōmongi* (visiting kimono) that were meant to
be worn for festive occasions. If they did, they were subject to criticism for bad taste, for showing a lack of respect for the dead; some of
the critics might even accuse the mother of using a sad occasion to
show off her daughter's elegant kimono.

Usually, however, the problem was simply one of finding something that wasn't too tattered or faded for the children to wear in
public. When Haruno Tazawa's husband suddenly died in 1928 and
she found herself a thirty-one-year-old widow with four children
aged from two to nine, and only thirty-five cents in her purse, she
felt devastated because she did not have any suitable kimono or
dresses for her daughters to wear to their father's funeral. Many,
many years later, the pain was still sharp; she told me:

> I was so desperate then. With only thirty-five cents, I could not
> afford to buy even a yard of white percale. I begged the plantation
> seamstress to make whatever she could, even if she had to use
> bleached rice-bag material, just so they could wear white. The
> seamstress made a simple A-line kappa dachi for each of my two
> girls, with openings for their heads and arms to go through. Some
> kindly neighbor had offered the bleached rice bags. My friends and
> neighbors banded together and pitched in and helped me with the
> funeral expenses. I can never forget the humiliation, nor the kind-
> ness of those who helped me face the most terrible ordeal of my
> life. For this reason, I do not have any desire to indulge in any lux-
> ury, even though I have enough pension money to afford some nice
> things. I cannot hold my head high and walk proudly down the
> street when I recall how all those kind people even helped me with
> the gratuity for the minister.

Haruno Tazawa's most prized possession today is the account of
offerings received for her husband's funeral in 1928. The average
offering was one dollar; some people gave a roll of incense sticks
along with the dollar, which was considered a very generous offering. "Giving a dollar was actually sacrificing a whole day's pay,"
Mrs. Tazawa said pensively.[18]

Mrs. Tazawa's story shows very clearly the respect shown to the
deceased and the concern and sympathy shown for the family by the

Haruno Tazawa and her children, taken several months after she became a widow. The two girls are dressed in the bleached-rice-bag dresses they wore for their father's funeral. 1928. Haruno Tazawa collection.

members of the Japanese immigrant community. It was important for the mother to attempt to dress her daughters properly for their father's funeral, and she did—even though the little girls had to wear dresses made of bleached rice bags. And it was important for friends and neighbors to band together and share whatever they had with the family in their time of need. The people who helped lived

barely at subsistence level themselves, yet they gladly helped the
young widow who was in even greater need. The issei people could
not have survived without this kind of care for each other.

Katami

Buddhists believe that the spirit does not leave the house until the
forty-ninth day; therefore, the personal effects of the deceased,
including clothing, are left undisturbed until that day. But after the
forty-ninth day, according to Japanese custom, the personal belongings of the deceased are divided and distributed among family members and close friends as *katami*, or keepsakes. This age-old custom
is still observed in Japan and by some of the Japanese in Hawaii
today.

Usually, cherished personal items are divided among the survivors according to the degree of closeness of the survivors to the
deceased. Clothes are considered the most important katami, as it is
believed that the spirit of the dead person who wore them remains
in them. The best garments are given to the children, brothers, sisters, or other close relatives of the deceased. A personal anecdote
will illustrate the meaning of katami. A few years ago, my only
cousin on my father's side died. I had developed a close relationship
with her during three trips to Japan, and her daughter-in-law sent
me three sets of exquisite hand-woven silk kimono and silk obi as a
katami from my cousin. These garments had been specially made
for my cousin in Kyoto. Every now and then I take them out to
admire their beauty and remember my cousin's warmth and kindness. She had been for me a bridge to my father's past, which I had
not known about or understood until I got to know her. I felt very
humbled and honored to receive these valuable items as a remem-
brance. I also have my late mother's black montsuki, which I cher-
ish. It is a reminder of my childhood and of the way my mother
brought me up. Now, as I look at that faded montsuki with the
hand-drawn design of pine, bamboo, and plum on the hemline, I am
grateful for the valuable lessons my mother passed on to me, which
are literally "bearing fruit" in my lifetime. Yes, to receive a katami,
no matter what it is, brings back fond memories of loved ones and
how they taught us to live.

The funeral photograph is another kind of katami, a souvenir of
the funeral itself. Many of the photographs taken at issei funerals in
Hawaii were destroyed during World War II. They were destroyed
because of the mounting fear that possession of anything that
showed a pride in one's Japanese heritage might be considered a sign

of disloyalty to the United States government. But some pictures have managed to survive. Most of them were recovered by families who were able to visit their ancestral homes in Japan after the war and bring back the precious photographs that had been sent by the issei in Hawaii to their relatives in Japan.

It may be hard to understand how the issei families could indulge in the luxury of souvenir funeral photography when they were having such a hard time trying to make their wages cover the barest necessities. A Buddhist minister gave me this explanation:

> It has always been traditional for a Japanese to die on his native soil and to die in dignity. For a Japanese to perish on foreign soil was lonesome and sad; this was even more so when one had to be taken home in ashes before he fulfilled his goal of acquiring wealth and success. Under such circumstances, the least one's kin or friend could do was to assure the parents and relatives back home how impressive the funeral ceremony was. The souvenir photograph served as evidence of how many people attended, thus giving some indication of how successful the deceased had been. Further, the adherence of the deceased to the Confucian value of filial piety was proven, in part, by the ritual of picture-taking. In the case of a son who died before his parents, the single photograph, more than words, assured the parents that their son had died in dignity.[19]

No photographs are available for the period from 1885 to 1890, since none of the issei owned a camera in those early years. But we have fairly comprehensive photographic records of Japanese plantation funerals from the late 1890s until 1941. These photographs were taken by professional issei photographers, who went into business to meet the demand for funeral photographs for family katami.

As the lives of the Japanese immigrants became more stable and economically secure, their circles of friends and acquaintances expanded and funerals became larger and more elaborate. Funeral photographs of the type taken in the late 1890s, which had measured eight by ten inches, were no longer able to include the whole funeral party; larger photographs were needed. And the demand for larger funeral photographs stimulated the use of panoramic photography. Sakae Morita of Waipahu was one of the first photographers to use a panoramic camera; he used it for the first time in 1907. Panoramic photographs were from twenty-four to thirty-eight inches wide and from eight to ten inches high and were therefore able to include in one photograph everyone who was present at the funeral service. Mr. Morita was in such demand as a panoramic photographer that he traveled throughout the islands—to the Big Island, Maui, Kauai, Lanai, and Molokai as well as on Oahu—to photo-

A section of a panoramic photograph of Torasaku Oyama's funeral, taken at the Soto Mission Temple in Waipahu on July 17, 1928, by Sakae Morita.

graph issei funerals, family groups, weddings, and historical planta-tion landmarks.[20] Other issei photographers appeared later who used similar types of techniques and equipment, but Mr. Morita is considered the pioneer of panoramic photography in the Hawaiian Islands.[21]

Funeral photography flourished from about 1907 to 1941. But World War II put an abrupt stop to it, for two reasons. First, at the start of the war all photographic equipment was confiscated from those whom the United States government considered "Japanese aliens," and that category included most of the professional photog-raphers who did business with Japanese plantation people; they were issei men who had succeeded because they could communi-cate in their native language with their clients. Second, during the war picture-taking in general in Hawaii was banned by the United States government for security reasons. After the war, picture-tak-ing with the panoramic camera resumed. But it never regained its popularity. In fact, demand for funeral photography declined to such an extent that production of the panoramic camera was eventually discontinued. Production of film for the panoramic camera was, of course, also discontinued, and any film substitute had to be wound by hand, which meant a lot of extra work for the photographer.[22] The wartime perception that "loyal" Americans should have no contact with Japan certainly contributed to the decline in souvenir funeral photography. Another reason for the decline was the soaring cost of funeral rites and services. Still another was the fact that nisei children were assimilating American values and attitudes and were

losing interest in some of the old Japanese customs. But perhaps the main reason was the fact that the parents of the nisei children were in Hawaii with them, not separated from them by miles of ocean, and there was, therefore, no need for the nisei children to send pictures to their parents to show how impressive a funeral ceremony had been.

10
Conclusion

The Japanese immigrants who came to Hawaii in a steady stream beginning in 1885 brought with them a rich cultural heritage, and their traditional clothing was an important part of that heritage. These immigrants had been exposed to little, if any, Western culture in their native Japanese villages. Not one of the women I interviewed for this study arrived in Hawaii wearing a Western dress; they all wore their native kimono. A few of the men did have Western suits, but a majority of them also wore kimono.

At first the issei men and women began working in the fields in the rustic cotton kimono they had brought with them from their villages. But those kimono were ill-suited for work in sugarcane and pineapple fields. And so, very soon, the issei women began to take apart their cotton kimono and remake them into more suitable work garments.

The Japanese have been known to be great cultural borrowers—ever since the Nara Period (618–794), when much of their clothing and many other elements of their culture were borrowed from the Chinese culture of the T'ang Dynasty (618–907) and gradually modified to suit Japanese tastes and the Japanese way of life. And this pattern was repeated in Hawaii as the Japanese worked and intermingled with Hawaiian, Chinese, Portuguese, Spanish, and Filipino laborers.

The issei men readily accepted the standard work clothing worn by the other ethnic groups who were already working on the plantations to which the issei came, and soon their work clothing was indistinguishable from that of the men of other ethnic groups; all the men doing field work on the plantations wore the same kinds of ahina jackets and pants. And once the issei men had adopted this standard work attire, they were not interested in any changes in style. As long as a garment was affordable, comfortable, and sturdy and served its purpose, they were satisfied with it. Almost the only changes seen in issei men's work wear in the early years were in the variety of straw hats and bright red and blue bandannas adopted from Spanish, Filipino, and Portuguese co-workers. Later, in the 1920s, when palaka jackets became popular among the other groups in Hawaii, the issei men readily adopted them also; they liked the palaka cloth because the plaid pattern resembled the checked design used on their cotton kimono and thus evoked memories of village life in their homeland.

For wear on formal occasions the issei men immediately adopted the Western suit. An issei man usually purchased a dark wool suit early in his settling-down period, and it lasted him a lifetime. He wore this one dark suit for all special occasions such as weddings and funerals and sometimes for his final journey into the next world.

The issei women were more selective and more inventive. As they came in contact with the diverse ethnic groups in Hawaii, they found useful ideas in the dress of other cultures. By assimilating these new ideas and combining them with their own traditional ideas, these women fashioned a unique style of clothing.

The issei women fashioned this new style of clothing to meet the needs of their new environment and their new way of life. Economic necessity dictated some of the changes. So did the need for protection against the tropical sun, dust, mud, the serrated edges of the sugarcane stalks, the sharp, tough leaves of the pineapple plants, and the stings of centipedes, scorpions, and yellow jackets. But the changes also demonstrated the issei women's flair for innovation and their desire to express their individuality. The issei women's attire left a strong visual imprint on the plantation landscape and its people. Some members of other ethnic groups who worked beside them still retain vivid memories of the issei women as the "Mamasan group who wore the fancy kasuri outfit with the straw hat, arm guards, leggings, and tabi."[1]

The clothing the issei women developed retained many features of their traditional Japanese clothing. The arm guards and leggings that the issei women learned to make out of sturdy ahina cloth were similàr to the protective garments used on their farms back home. The wide, cummerbund-like sashes that held their work outfits together were a strong reminder of their Japanese folk culture: back in their home villages, they had always worn wide sashes over their kimono. The issei women liked the comfort and security of the wide black sash tied firmly around the waist. Some of them even said it gave them the strength to endure the hard work on the plantation. And often, when they were hungry, the tightness of the sash helped to overcome the pangs of hunger. The indigo-dyed kasuri fabric that they used for their work jackets was another link with the past: it was precious to the issei women in part because it had been favored for work clothing in their home villages.

Originally, the distinctive differences in the women's work jackets were differences in the kasuri patterns brought from the various prefectures of Japan. During the early settling-down period, the issei women could tell what prefecture a woman came from simply by looking at the kasuri pattern on her jacket. Later, however, as kasuri fabrics were imported from various prefectures of Japan and sold in Japanese dry goods stores in Honolulu, it became impossible to make such identifications.

The issei women certainly did not try to stay as close as possible to their traditional styles in all respects, however; when innovations seemed useful to them, they borrowed freely from women of other ethnic groups. The jacket style came from the Chinese women; various types of skirts came from the Hawaiian, Spanish, and Portuguese women; and slat sunbonnets came from Spanish, Portuguese, and Puerto Rican women. And the issei women even began to purchase American fabrics instead of their beloved kasuri fabrics when it became clear to them that the American fabrics were a better buy: the American fabric cost about a third less than kasuri fabric, and it took less effort to cut and sew because it was much wider than the kasuri fabric.

The issei women were relatively slow to discard their traditional kimono for casual wear around the house and for wear on social occasions. But once they had an opportunity to find out how comfortable simple A-line dresses and Hawaiian mu'u mu'u were and what freedom they afforded, they enthusiastically adopted those styles of dress. As with everything else they adopted, however, they often made changes to suit their tastes—for example, they tended to use fabrics that were similar in color and pattern to traditional Japanese fabrics.

Over the years the issei women continued to make changes in clothing that gave them greater freedom and comfort. By the late 1930s, there were few issei women workers left on the plantations, but those few began wearing the same kind of blue-and-white-plaid palaka jackets and the same kind of ahina pants that their male counterparts wore. These outfits were comfortable and took much less time to put on than the cumbersome layers of clothing and the tight sashes that the issei women had been wearing. One issei woman, the last to retire from the wahine gang in Waipahu in 1964, said to me: "To think that we got dressed in layers of clothing and many accessories at 4:30 in the morning while preparing breakfast and packing two lunch bags (my husband's and my own) is unbelievable. Look how easy it is to step into denim pants and to put on my palaka jacket!"[2]

As the issei women changed their outer image, they changed their inner image as well. For, as Ingrid Brenninkmeyer has said, "Clothing is symbolic of the values and aspirations of a society and its culture."[3] By the time the issei women had adopted the same kind of work clothing their male counterparts wore, some of them had risen to the rank of luna and had outdone their husbands in work performance. The issei women had become independent and aggressive; they were no longer the shy picture brides who had come to Hawaii to marry men sight unseen.

But neither the issei men nor the issei women changed completely. They never abandoned the values and beliefs that had been such an important part of their childhood in Japan; they still respected and valued their cultural heritage. And perhaps that is the real reason why so many of them held on to their traditional Japanese kimono and their kasuri jackets long after they had ceased to wear them.

Appendix A
Kamon

Kamon (family crests) in Japan have been more than merely decorative emblems; they have played an important role in Japanese culture. And the Japanese immigrants continued their traditional uses of crests in Hawaii.

The origin of family crests in Japan dates back to the Nara Period (710–794) and the Heian Period (794–1185) and is closedly linked to the history of the T'ang Dynasty (618–907) in China. The rich culture of the T'ang Dynasty had a profound influence on many aspects of Japanese culture, and during the golden age of the dynasty the T'ang court costumes were introduced in Japan. These court costumes were worn by the high-ranking nobles of the imperial court in Japan, and designs woven into the silks captured the interest of the noble class.

These designs were borrowed and used to embellish ox-drawn carriages and personal belongings of the nobility in Japan. And, whenever there were special functions that created heavy traffic, these motifs painted on the carriages helped to distinguish the different families. But during the Nara and Heian Periods the emblems were used primarily for their aesthetic value; they had not yet become family crests.

Some of the early designs found in textiles and on personal possessions favored by the nobility were the arabesque, China flower *(karabana)*, brocade flower *(fusenryō)*, peony, chrysanthemum, paulownia, wisteria, plum blossom, gentian, bamboo, iris, melon, and maple leaf and geometric shapes such as diamonds, hexagons, and triangles. Tortoises, phoenixes, and circular cranes were introduced as patterns on textiles as early as the Nara Period. In the late eleventh century, as relations with China waned, the Japanese nobles began to create designs incorporating flowers and birds from their own environment, such as cherry blossoms, reeds, clovers, mistletoes, pigeons, and sparrows.[1]

By the late twelfth century, the nobility in Japan had been overrun by the powerful military class; with the Kamakura Period (1185–1333) the era of feudalism had begun. It continued for the next five hundred years and was marked by many rebellions, revolts, civil wars, and changes of rulers. Warriors of high rank, who were constantly engaged in battles against one another began to mark their banners, flags, weapons, and armor with large emblems in simple but bold abstract designs such as the first characters of their names, vertical stripes, crossed bars, or images of falcon feathers. These bold emblems made it easy to distinguish between friend and foe on the battlefield. These insignia were also painted on curtains and lanterns to identify a general's camp. And the lord *(daimyō)* often rewarded loyal subordinates and retainers, and even lesser-ranking samurai who had performed meritorious feats, by giving them the right to use his insignia. Thus, the elite warrior class during the Kamakura Period initiated the use of emblems as family crests.[2]

As the warrior clans increased in size and power and split into smaller units, each unit adopted a place name as its identifying name. This was the origin of the surname *(myōji)*, and the emblem that had been adopted by each of these smaller units became the family crest. The basic design of the crest was varied slightly to represent new branches and individual families. For example, the warrior descendants of the Fujiwara clan selected the wisteria *(fuji)* to mark their carriages and belongings during the Heian Period; this emblem later was designated as the family crest. As the family expanded and even the concubines' children and the children gained by adoption for political reasons had to be taken into account, the family lineage became very complicated. It became necessary to create new variations of the original wisteria crest to represent the new expanded family groups, and the family crest of the great Fujiwara clan was transformed in hundreds of ways.

As the warrior-class families expanded and branched out, the uses of crests also expanded: they were placed on tombstones and on everyday objects. And soon the men and women of the samurai class began to use their family crests on their formal kimono as well as on their banners and armor and the like. The court nobles had originated the idea of using Chinese motifs as patterns on their fine costumes, but those motifs had not been family crests. One of the first official garments that had a distinct family crest was the *daimon* (great crest) robe, a kimono with wide, billowing sleeves. The daimon was first seen sometime between 1338 and 1568. The daimon was identical to the *hitatare*, except that the latter was of less-expensive material and lacked crests. The daimon robe was made of linen and had five kamon—two on the chest, two on the sleeves, and one at the neck in the back center. When this costume was designated as formal ceremonial attire, the use of crests for formal attire began.[3]

From the fourteenth to fifteenth centuries, more and more agreements were made between lords and retainers about the use of specific crests. Consequently, even crests from obscure genealogies became objects of political and social exchange. They were bestowed on inferiors, shared with equals, and seized from defeated foes. During the second decade of the Muromachi Period (1336–1573), a list of about 255 crest patterns, complete with names, was compiled from the Kyoto and Osaka regions alone.[4]

It was during the early Edo Period (1603–1868) that the family crests became popular among commoners. After the Tokugawa regime had restored peace to the land, there was no need for emblems in warfare. Once again the family crests were used for aesthetic purposes. Symmetrical designs were favored. Enclosing the motifs in a white circle became popular. People began creating new designs incorporating things that were familiar to them, such as snowflakes, wild geese, rabbits, sailboats, oars, spools, sickles, hand drums, spinning tops, rice pounders, ladders, and mountains in mist.[5] Some of these motifs were already in use.

During the Edo Period (1603–1868), the sleeveless robe that had been known as a *kamishimo* was designated as the official garment of the samurai; this robe featured the family crest on its front lapels and back bodice. It was also during the Edo Period that the practice of using five family crests on formal kimono and three crests on haori became firmly established. These crests were usually about an inch and a half in diameter.[6]

The crests that had been put on carriages, lanterns, samurai banners, and the like were all painted on. And when crests were put on clothing, they were also painted on, usually with the aid of a stencil. The painting of crests on kimono became a specialized, important, and highly respected art.

There was another type of crest, however: the *nuimon* (embroidered family crest), also called *keshinui* (from *keshi*, to erase, and *nui*, to sew; that is, to erase the white dotted lines of the design as one embroiders the crest) which was introduced during the Edo

Period.[7] I have seen two of these intricately embroidered crests, both done with white silk thread. One example was on Ko Shigemura's formal black haori, which she brought to Hawaii in 1904 from Yamaguchi Prefecture. The crest, embroidered on the center back of the haori, depicted a single butterfly with raised wings. Mrs. Shigemura had done the embroidery herself.[8] The other embroidered crest was on my mother's black silk haori; it was my father's family crest. The delicate stitching looks like tiny beads; only skilled hands could have done this fine embroidery on delicate silk crepe. The embroidering of crests was obviously a very demanding art, and men as well as women specialized in it.

In the Meiji Period (1868–1911), many commoners obtained family crests. In 1870, when the Meiji government decreed that commoners should have family names as did members of the upper classes, many chose names that indicated where they lived. And, after surnames were chosen, a motif could be recognized as a family crest. Approximately three hundred to five hundred designs have been accepted as crests, and several thousand variations exist in Japan today. These designs are based on various animals, plants, natural phenomena, and geometric forms. Often the family selected a crest that featured something associated with the prefecture in which it lived. For example, Fukuoka Prefecture is famous for its plums, so the plum crest is very popular in Fukuoka. And Wakayama is known for its fishing villages and beautiful coastline, so fish, boats, oars, and waves are commonly used for its crests.[9] The only crests that commoners were not allowed to use were the asarum, paulownia, chrysanthemum, and peony, the four most prestigious crests in Japan. Many commoners chose patterns favored by kabuki actors and prostitutes, who had already adopted patterns for their own use as trademarks. Some changed an earlier motif to a more elegant one; some added enclosures to their designs to distinguish their main and branch families. Merchants identified their businesses with simple designs marked on their shop curtains and on the happi of their employees.

In 1868, when Japanese immigrants first came to Hawaii, some of the immigrants had surnames, and these surnames were entered in the immigration records. Others were identified in the records by a first name followed by the person's birthplace. By 1885, when the first large wave of Japanese immigrants came to Hawaii, all of the immigrants had surnames. But not all of them had family crests.

The family crests that were brought by the Japanese immigrants to Hawaiian plantations on their kimono were a direct link to their families as well as to the culture and history of Japan; bringing their crests was one way of bringing their family with them as they started a new life in Hawaii. And most of those who did not bring crests with them soon selected crests. Shizu Kaigo, a bridal consultant who dressed hundreds of nisei brides before World War II, kept a special book of crest designs, and many people who did not have family crests chose designs from this book. Sometimes two friends would order the same designs for their formal kimono.[10]

Douglas Nakaguma, who engraved tombstones for Hawaii Marble and Granite Company, was able to tell me a good deal about the way Japanese immigrants to Hawaii selected crests to be engraved on tombstones for members of their families. If the family had a family crest that had been handed down for generations and was used on its formal kimono, then that crest—or some variation of it—was, of course, used for the tombstone. If the family did not have such a crest, it would select a crest that was associated with the prefecture from which the family came or a clan from which it was descended. Or the family might select a crest motif associated with the religious sect to which it belonged.[11]

The Okinawan immigrants who arrived in 1900 did not have family crests on their kimono. For them, this was a new idea. But after they had mingled with the naichi in Hawaii for a while, they adopted the idea enthusiastically. In Okinawa, only the members of the royal family had worn a family crest on their kimono. Their crest was the "left-rotating three commas" *(hidari mitsu-domoe)*, which was adopted by King Shō Toku as the family crest for the royal house of Okinawa. Some families in Okinawa had a *yaban* (household seal or stamp) that they put on household furniture, dishes, and other articles of significance. But even these families did not pass it down unchanged from generation to generation to all members of the family the way the naichi families did: the first son had the right to use the yaban, but when the second son got married and set up his own household, he had to have a new motif designed for his family's furniture.[12] And only the members of the royal family ever wore a family crest on their kimono. There are a few Okinawan families in Hawaii who trace their lineage to the royal family and they adopted variations of the "comma" patterned crests. But other families chose other motifs—usually from nature (the crescent moon, for example)—and used those as family crests for their black formal kimono.

The wearing of the family crest was traditionally tied in with the observation of all of the life-cycle ceremonies in all areas of Japan except Okinawa. For example, the crests were seen on children's ceremonial kimono when a newborn baby was taken to the Shinto shrine (on the thirtieth day for girls and on the thirty-first day for boys).[13] Japanese immigrants continued this tradition after they were settled on the plantations. It was discontinued at the outbreak of World War II, when the Shinto shrines were closed and the priests were interned, but it has been revived again; I have seen some third- and fourth-generation Japanese women at a Shinto shrine with new-borns dressed in ceremonial kimono.

Today, however, family crests are used primarily as designs for pendants, rings, and wall hangings. And today very few families can claim to have a historically authentic family crest without doing some research in Japan at their ancestors' village office, the original temple that has preserved their family history, or their ancestors' graves.

I first became fascinated with the intricately drawn crests while growing up in the plantation town of Waipahu. I was accustomed to seeing my mother dressed in a faded gray cotton dress, wearing wooden clogs and bending over a washboard. On the rare occasions when she donned her five-crested black kimono to attend weddings or funerals, she looked like an altogether different person to me. Because she did not have a black obi, she wore a dull gold-brocaded obi. Underneath her kimono, she wore a white silk underkimono. She looked elegant—even regal, I thought. Traditionally, men were the ones who represented the family at such affairs, but my father had died early and so my mother attended these functions in his place.

The crest on my mother's kimono consisted of three oak leaves enclosed in a white circle *(maru ni mitsu gashiwa)*, a crest that had been in our father's family since the seventeenth century. When I first visited my father's ancestal home, in 1972, my cousin took me to a Soto Zen temple that was more than five hundred years old, the oldest in the village. It was surrounded by old tombstones of the Oyama family, some of which dated back to the time the temple was built. My cousin showed me a weathered tombstone with the three-oak-leaves-in-a-circle crest engraved at the top and the name of the first of our ancestors who settled in that village. As I knelt there to pray, a black snake came out of nowhere and circled the tombstone. I was frightened, for I had never seen a snake before. But my cousin, who said this was the first time he had ever seen a snake at the ancestral grave, interpreted the appearance of the snake as a good omen: he said that the ancestral spirits were happy that I had come back to pay repects to my ancestors.

On my mother's side, the ancestral motif was a sword blade and wood sorrel *(ken katabami)* in a white circle. This motif dates back to the feudal period and is engraved on our ancestors' tombstones in my mother's village. I had never seen this crest on any of my mother's formal kimono, for she had adopted my father's family crest after her marriage. Perhaps she did so because her family considered the sword motif too masculine for a daughter to use. But this was not necessarily the reason; in many families it was customary for a daughter to wear her husband's family crest after marriage. More often, however, the matrilineal crest design was handed down from mother to daughter. This custom of taking the mother's family crest was common among the nisei brides in Hawaii. If, as was common, the bride changed her kimono two or three times during the wedding ceremony, the first formal kimono she wore would most likely be the one that had been given to her during the exchange of betrothal gifts and would have her husband's family crest on it, but the second formal kimono she wore would bear her mother's crest. And there were some brides, like my older sister, who took their father's family crest rather than their mother's. My older sister, who was married in 1936, in the exchange of betrothal gifts received a bridal kimono with the groom's family crest on it, and she wore this first at the wedding reception. But all her other formal kimono were decorated with my father's family crest, and so were the coverlets *(yutan)* for the furniture in her dowry. Her dowry included a Singer sewing machine, a *kyōdai* (a low dressing table with a long mirror), and a six-foot-tall Japanese-style clothes closet with a five-drawer chest of drawers. Each piece was covered with a yutan made of royal-blue cotton (with slit openings in each corner that were fastened with narrow red ties), and in the center of each yutan, appliqued in white cotton, was my father's family crest, twelve inches in diameter. These crests had been appliqued by Ko Shigemura.

Shizu Kaigo and Ko Shigemura were exceptional issei women who acquired the skill of drawing crest designs. Another expert was Hanzo Shinokawa, who had been trained as an artist in Japan and who, after he came to Hawaii to work on the plantations, saw the need for crest-drawing for the nisei girls' bridal costumes. One of his daughters, Yuri Tsunehiro, told me that the family has carefully preserved the implements he used for drawing crests.

Fusao Iwahori, a nisei who studied in Kyoto and returned to Hawaii in 1938 to start a business in crest-drawing, gave me many insights into the rigorous training required of crest artists in Japan. Mr. Iwahori was born in Kawailoa, Oahu, on January 16, 1919. His mother, who had been a picture bride from Shizuoka Prefecture, took him to Japan for medical treatment when he was a young boy. There his uncle encouraged him to become an artist and, when he

A nisei bride's dowry, photographed in the 1930s. The crests on the yutan were stenciled on by Shizu Kaigo. Shizu Kaigo collection.

was thirteen and had completed the eighth grade at the village school, sent him to Kyoto to become an apprentice under a Mr. Uesugi, an established crest artist. During his first two years as an apprentice, he spent most of his time baby-sitting, doing household chores, running errands, and delivering the finished products. (For deliveries, the garments were wrapped in a large *furoshiki* [wrapping cloth] and tied to his back.) In the third year, after he had acquired skill with the brush-tipped compass and other fine brushes, he was allowed to do touch-ups on small sections of the design. The work continued late into the night, and Fusao often dozed off with brush in hand. He told me that when he was finally allowed to draw a design on silk cloth for the first time, he held his breath until the drawing was finished. As he became more experienced and confident, he was allowed to work on expensive fabrics, including fine silks such as kinsha, chirimen, habutae, and tsumugi. Ordinarily it took an apprentice ten years to become a skilled craftsman in this field, but Fusao was eager to return to Hawaii and he did so after his fourth year. The timing was perfect, for many nisei girls were then getting married in the five-crested formal kimono. He immediately started doing business with the Hata, Nagao, Oomi, Musashiya, and Marumiya stores, which specialized in Japanese bridal wear, accessories, and furniture, and the stores gave him more work than he could handle. He charged 50 cents apiece for each design and with five crests on each kimono that totaled $2.50 per garment, so he earned about $200.00 to $300.00 a month (which was considered a

Ko and Saburo Shigemura, dressed in their montsuki. Ko had many talents: she was a fine seamstress, excelling in both Western sewing and the sewing of kimono; she operated a successful sewing school; she was an expert at drawing crests on formal kimono and yutan. 1935. Grace Kiyoko Shigemura collection.

good salary at that time). In addition to stenciling crest designs on kimono, Mr. Iwahori also drew large-sized crests for the yutan used for the bride's furniture.

Mr. Iwahori told me that one of the most important things he learned in his study of crest-drawing was the technique for removing spots. Drawing the intricate design with a fine brush is painstaking work and, no matter how cautious one may be, errors are bound to be made; sometimes the design is even drawn upside-down or the wrong motif is drawn in or the crest faces the wrong way. If such errors were made, Mr. Iwahori said, the apprentice was held responsible and required either to pay the cost of replacing the fabric or to erase the error without leaving any smudges. Every precaution had to be taken not to ruin the fabric. Nightingale dung was first rubbed on the design; it was allowed to set and then removed. A whitening agent was applied to remove all traces of ink. Then the white powder was washed off; the fabric was rinsed repeatedly, using as little water as possible, to return it to its former condition. The process took hours and caused a great deal of anxiety.

Mr. Iwahori's patience and perseverance paid off; his business was very successful. And after he stopped painting crests on kimono, he was kept busy designing gold pendants and rings that featured family crests; he also designed individual crests to use as wall hangings.[14]

The use of the crest "as a specific mark of identification" helped to establish the family system in Japan.[15] And for the Japanese immigrants who settled in Hawaii, the use of the family crest has been one way of establishing links with relatives in Japan and preserving the family's heritage.

Appendix B
Preservation and Care of Clothing

Clothes are made to be worn, and eventually most of them are discarded. But some garments should be preserved, for it is certainly true that, as Karen Finch and Greta Putnam have observed, textiles "can . . . be things of great beauty, historical interest or sentimental value."[1] And many of the garments that the Japanese immigrants brought to Hawaii deserve to be preserved—some for aesthetic reasons, some for historical reasons, some for sentimental reasons, many for all three reasons.

Most of the early Japanese immigrants who came to Hawaii were poor peasants who had only a few belongings, but there were some who brought collections of treasured kimono with them. The great majority of both the men and the women began working in the fields within a few days after their arrival, and they quickly remodeled the cotton kimono they had brought into clothing suitable for field work. But they had very little opportunity to wear the more elaborate silk kimono they had brought. Many of these garments were simply stored; they were seldom, if ever, taken out of their original storage places. And some of these kimono survived remarkably well.

The oldest kimono in my collection were brought to Hawaii in 1898 by Kimiyo Hamamura Okuno. Because these kimono were kept in a sea chest, they were unsoiled, except for a few brown age spots in the linings. They have miraculously retained their original color, design, and texture. I was surprised to find out that these fine garments, while stored in the chest, had been wrapped in Japanese newspapers. This practice would be unthinkable today because the carbon and oil used in today's newsprint easily rub off on contact with clothing and other articles. But I learned that the ink used in the old newpapers did not stain clothing or other personal posses-sions.[2] Gary Woodard of the California Ink Company told me that until about 1920 newspapers were printed by the "litho-stone" pro-cess, a process that used only ink and water. Only a few copies could be printed at a time, but because no oil was used, the ink dried quickly and did not stain other materials on contact.[3] This explains why newspapers could be used in those days for wrapping clothing, foodstuffs, and almost anything else one can think of. Japanese women who did the laundry for the plantation bachelors even wrapped the clean garments in old newspapers for delivery.

Saburo Shigemura and his wife, Ko, brought a fine collection of traditional Japanese clothing with them to Hawaii. Both came from Yamaguchi Prefecture—Saburo in 1892, Ko in 1904. Mr. Shigemura first worked on the Lyman Estate in Kapoho, on the Big Island, as a cook; when Ko arrived, she did sewing and helped with household chores. After Saburo was thrown from a horse and injured his leg, he moved to Oahu and eventually settled in Waipahu, where he worked for the Oahu Sugar Company as a maintenance man until his retire-ment. Mrs. Shigemura operated a large sewing school in Waipahu.

Despite their various moves, the Shigemuras kept their collection of traditional clothing intact. Mr. Shigemura had a formal five-crested black habutae kimono, a three-crested half-coat of habutae, and two silk hakama for formal wear. Ko kept these garments wrapped in ecru cotton cloth. One of the Shigemuras' daughters, Grace, later put them in a metal chest lined with paper. And there they remained for many years. When the chest was finally opened, only the habutae half-coat showed signs of deterioration; once it was exposed to air and heat, it began to split in the center back and on the shoulder line.

This formal half-coat had Mr. Shigemura's family crest, the *kikkō ni gohon bone no ōgi* (five-boned fan enclosed in a hexagon), drawn on it in three positions; these crests are still well preserved and have not split or faded. The crest design had been handed down for gener-ations, along with a valuable family history. (The Shigemura family is one of the few immigrant families in Hawaii that have a well-documented genealogy [*keizu*] written in calligraphy on rice paper; this is the original document, handed down in Mr. Shigemura's fam-ily since the fifteenth century. The paper has turned brown with age and is very fragile, but the pages are still intact.)[4]

Kichizo Sugimoto brought a hakama and a black habutae mon-tsuki (with a cherry-blossom crest) with him when he came to Hawaii on November 16, 1916. They are still stored in the original sea chest in which the clothing was packed for his journey to Hawaii. And they are still in perfect condition.[5]

An elegant collection of pure silk kimono and patterned silk brocade obi that once belonged to Hisa Kawakami, who came from Fukuoka Prefecture and settled in Eleele, Kauai, in the late 1880s, has been carefully preserved in the original sea chest by her daughter, Mabel Hashisaka. The kimono and sashes are unwrinkled and in excellent condition. The sea chest, the finest I have ever seen, is made of wood and has ornate metal fittings; the interior is lined with green silk. In the chest, along with the garments, are some embroidered pieces, including some *furoshiki* (wrapping cloths) that Mrs. Kawakami had embroidered with floral patterns and the Kawakami name. This elegant collection of clothing and embroidered pieces is a perfect example of katami passed down from mother to daughter.[6]

In Japan, dressy silk kimono are usually taken apart before being washed, rinsed, and carefully stretched on a wooden frame to dry; the pieces are then sewn back together by hand.[7] But in Hawaii most of the Japanese women worked in the sugarcane or pineapple fields and could not spare the time for such tasks. They had very little time for socializing either and, therefore, except during occasional visits to Honolulu to see off relatives or close friends who were returning to Japan, had very few opportunities to wear their dressy kimono. Probably the last time any of the immigrants' dressy kimono and silk obi were worn was shortly after the outbreak of World War II when some issei mothers wore their silk kimono to bid their sons farewell when they left to serve in Europe with the 100th Battalion and 442nd Regiment of the United States Army. This was the traditional manner of showing respect to soldiers who were going off to war. (Fathers wore their dark suits.) After this, the kimono were wrapped and put in storage. Japanese women were afraid to be seen in their kimono during the war; in fact, when neighbors were interned, some people burned their Japanese kimono and Japanese artifacts out of fear. Fortunately for me, my mother saved all her kimono, and hers were made of an unusually large variety of silk and wool fabrics.

As a child growing up on the plantation, I saw the precautions my mother took to preserve her silk kimono. She would air them out about once a year, on the spacious veranda, away from the sunlight. She always warned us not to touch them or brush our heads against them because we might soil them. Whenever she wore her formal black kimono, she aired it out for a few days afterward. Then she folded the kimono neatly and smoothed out every wrinkle, wrapped it carefully in bleached rice bags, put it away in a drawer, and placed fresh camphor balls, wrapped in rice paper, in each corner of the drawer. If the folding was done properly, the kimono never needed ironing; there were no wrinkles.

Most of the work garments worn by the early Japanese women were worn until they were made into rags. Field work was hard on clothing. And so was the brown soap that was used to remove the red dirt embedded in the work clothing. This soap, which came in oblong bars, was very strong; if left in a garment a long time, it could cause the fiber to deteriorate. Nevertheless, some of the issei women preserved some work garments. Kin Watanabe wore her kasuri work clothing and accessories until 1921 and then put the garments away in a cardboard box. When her daughter, Elaine Yokota, gave them to me, a few years ago, they were still in excellent condition. Elaine told me that her mother had used the brown soap on them,[8] so I carefully hand-rinsed the garments to make sure no soap residue was left. Obviously Mrs. Watanabe had done a good job of rinsing; my rinse water was clear.

Another kasuri work jacket that was carefully preserved is one that Haruno Tazawa made from a kimono she brought from Fukushima Prefecture in 1917. Mrs. Tazawa carefully wrapped this jacket and her other work clothing in bleached rice bags and put them in the kōri she had originally brought to Hawaii. The jacket is patched with so many scraps of kasuri from other garments that the design of the original kasuri can hardly be made out. When I asked Mrs. Tazawa what had inspired her to save this particular garment, she told me that she had followed the example of her niece's husband: in 1939, when she had returned to Japan for the first time, she had visited her niece and her niece's husband in Tokyo; in their home she saw an unusual white box placed on their Shinto shrine; when she asked about it, her niece's husband told her that the box contained his old work clothes, which had become symbolic of everything that he had endured. He said:

> When I emigrated to Brazil and worked on the plantation, life was so tough that I often had to go without food for days. I did not have much in the way of clothing except for one pair of pants and a shirt to wear to work. Somehow I scraped up enough money to return to Japan, and I came home wearing that one set of clothing. I felt so thankful to return safely to Japan. I believed that, if I could endure all that hardship, I could survive anything in this world. As a reminder of that ordeal, I preserved that clothing in the white box and placed it on the shrine. Another reason was to show gratitude for being able to come safely to the mother country.

Inspired by his example, Mrs. Tazawa decided to preserve her own work garments, the ones she had worn on the Ewa Plantation during the hardest years of her life.[9] When her tattered jacket was exhibited at the Neal Blaisdell Cultural Center during the 1985 Japanese Immigrant Centennial Celebration, many people, including young students, were drawn to it. The jacket itself told the story of a courageous woman who had overcome great odds.

These examples show that some of the Japanese immigrants took a great deal of care to preserve the garments they valued. In general, they followed the well-established basic principles for the preservation of textiles, principles that may be summarized as follows:

> Fine textiles should be protected from excessive heat; garments should be stored in a cool place.
> Excessive dryness should be avoided. On the other hand, dampness can rot the fibers and cause mold to grow. Therefore, low humidity should be maintained in the storage area.
> Light should be avoided—fluorescent light as well as sunlight.
> Textiles should be kept in a clean place, protected from dust and grease. And, of course, they should be clean when they are stored away.
> Fine textiles should be aired out, in the shade, before being put away, and they should be aired out at least once a year while they are being stored.

When I visited my cousin in Wakayama Prefecture, I was impressed with her beautiful collection of silk kimono, all of which had been made to order in an old shop in Kyoto where she selected her own fabrics and her own colors for dyeing. She told me that she spot cleaned her kimono each time she wore them. In Japan, the dry cleaners are well equipped and thoroughly trained to handle the finest of silks. Because kimono are hand-sewn and many of them are still hand-dyed, dry cleaners take extra precautions when cleaning kimono. It is possible to remove spots at home using benzine or other good-quality products found at reputable stores, but caution must be taken not to leave any ring marks: the cleaning fluid has to be dabbed on carefully with gauze, a soft towel, or a cotton ball, a little at a time; a clean white towel must be placed between the layers of the garment so the fluid does not penetrate to other parts of the garment; the ring that forms at the outer edge of the fluid must be rubbed off gently with gauze or a cotton ball. Japanese kimono dyes react differently from other dyes, so it is best to do a test on the back lining or on an inconspicuous part of the kimono before using any cleaning fluid on the main surfaces.

It is important to fold textiles carefully and wrap them properly before storing them. Because kimono are made with straight lines, they can be folded flat and smooth. Folding helps to prolong the life of the kimono. If a kimono is hung on a hanger like a Western dress, the shoulder area will fade and deteriorate faster than the other parts of the garment. Brocaded obi, however, should be rolled around paper-towel rolls or rolls from wrapping paper when they are stored. Some brocaded obi that were brought to Hawaii by picture brides in the early 1900s were, sadly, falling apart when they were taken out of their storage places. In the old days, Japanese women wrapped their folded kimono in old newspapers, bleached rice bags, or muslin or silk furoshiki. Now there are special wrapping cases made of stiff paper, with strings attached to hold garments neatly in place. These cases also protect the fine silks from rubbing against other garments and keep them free of wrinkles. I have wrapped kimono in acid-free paper and stored them in acid-free boxes.

Whatever paper is used, silverfish and the tiny, almost transparent insects known as book lice may breed on the paper. According to Bishop Museum technologists, book lice do not harm textiles but silverfish may feed on the starch used for decorations on clothing and sashes. Therefore, even acid-free paper has to be aired out once in a while to get rid of the insects that breed on the paper.

The Honolulu Academy of Arts and other museums use old sheets donated by hotels to wrap their valuable clothing and textile collections. Old sheets, old pillowcases, lengths of muslin, or flour bags—if free of any detergents—can be safely used. If the proper precautions are taken, valuable garments can be enjoyed and appreciated by many people for many years.

The tattered work jacket preserved by Haruno Tazawa. Blanche Klim. Barbara Kawakami collection.

Notes

Chapter 1

1. James H. Okahata, ed., *A History of Japanese in Hawaii* (Honolulu: The United Japanese Society of Hawaii, 1971), p. 41. For information about the Gannen Mono, I have relied primarily on Okahata, pp. 39–62.

2. Ibid., p. 47.

3. For information about Japanese immigration to Hawaii after 1885, I have relied primarily on Bishop Museum, Hawaii Immigrant Heritage Preservation Center.

4. Robert K. Sakai and Mitsugu Sakihara, "Okinawa," in *Kodansha Encyclopedia of Japan* (New York: Kodansha International, 1983), vol. 6, p. 87.

5. Mitsugu Sakihara, "A History of Okinawa," in *Uchinanchu: A History of Okinawans in Hawaii*, Ethnic Studies Oral History Project, United Okinawan Association of Hawaii (Honolulu: University of Hawaii Press, 1981), pp. 14–15.

Chapter 2

1. Gail Miyasaki, "Contributions of Japanese Women in Hawaii," in *Montage: An Ethnic History of Women in Hawaii*, ed. Nancy Foon Young and Judy N. Parrish (Honolulu: College of Education, University of Hawaii, 1977), p. 46.

2. Hiroshi Wagatsuma and George DeVos, "Attitudes toward Arranged Marriages in Rural Japan," in *Selected Readings on Modern Japanese Society*, ed. George K. Yamamoto and Tsuyoshi Ishida (Berkeley, California: McCutchan Publishing Corporation, 1971), pp. 16–17.

3. Taga Toki, interview, March 8, 1985.

4. Unidentified interviewee on Radio KOHO (Japanese-language radio station, Honolulu), 1981.

5. Taniyo Tanimoto, interview, April 27, 1979.

6. Kana Higa, interviews, May 25, 1985, and October 9, 1987.

7. Karin C. Nelson, "Okinawan Textiles," in *Kodansha Encyclopedia of Japan* (New York: Kodansha International, 1983), vol. 6, p. 91.

8. Sae Tachikawa, interview, November 12, 1979.

9. Mock Joya, *Things Japanese* (Tokyo: Tokyo News Service, 1971), p. 342.

10. Ibid., p. 347.

11. Kana Tsukayama, interview, February 17, 1988.

12. Ryuzo Saito, *Japanese Coiffure* (Tokyo: Japan Tourist Bureau, 1939), p. 62.

13. This silk floss cap was originally worn by the women of the Ikko Sect when they visited Buddhist temples; it was a symbol of a desire to suppress feelings of jealousy. The cap later became part of the traditional bridal costume. See Joya, pp. 365–366.

14. Torajiro Sato, interviews, November 1, 1984–January 26, 1989.

15. Tei Saito, interview, March 10, 1980.

16. Ushii Nakasone, interview, March 15, 1985.

17. Sagami Shinozawa, interview, May 28, 1985.

18. Ushi Tamashiro, interview, April 22, 1985.

19. Norio Yamanaka, *The Book of Kimono* (Tokyo: Kodansha International, 1982), p. 40.

20. John Dower, *The Elements of Japanese Design* (New York: Walkers-Weatherhill, 1971), p. 48.

21. Shizu Kaigo, interview, February 19, 1985.

22. Haruno Tazawa, interview, January 15, 1984.

23. Ayako Kikugawa, interview, April 4, 1985.

24. Alma Ogata (daughter of Sadahiko and Tsugi Sonoda), interview, September 22, 1982.

25. Ima Ohashi, interview, January 10, 1986.

26. Tsuru Omine, interview, November 6, 1987.

27. Kama Asato, interview, May 28, 1985.

28. Nobuichi Higaki, interview, June 6, 1987.

29. Yasu Sato, interview, July 13, 1984.

30. Kaichi Abe, interview, July 9, 1984.

31. Kaichi and Miki Abe, interviews, July 9 and 10, 1984.

32. Tatsuno Ogawa, interviews, 1985–1990.

33. Taga Toki, interview, November 2, 1986.

34. Kamezo and Taga Toki, interview, November 2, 1986.

35. Amy Umeko Sugimoto, interview, June 28, 1987.

36. Raku Morimoto, interview, July 20, 1986.

37. Masaki Tabusa, interview, August 3, 1987.

38. Masaki and Ayako Tabusa, interview, August 3, 1987.

39. Dr. Dorothy Matsuo (daughter of Asaichi and Hayame Nekomoto), interview, April 12, 1986.

40. Ryoto and Kimiyo Yasui, interview, August 1, 1987.

41. Robert Shigeo and Shizume Muroda, interview, August 6, 1984.

42. Takayo Kobayashi, interview, December 22, 1987.

Chapter 3

1. Chinzen Kinjo, the leader of the first group of Okinawan immigrants, in an interview published in the *Hawaiian Reporter*, May 2, 1960.

2. Kaku Kumasaka, interview, July 4, 1979.

3. Kameko (Kay) Arakawa, interview, July 7, 1979.

4. Haruno Tazawa, interview, June 15, 1984; Gijun Funakoshi, interview, October 1, 1983.

5. Arthur Kaneshiro, interview, June 12, 1985.

6. Alfons L. Korn, "Some Notes on the Origin of Certain Hawaiian Shirts: Frock, Smock-Frock, Block, and Palaka," *Oceania Linguistics*, vol. 15,

Spring–Summer, 1976, pp. 14–38. Also, interview with Professor Korn, January 6, 1986.

7. Bob Krauss, Edward McGrath, and Kenneth Brown, *Historic Waianae: A Place of Kings* (Australia: Island Heritage, 1973), pp. 38–39.

8. Hawaiian Sugar Planters' Association (HSPA), item in file from the United States Bureau of Immigration's *Reports on Immigration, 1866 to 1914.* Also, telephone interview with Harriet Iwai, Archivist for HSPA, January 1989.

9. Kaku Kumasaka, interview, July 4, 1979; Kiku Yoshida, interview, July 12, 1979.

10. Gijin Funakoshi, interview, August 14, 1983.

11. Ernest Malterre, Jr., interview, September 8, 1979. One of the Chinese women who were especially skilled in weaving lau hala hats was Anchoi Liu.

12. Masao (Cranky) Watanabe and Ernest Malterre, Jr., interviews, 1981.

13. Kaku Kumasaka, interview, July 4, 1979.

14. Ernest Malterre, Jr., interview, September 8, 1979.

Chapter 4

1. Ronald Takaki, *Pau Hana: Plantation Life and Labor in Hawaii* (Honolulu: University of Hawaii Press, 1983), pp. 77–78.

2. Ibid., p. 25.

3. Kaku Kumasaka, interview, July 4, 1979.

4. Haruno Tazawa, interview, August 6, 1979; Kaku Kumasaka, interview, July 4, 1979.

5. Takaki, p. 17.

6. Alice Kuroiwa Schwartz, interview, January 16, 1986. Alice also gave me a skirt of black and white stripes, a type of skirt that was popular in the picture-bride period.

7. Elaine Haruko Yokota, interview, August 6, 1979.

8. Kaku Kumasaka, interview, July 4, 1979.

9. Kiku Yoshida, interview, August 8, 1979.

10. Norio Yamanaka, *The Book of Kimono* (Tokyo: Kodansha International, 1982), pp. 44–45.

11. Taniyo Tanimoto, interviews, July 25 and August 16, 1979.

12. Kiku Yoshida, interview, August 8, 1979.

13. Haruno Tazawa, interviews, July 25 and August 16, 1979.

14. Kaku Kumasaka, interview, July 4, 1979.

15. Kiku Yoshida, interview, August 8, 1979.

16. Haruno Tazawa, interview, June 15, 1984; Kaku Kumasaka, interview, July 4, 1979.

17. Kiku Yoshida, interview, August 8, 1979.

18. Kaku Kumasaka, Taniyo Tanimoto, Tei Saito, and Haruno Tazawa, interviews, 1979 and 1984.

19. Kaku Kumasaka, interview, July 4, 1979; Sagami Shinozawa, interview, May 28, 1985.

20. Sarah Lindsey, interview at Waipahu Cultural Park, August 22, 1979.

21. Sueno Koga, interview, August 29, 1979.

22. Taniyo Tanimoto, interviews, July 25 and August 16, 1979.

23. Alice Morse Earle, *Two Centuries of Costume in America, 1620–1820* (New York: Dover, 1970), p. 582.

24. Margaret Schleif, interview, August 17, 1979.

Chapter 5

1. Kay Arakawa, interview, July 18, 1979.
2. Yoji Takahashi, compiler, *Washi* [Japanese Paper] (Tokyo: Heibonsha, 1982), No. 40, Autumn, p. 48.
3. Chie Koike, "Raingear," in *Kodansha Encyclopedia of Japan* (New York: Kodansha International, 1983), vol. 6, p. 280.
4. Takahashi, p. 48.
5. Koike, p. 280.
6. Kay Arakawa, interview, July 18, 1979.
7. Kay Arakawa gave me a rare photograph of the crowded tailor shop.
8. Taniyo Tanimoto, interview, April 27, 1979.
9. Robert Muroda, interview, August 6, 1984.
10. Kazuma Oyama, interview, July 14, 1984.
11. Rikio Anzai, interview, February 28, 1987.
12. Robert Muroda, interview, August 6, 1984.
13. Kimiko Yahiro, interview, June 23, 1986.
14. Mr. Mukai later donated his ashigappa to the Waipahu Cultural Garden Park's plantation-clothing collection.
15. Robert Mukai, interview, April 21, 1988.
16. Ernest Malterre, Jr., interview, September 8, 1979.
17. Kazuma Oyama, interview, August 20, 1979.
18. Ernest Malterre, Jr., interview, September 8, 1979.
19. Kay Arakawa, interview, May 6, 1987.
20. Robert Mukai, interview, June 12, 1985.
21. Kaku Kumasaka, interview, July 4, 1979; Kiku Yoshida, interview, August 8, 1979; Tei Saito, interview, August 1, 1979; Haruno Tazawa, interview, June 15, 1984.
22. Elaine Haruko Yokota, interview, April 6, 1979.
23. Taniyo Tanimoto, interview, April 27, 1979.
24. Haruno Tazawa, interview, June 15, 1984; Tei Saito, interview, August 1, 1979.
25. Kay Tanoura, interview, May 5, 1985.
26. Matsue Yoneji, interview, March 3, 1988.
27. Mikiko Hirohata, interview, July 22, 1987.
28. Alice Kuroiwa Schwartz, interview, January 16, 1986.
29. Gijun Funakoshi, interview, October 1, 1983.
30. Sueno Koga, interview, April 9, 1988.
31. Taga Toki, interview, March 8, 1985.
32. Yasu Sato, interview, July 13, 1984.
33. Ernest Malterre, Jr., interview, September 8, 1979.
34. Taniyo Tanimoto, interview, July 25, 1979; Kaku Kumasaka, interview, July 4, 1979.

Chapter 6

1. Kimiko Yahiro, interviews, June 23, 1986, and July 5 and 16, 1987.
2. Ruth Higa Oshiro, interview, November 6, 1987.
3. Matsue Oshiro, interview, November 3, 1987.
4. Kaku Kumasaka, interview, July 4, 1979.
5. Sueno Koga, interview, August 29, 1979.
6. Yasuyo Kuwahara, interview, November 11, 1987.

Chapter 7

1. Mock Joya, *Things Japanese* (Tokyo: Tokyo News Service, 1971), p. 18.
2. Patricia Massy, *Sketches of Japanese Crafts and the People Who Make Them* (Tokyo: The Japan Times, 1980), p. 123.
3. Joya, pp. 47–48.
4. Marie C. Neal, *In Gardens of Hawaii* (Honolulu: Bishop Museum Press, 1965), p. 88. Also Dr. Horace Clay, interview, August 1982.
5. James and Miyake Ochikubo, interview, June 3, 1983.
6. Kenichi Tasaka, interview, June 4, 1985.
7. Franklin Odo and Kazuko Sinoto, *A Pictorial History of the Japanese in Hawaii, 1885–1924* (Honolulu: Bishop Museum Press, 1985), p. 112.
8. Hisako Yamasaki, interview, April 16, 1986.
9. Mrs. Silva (given name not known), one of his neighbors, in an interview at the Japanese Centennial Cultural Exhibit on March 27, 1985.
10. Patsy Ochikubo Hiyane, interview, June 6, 1983.
11. Kaku Kumasaka, interview, August 22, 1979.
12. Kay Arakawa, interview, July 7, 1979.
13. Kaku Kumasaka, interview, August 22, 1979.
14. Haruno Tazawa, interview, June 15, 1984.
15. Wasaku Suzuki, interview, August 1979.
16. Sahichi Kumasaka, interview, July 4, 1979.

Chapter 8

1. Tei Saito, interview, August 1, 1979.
2. Tatsuno Ogawa, interview, March 2, 1985.
3. Ibid.

Chapter 9

1. Bishop Gyokuei Matsuura, interview, January 20, 1988.
2. The Reverend Shugen Komagata, interview, August 3, 1984.
3. Mock Joya, *Things Japanese* (Tokyo: Tokyo News Service, 1971), pp. 20–21.
4. Henry Uyehara, interview, March 17, 1988.
5. Suye Kubo, interview, November 11, 1987.
6. Ibid.
7. Kaoru Matsunaga, interview, June 23, 1986.
8. Gijun Funakoshi, interview, December 11, 1988.
9. Kaichi Abe, interview, July 9, 1984.
10. Noriyu Koga, interview, August 29, 1979.
11. Ise Wakasa, interview, April 10, 1988. When the Chinese tailor from whom she had learned the art of tailoring retired, Ise bought from him a one-hundred-year-old combination lint chaser and clapper; she later gave it to me.
12. Kaichi Abe, interview, July 9, 1984.
13. Robert Sato, interview, July 10, 1988.
14. Kaichi Abe, interview, July 9, 1984.
15. Ise Wakasa, interview, April 10, 1988.
16. Kaichi Abe, interview, July 9, 1984.
17. Yukie Okuno Kawana, interview, June 12, 1985.
18. Haruno Tazawa, interview, January 15, 1984.

19. The Reverend Shugen Komagata, interview, August 23, 1984.

20. Gaylord Kubota, who is now director of the Alexander and Baldwin Sugar Museum in Puunene, Maui, and was formerly director of the Hawaii Immigrant Heritage Preservation Center at the Bishop Museum in Honolulu, has done extensive research on the early issei commercial photographers. He has emphasized the value of their work in recording the "technological and social history of plantation towns and outlying areas." See Gaylord Kubota, "The Shashinya-san [The Photographer]," in *Kanyaku Imin: A Hundred Years of Japanese Life in Hawaii* (Honolulu: International Savings and Loan Association, 1985), pp. 36–37.

21. Shizuko Morita, interview, August 12, 1979.

22. Henry Uyehara, interview, March 17, 1988.

Chapter 10

1. Violet Fernandez, interview, April 6, 1980.

2. Kaku Kumasaka, interview, August 22, 1979.

3. Ingrid Brenninkmeyer, *The Sociology of Fashion* (Paris: Libraire du Recueil, 1963), p. 87.

Appendix A

1. John W. Dower, *The Elements of Japanese Design: A Handbook of Family Crests, Heraldry and Symbolism* (New York: Walkers-Weatherhill, 1971), pp. 3, 29. Also, Motoji Niwa, *Kamon Daizukan* [The Big Book of Family Crests] (Tokyo: Akita Publishing Co., 1986), p. 13.

2. Norio Yamanaka, *The Book of Kimono* (New York: Kodansha International, 1982), p. 131.

3. Dower, pp. 7–15; Yamanaka, pp. 36–37.

4. Dower, p. 10.

5. Fumie Adachi, *Japanese Design Motifs: 4260 Illustrations of Heraldic Crests* (New York: Dover Publications, 1972), p. vi.

6. Dower, pp. 10–15.

7. Adachi, p. vi.

8. Mikiko Hirohata, interview, March 12, 1987.

9. Douglas Nakaguma, interview, January 14, 1989. Sugawara Michizane, a court scholar who was exiled to Dazaifu, Fukuoka, loved the *ume* (plum) blossom. After his death, people in Fukuoka erected the Tenmangu Shrine and used the plum blossom crest. His admirers later adopted the same crest.

10. Shizu Kaigo, interview, July 28, 1987.

11. Douglas Nakaguma, interview, January 14, 1989.

12. Gijun Funakoshi, interview, October 1, 1983.

13. Mock Joya, *Things Japanese* (Tokyo: Tokyo News Service, 1971), p. 116.

14. Fusao Iwahori, interviews, February 1987–November 1989.

15. Dower, p. 10.

Appendix B

1. Karen Finch and Greta Putnam, *Caring for Textiles* (New York: Watson-Guptill Publications, 1977), p. 9.

2. Rhoda Komuro, interview, August 10, 1985.

3. Gary Woodard, telephone interviews, November 1–7, 1989.

4. Grace Kiyoko Shigemura, Sumiko Kubota, and Mikiko Hirohata (daughters of Saburo and Ko Shigemura), interviews, 1987–1989.

5. Amy Umeko Sugimoto, interview, March 25, 1984.

6. Mabel Hashisaka, interview, March 25, 1988.

7. Susan Barberi, "Textiles: Care and Preservation of Clothing," in *Kodansha Encyclopedia of Japan* (New York: Kodansha International, 1983), vol. 8, p. 20.

8. Elaine Haruko Yokota, interview, June 8, 1984.

9. Haruno Tazawa, interview, November 10, 1984.

Glossary

ahina	Hawaiian word meaning blue dye; the usual word in Hawaii for American blue denim.
ai	Japanese term for vegetable indigo dye.
apuron	Japanese pronunciation of "apron."
apuron pansu	Japanese pronunciation of "apron pants"; another term for *ashigappa*.
ashigappa	Literally, "*kappa* for the legs," or "leg covering"; sometimes called apron pants.
atsuita	A stiff, heavy brocade.
bashōfu	A cloth made from banana plantain fiber.
bentō	Packed lunch taken to work, school, picnics, etc.
bentō bukuro	Bag in which *bentō* was carried.
bon	Same as *Obon*; the initial *o* in *Obon* is simply an honorific prefix.
capa	Portuguese word for rain cape.
chanchanko	A sleeveless kimono jacket for toddlers.
chirimen	Silk crinkle crepe.
daimon	"Great crest" robe, a formal costume with five family crests—two at the front chest, two on the sleeves, and one at the neck in the center back.
daimyō	Lord; leader of a clan in a province.
datemaki	Narrow sash that is worn under a dressy obi to hold a kimono in place. In Hawaii, it was often worn by women as a waistband for a *yukata*.
Doitsu ahina	Blue denim imported from Germany. (*Doitsu* is the Japanese term for Germany; *ahina* is the Hawaiian term for blue denim.)

dongorosu   Japanese pronunciation of "dungarees," the word used by Portuguese and Spanish field workers for a type of work hat made from dungaree, the "duck" or lightweight canvas that is used to make the work trousers known as dungarees.

egasuri   Pictorial *kasuri;* splash-pattern designs of birds, flowers, leaves, and a variety of geometric figures. The designs differed from region to region.

furoshiki   A square piece of cloth measuring about twenty-seven inches on each side, used for wrapping various things.

fuji   Wisteria.

futon   Cotton-filled bedding. Thin *futon* were used for coverlets; thick ones, for mattresses.

gaijin   An "outside person"—that is, a person not of one's own ethnic group; the usual Japanese term for a Caucasian.

Gannen Mono   The "First-Year People," that is, the Japanese who migrated in the first year of the Meiji Era, 1868. They were the first group of Japanese immigrants to Hawaii.

geta   A wooden clog (basically, a wooden platform on two wooden stilts) that is held on the foot by a thong that passes between the first and second toes.

gobanji   A plaid, or check, pattern. Issei often used this term to refer to *palaka.*

gogurosu   Goggles worn for field work; Japanese pronunciation of the English word goggles.

habutae   A glossy, lightweight pure silk.

hachimaki   A sweatband; a *tenugui* wrapped around the head and tied in front.

hada juban   A short undershirt with sleeves, made of lightweight cotton, worn next to the body.

hakama   A divided, ankle-length skirt, with deep pleats at the waist, worn over the kimono; paired with *haori* for men's formal wear.

Hakata shibori A style of tie-dyeing that originated in Hakata, in Fukuoka Prefecture, and produces a cotton fabric covered with striking floral patterns in white on an indigo blue background.

Hakata weave   A heavy ribbed weave, usually of silk, used for obi.

hakoseko   A brocaded ornamental purse that is tucked into the neckline of the kimono above the sash; a bridal accessory.

haole   Hawaiian term for white person, Caucasian.

haori   Short, medium, or three-quarter length coat worn over a kimono.

hapai kō   Hawaiian term meaning to carry bundles of sugarcane. The laborers who did the heavy manual work of carrying bundles of cut sugarcane on their shoulders to the train cane-cars were called *hapai kō* gangs.

happi	Workman's livery coat. This type of short coat is also worn by participants in certain festivals.
haze	Same as *kohaze*.
heko obi	Men's soft sash in crepe or cotton; about thirteen inches wide and three yards long.
hetchi pansu	"Button-on pants"; short pants, worn by young boys, that were made of either khaki or navy cotton twill and had buttonholes at the waist through which buttons attached to the boys' shirts were passed.
hidarimae	With the right front panel (of the kimono) overlapping the left front panel—the opposite of the traditionally prescribed manner. The kimono shroud is placed on a dead person in this manner. For a living person to wear a kimono in this manner is considered an omen of misfortune.
Hinamatsuri	Doll Festival—that is, Girls' Day.
hitatare	Kimono with wide sleeves worn with long trousers; one of the earliest ceremonial garments to have a crest on it (fourteenth century).
hiyoku	An underkimono that is single and unlined but looks like a double- or triple-layered kimono because of the color contrast added at the sleeve opening and at the hemline.
holoku	A Hawaiian mu'u mu'u that features a train.
hōmongi	Visiting kimono; a dressy silk kimono with designs painted on the lower front panels; usually worn for special occasions such as weddings, tea ceremonies, or music recitals.
iriko	Small dried sardines.
issei	First-generation Japanese in America (that is, Japanese born in Japan).
jika tabi	Thick, rubber-soled canvas footwear worn by field workers or fishermen in Japan.
jōfu	A fine hemp, or ramie, cloth.
kakishibu	Persimmon tannin.
kaku obi	Men's stiff, narrow sash, about five inches wide, made of satin, brocade, or cotton.
kalua pig	Whole pig roasted Hawaiian-style in an underground oven (*imu*).
kamishimo	A sleeveless robe that featured the family crest on its front lapels and back bodice; during the Edo Period it was designated as the official garment of the samurai.
kamon	Family crest.
kampū	Okinawan hairstyle that features a topknot.
kanaka	Hawaiian word for a Hawaiian.
kanakagi	Loose-fitting simple dress (literally, "Hawaiian wear" [*kanaka* is the Hawaiian word for "Hawaiian"; *gi* is the Japanese word for "wear" or "clothing"]).

kanoko

Ka means deer and *ko* means child; therefore, *kanoko* means fawn. The word is used to describe a dappled pattern that resembles the coat of a fawn.

kappa

Raincoat made of muslin that has been treated to make it water-repellent.

kappa dachi

Literally, "simple cut"; a simple A-line dress.

karanko geta

A dressy *geta* in which either the platform is made thicker and the stilts eliminated entirely or the front of the platform is made thicker, eliminating the front stilt, and the back stilt is made heavier to provide balance. The word *karanko* is an attempt to reproduce the sound these *geta* make when the wearer walks.

kari fūfu

"Borrowed spouse," or "temporary spouse." To come as a *kari fūfu* was one way an issei could gain entry into the United States or its territories during the Restricted Immigration Period (1908–1924), when unmarried persons were not allowed to enter unless they were related to earlier immigrants. After the temporarily wedded couple entered Hawaii, they applied for a divorce and waited a year until they were free to remarry.

kasuri

Cotton, silk, or linen fabric with a "splash pattern" produced by tying and dyeing the yarn before weaving.

katami

Keepsakes—specifically, the belongings of a deceased person that are distributed to family members and close friends as keepsakes.

kendō

Japanese art of swordsmanship, fencing.

keshinui

Embroidered family crest. *Keshi* means to erase, and *nui* means to sew; together, they describe the embroidered family crest as "sewing that erases [the white lines with which the crest is drawn on the fabric]." In Kyoto, it is known as a *nuimon* (embroidered crest).

kimono

A long, loose, straight-cut garment with long sleeves. The word literally means clothing: *ki (ru)* means to wear; *mono* means thing.

kinsha

Fine silk fabric, smooth and soft.

Kintarō outfit

The diamond-shaped bib and headband associated with the legendary boy warrior Kintaro.

kohaze

A copper fastener that was sewn into the seam line; it was usually called a "coin-shaped button" because its shape (an oval with one of the short ends cut off straight) was similar to that of a Japanese coin that was used during the Tokugawa Period.

kon-gasuri

A cotton kasuri dyed with *ai* (vegetable indigo dye).

konpan

The Japanese pronunciation of the English word "company." It referred to a group of people who formed a partnership under the leadership of one person and worked a designated area of sugarcane or pineapple land. The members of the group shared the profits; the group leader was paid more than the others because he assumed greater responsibility.

konpan papale	*Papale* is the Hawaiian word for hat, so the phrase means *konpan* hat—that is, the hat worn by *konpan* workers. Another name for *dongorosu*.
kōri	Wicker trunk; woven of strips of willow-vine or bamboo.
koseki	Family register.
koshimaki	Wrap-around underskirt worn under the kimono by women.
kukui	Hawaiian word for candle nut tree *(aleurites moluocana)*.
kumpang	Filipino equivalent of *konpan*.
Kurume-gasuri	Kasuri with a distinctive design that originated in Kurume, Fukuoka Prefecture, Japan.
kyahan	Leggings.
kyōdai	A low dressing table with a long mirror.
lau hala	Hawaiian word for pandanus leaf, especially as used in plaiting.
luna	Hawaiian term for foreman or overseer.
maedare	A small apron that a woman field worker wore over her dirndl skirt and under her full-length denim apron.
maekake	A regional variant of the word *maedare*.
make	Hawaiian word meaning dead.
makura-gyō	Literally, "pillow prayer"; recited by Buddhist priest after a person dies.
mama-san	A combination of the English word *mama* and the Japanese suffix *san*, a suffix that indicates affectionate familiarity.
marumage	Rounded coiffure reserved for married women.
maru obi	A sash made of twenty-six-inch-wide brocade, satin, or damask folded in half lengthwise.
megane	Japanese term for eyeglasses; sometimes used by issei to refer to field goggles.
meisen	An especially fine silk, usually striped.
mikoshi	Portable shrine used in festivals.
miso	A food paste made of soybeans, salt, and, usually, some fermented grain.
mizuhiki	Decorative paper cords in silver and gold or red and white are used for auspicious occasions. Pure white and black are used for solemn events.
mofuku	Mourning wear.
momohiki	Knee-length breeches, or pantaloons; men's fitted work pants. In Japan *momohiki* were worn over the kimono to protect it and allow greater freedom of movement; in Hawaii issei women wore them as underpants under their full skirts.
Momo no Sekku	Peach Blossom Festival—that is, Girls' Day.
mon	Crest.

montsuki	Formal five-crested kimono.
mori mono	An assortment of foods that include sliced fishcake, sweet beancake, sweet potato fritters, cluster of grapes, and whatever one wishes to add. For happy occasions, an uneven number of foods are used; for funerals, an even number.
mugiwara bō	Straw hat. In Japan the term denoted the hats woven out of barley straw that were worn in Japanese villages; the Japanese in Hawaii broadened the meaning to include all types of straw hats.
mansuji	Literally, "ten thousand lines." Same as *sensuji.*
mu'u mu'u	Hawaiian term for the long, loose, flowing gown that the missionary wives taught the Hawaiian women to sew and wear.
myōji	Surname.
naga juban	A long underkimono.
naichi	Japanese from the main islands of Japan.
nakōdo	Marriage go-between.
nekutai	Issei pronunciation for necktie.
nisei	Children born to the issei; second-generation Japanese-Americans.
nishime	A dish of meat or poultry with vegetables seasoned with sugar and shoyu.
obi	Sash worn with a kimono.
obi-age	Bustle sash.
obi-jime	Silk, satin, or brocade cord used on top of the wide obi to hold the obi in place.
Obon Festival	Festival for the Ancestors.
Obon season	Period from June 15 to August 15, the period when, according to traditional Buddhist beliefs, the souls of the deceased return to their homes.
ōgi-taiko	Drum bowknot.
omeshi	Pebble crepe.
otsuya	Wake service.
palaka	Originally a transliteration into Hawaiian of the English word "frock," the term used for the loose-fitting work shirts worn by the British and American sailors who came to Hawaii; the word came to be used to mean the fabric from which these shirts were made—a heavy cotton cloth woven in a white plaid pattern with a dark blue background.
papale	Hawaiian word for hat.
pa'u	Hawaiian word for wrap-around skirt, or sarong.
pit-chin	Metal snaps used for closing a placket or other opening in clothing. The issei women gave the fasteners this name because it approximates the sound of the snaps closing.

pokkuri	Dressy lacquered *geta* for girls, formerly called *karanko geta*. The word *pokkuri*, like *karanko*, is an attempt to reproduce the sound these *geta* make when the wearer walks.
pulapula	The Hawaiian word for seedlings. The laborers who did the heavy manual work of cutting sugarcane seedlings were called *pulapula* gangs.
Ryūkyū-gasuri	An Okinawan silk kasuri.
sakana tabi	Same as jika tabi.
sake	Rice wine.
samurai	Japanese warrior.
sanjaku-obi	Literally, three-foot-long sash; men's dressy kimono sash.
sansankudo	The exchange of nuptial cups by the bride and groom to seal their marriage vows.
sansei	Children of nisei; third-generation Japanese-Americans.
sarashi	Unbleached muslin.
sarashi nuno	A white, lightweight cotton fabric that looks something like fine cheesecloth; traditionally used to make the kimono shroud.
sashimi	Thinly sliced raw fish.
satogaeri	A bride's ceremonial visit to her parents' home a few days after the wedding.
Sendai Hira silk	A stiff, flat-weave silk in which the warp is a fine glossy silk and the woof is a moistened, untwisted raw silk; made on the Sendai Plains.
sensuji	A heavy-duty cotton fabric—resembling a lightweight canvas—used for work jackets. The word literally means "a thousand lines"—a reference to the large number of white stripes running lengthwise in the fabric against a gray background.
shibori	Usually translated as "tie-dyeing." The word is used for a variety of ways in which fabric is manipulated (for example, folded, stitched, twisted) and then secured before dyeing.
shichi go san	Literally, "the lucky numbers of seven, five, and three"; a time in late October when children who have reached these ages are taken to a Shinto shrine to offer gratitude for their blessings.
shigoki obi	A white crepe or white cotton sash.
shijū kunichi	The mourning period—that is, the forty-nine-day period from the day of death.
shiromuku	Pure white silk bridal kimono.
shōchikubai	The pine, bamboo, and plum designs that are said to symbolize the virtues of physical and spiritual discipline and endurance.
splash-pattern	The type of design produced by *kasuri* (tie-dyeing) techniques.

suji	Lines or stripes.
sushi	Rice seasoned with vinegar, salt, and sugar.
suso moyō	Designs painted or embroidered on the front panels of a kimono.
sutra	Buddhist scriptures.
tabi	Cotton socks that have a division between the big toe and the other toes and are closed at the ankle by buttons of some type.
taiko obi	Drum-shaped obi worn by married women.
Takasago	Noh song or ballad sung at weddings until World War II.
takashimada	Formal bridal hairdo.
Tango No Sekku	Feast of the Horse—that is, Boys' Day.
tanmono	A roll of cloth about twelve to fourteen inches wide and twelve yards long.
tanomoshi	A mutual financing system into which many issei put half their monthly pay.
tanzen	A cotton-padded kimono worn by people in northern Japan during the winter months.
tasuki	A narrow cord used in Japan to hold kimono sleeves behind the back while working.
tekkō	A hand protector; basically, a mitten with the fingertip sections cut off.
tenugui	A soft cotton towel that measures about thirteen inches in width and thirty-two inches in length.
teoi	A regional variant of the word *tesashi*.
tesashi	Elbow-length arm protector made of denim. It extended to the knuckles and had a loop hooking it onto the middle finger; it covered the back of the hand, but not the palm.
tokoromon	A colloquial, affectionate shortening of the proper term *tokoromono*, which means "a person from the same place," or "fellow villager."
tomobiki	A day considered unlucky for funerals.
tsumugi	Pongee.
tsumugi-gasuri	A hand-spun *kasuri* made from the cocoons left over after the best silks have been sold to the markets.
tsunokakushi	Literally, "horn concealer," a white silk band lined in red that replaced the silk floss cap.
tutu mu'u	loose-fitting gown with high neckline, yoke, and gathered bodice; may be either floor length or knee length.
uchikake	Long outer robe, heavily padded at the hemline and made of brocade, satin, or other rich silk; it is worn over the bridal kimono.
ume	Pickled plum.
ushinchi style	The traditional Okinawan way of wearing a kimono—that is, without a sash, with the kimono tucked firmly, but with ample looseness, into the waistcord of long cotton

	underpants worn under the kimono; this gives a graceful blouson effect.
wahine	Hawaiian word for woman.
wahine luna	Hawaiian term meaning female overseer.
wara	Straw.
waraji	Straw sandals.
washi	Paper produced from mulberry bark: *wa* means Japanese, *shi* means paper.
watabōshi	Silk floss cap worn by brides, traditionally regarded as a symbol of the bride's desire to curb any tendency toward jealousy.
Yaban	Stamp or seal used for individual household.
yobiyose	Someone who was summoned to Hawaii by relatives during the Restricted Immigration Period.
Yobiyose Jidai	"Summoning by Relatives Period," or Restricted Immigration Period, 1908-1924.
yūkan	The bathing of the body of the deceased, a Buddhist purification rite.
yukata	Unlined kimono made of printed cotton.
yutan	A coverlet for furniture.
yūzen	A silk or cotton that is dyed by a starch-resist technique and hand-painted with designs in brilliant colors.
zabuton	Square cotton-filled floor cushion.
zōri	The Japanese slipper, or sandal; it consists of a flat sole that is held on the foot by a thong that passes between the first and second toes. It may be made of various materials —including straw, bamboo sheaths, and cloth.

Sources

Printed Materials

Adachi, Fumie. *Japanese Design Motifs: 4260 Illustrations of Heraldic Crests.* New York: Dover Publications, 1972.

Adams, Romanzo Colfax. "Japanese Migration Statistics." *Sociology and Social Research,* vol. 13, 1929, pp. 436–445.

———. "Some Statistics on the Japanese in Hawaii." *Foreign Affairs,* vol. 2, 1923, pp. 310–318.

Adaniya, Ruth, Alice Njus, and Margaret Yamate, eds. *Of Andagi and Sanshin: Okinawan Culture in Hawaii.* Honolulu: Hui O Laulima, 1988.

Akita, Sadami, compiler. *Utsukushii Kimono: Collection 91.* Tokyo: Fujin Gano Kabushiki Kaishi, n.d.

Ayer, Jacqueline. *Japanese Working Costume.* New York: Scribner and Sons, 1975.

Baker, Ray Jerome. *Hawaiian Yesterdays: Historical Photographs by Ray Jerome Baker.* Edited by Robert E. Van Dyke; text by Ronn Ronck. Honolulu: Mutual Publishing Co., 1982.

Barberi, Susan. "Textiles: Care and Preservation of Clothing." In *Kodansha Encyclopedia of Japan.* New York: Kodansha International, 1983. Vol. 8, p. 20.

Beechert, Edward D. *Working in Hawaii: A Labor History.* Honolulu: University of Hawaii Press, 1985.

Blackmore, Frances. *Japanese Design through Textile.* New York: Weatherhill, 1978.

Brandon, Reiko Mochinaga. *Country Textiles of Japan: The Art of Tsutsugaki.* Honolulu: Academy of Arts, 1986.

Brenninkmeyer, Ingrid. *The Sociology of Fashion.* Paris: Libraire du Recueil, 1963. Thesis completed at University of Fribourg.

Broby-Johansen, Rudolf. *Body and Clothes.* London: Faber and Faber, 1968.

Bryan, William S., ed. *Our Islands and Their People as Seen with Camera and Pencil.* Narrative by Jose De Olivares. Vol. 2. New York: N. D. Thompson Publishing Co., 1899.

Chong, Douglas D. L. *Reflections of Time: A Chronology of Chinese Fashion in Hawaii.* Honolulu: Hawaii Chinese Historical Center, 1976.

Conde, Jesse. *Sugar Train Pictorial.* California: Glenwood Publishers, 1975.

Conroy, Francis Hilary. *East across the Pacific: Historical and Sociological Studies of Japanese Immigration and Assimilation.* Santa Barbara: Clio Press, 1972.

———. *The Japanese Frontier in Hawaii, 1868-1898.* Berkeley: University of California Press, 1953.

Contini, Mila. *Fashion: From Ancient Egypt to the Present Day.* New York: Crescent Books, n.d.

Cunnington, Phyllis, and Catherine Lucas. *Costume for Births, Marriages and Deaths.* New York: Barnes, 1972.

———. *Occupational Costume in England: From the Eleventh Century to 1914.* London: Adam & Charles Black, 1976.

Dan River, Inc. *A Dictionary of Textile Terms.* New York: Dan River, Inc., 1976.

Dower, John W. *The Elements of Japanese Design: A Handbook of Family Crests, Heraldry and Symbolism.* New York: Walkers-Weatherhill, 1971.

Earle, Alice Morse. *Two Centuries of Costume in America, 1620-1820.* New York: Dover, 1970.

Feher, Joseph. *Hawaii: A Pictorial Review.* Honolulu: Bishop Museum Press, 1969.

Finch, Karen, and Greta Putnam. *Caring for Textiles.* New York: Watson-Guptill Publications, 1977.

Fluger, J. C. *A Psychology of Clothes.* London: Hogarth Press, 1966.

Fujimoto, Lore F. *Obon: A Buddhist Memorial Celebration.* A Tape-Slide Program. Produced and distributed by Lore Fujimoto, 1975.

Gee, Emma. "Issei: The First Women." In *Asian Women.* Berkeley: University of California Press, 1971. Pp. 8-13.

Hashimoto, Sumiko. *Japanese Accessories.* Tokyo: Japan Travel Bureau, 1962.

Hauge, Victor and Takako. *Folk Traditions in Japanese Art.* Tokyo: Kodansha International, n.d.

Hawaiian Sugar Planters' Association. *A Brief History of the Hawaiian Sugar Industry.* Honolulu: Hawaii Sugar Planters' Association, 196

Hawaii State Archives. Photograph Collection. Honolulu, Hawaii.

Hawaii Zairyū Kumamoto Kenjin Yakureki Shashin Chō [A Pictorial History of Japanese Immigrants to Hawaii from Kumamoto Prefecture]. Tokyo: Seiai Tokyo, 1927.

Hayashi, Tadaichi. *Kyodo no Fuzoku; Japanese Women's Folk Costumes.* Tokyo: Ie-no Hikari Association, 1960.

Hoverson, Martha, ed. *Historic Koloa: A Guide.* Kauai, Hawaii: The Friends of Koloa Community School Library, 1985.

Hunt, Barbara, Marion Kelly, and Kehua Lee. *Stories of Hawaii.* Honolulu: University of Hawaii, College of Education, Educational Foundations, General Assistance Center for the Pacific, 1975.

Hunter, H. Louise. *Buddhism in Hawaii: Its Impact on a Yankee Community.* Honolulu: University of Hawaii Press, 1971.

Ito, Masako, and Akiko Inoue. *Kimono.* Translated by Patricia Massy. Osaka: Hoikusha Publishing Co., 1982.

Japanese Coiffure. Tourist Library 28. Tokyo: Japan Tourist Bureau, 1984.

"The Japanese in Hawaii: 100 Years of Progress." *Honolulu Star-Bulletin Progress Edition,* February 19, 1985.

Joya, Mock. *Things Japanese.* Tokyo: Tokyo News Service, 1971.

Kamakura, Yoshitaro. *Craft Treasures of Okinawa: The National Museum of Modern Art, Kyoto.* Translated and adapted by Erika Kaneko. Tokyo: Kodansha International, 1978.

Kawakatsu, Kenichi. *Kimono.* Tokyo: Japan Travel Bureau, 1960.

Kerr, George H. *Okinawa: The History of an Island People.* Rutland, Vermont: C. E. Tuttle, 1969.

Kimura, Yukiko. "Psychological Aspects of Japanese Immigration." *Social Process in Hawaii,* vol. 6, 1940, pp. 123–128.

Kolander, Cheryl. *A Silk-Worker's Notebook.* Loveland, Colorado: Interweave Press, 1985.

Korn, Alfons L. "Some Notes on the Origin of Certain Hawaiian Shirts: Frock, Smock-Frock, Block, and Palaka." *Oceania Linguistics.* Vol. 15, Spring–Summer, 1976, pp. 14–38.

Krauss, Bob, Edward McGrath, and Kenneth Brown. *Historic Waianae: A Place of Kings.* Australia: Island Heritage, 1973.

Kubota, Gaylord. "The Shashinya-san [The Photographer]." In *Kanyaku Imin: A Hundred Years of Japanese Life in Hawaii.* Honolulu: International Savings and Loan Association, 1985. Pp. 36–37.

Leathers, Noel L. *The Japanese in America.* Minneapolis: Lerner Publications Co., 1967.

Maretzki, Thomas and Hatsumi. *Taira: An Okinawan Village.* New York: Wiley, 1966.

Martin, Linda. *The Way We Wore: Fashion Illustrations of Children's Wear 1870-1970.* New York: Scribner's, 1978.

Massy, Patricia. *Sketches of Japanese Crafts and the People Who Make Them.* Tokyo: The Japan Times, 1980.

Matsuda, Mitsugu. *The Japanese in Hawaii: An Annotated Bibliography of Japanese Americans.* Revised by Dennis M. Ogawa and Jerry Y. Fujioka. Honolulu: University of Hawaii Press, 1975.

Minnich, Helen Benton. *Japanese Costume and the Makers of Its Elegant Tradition.* Tokyo: Charles E. Tuttle, 1963.

Missionary Album Sesquicentennial Edition 1820-1970. Honolulu: Hawaii Children's Mission Society, 1969.

Miyabe, Kozo. *Japanese Couffure* [i.e., Coiffure]. Tokyo: Japan Tourist Bureau, 1970.

Miyasaki, Gail. "Contributions of Japanese Women in Hawaii." In *Montage: An Ethnic History of Women in Hawaii.* Edited by Nancy Foon Young and Judy N. Parrish. Honolulu: College of Education, University of Hawaii, 1977. Pp.45–49.

Moriyama, Alan Takeo. *Imingaisha: Japanese Emigration Companies and Hawaii, 1894-1908.* Honolulu: University of Hawaii Press, 1985.

Neal, Marie C. *In Gardens of Hawaii.* Honolulu: Bishop Museum Press, 1965.

Nelson, Karin C. "Okinawan Textiles." In *Kodansha Encyclopedia of Japan.* New York: Kodansha International, 1983. Vol. 6, p. 91.

Niwa, Motoji. *Kamon Daizukan* [The Big Book of Family Crests]. Tokyo: Akita Publishing Co., 1986.

Odo, Franklin and Kazuko Sinoto. *A Pictorial History of the Japanese in Hawai'i 1885-1924.* Honolulu: Bishop Museum Press, 1985.

Okahata, James H., ed. *A History of Japanese in Hawaii.* Honolulu: The United Japanese Society of Hawaii, 1971.

Okinawa Shiryō Shusei: Shizen Rekishi Bunka Fūdo [Compilation of Information about Okinawa: Nature, History, Culture, and Climate]. Tokyo, Green Life, 1975.

Onishi, Katsumi. "*Bon* and *Bon-odori* in Hawaii." In *Kalavinka—Voice of the Dharma.* Honolulu: Hawaii Buddhist Information Center. Vol. 4, No. 4, September 1980, pp. 1–3.

Picken, Mary Brooks. *The Fashion Dictionary: Fabric, Sewing, and Dress as Expressed in the Language of Fashion.* New York: Funk, 1939.

Pizzuto, Joseph J. *Fabric Science.* New York: Fairchild, 1977.

"Plantation Fashions of 1910." *Paradise of the Pacific,* May 1960, p. 18.

"The Romantic World of Weddings." *Japan Pictorial,* vol. 7, No. 4, 1984, p. 9.

Ryan, Mary Shaw. *Clothing: A Study of Human Behavior.* New York: Holt, Rinehart and Winston, 1966.

Saiki, Patsy. *Japanese Women in Hawaii: 100 Years of History.* Honolulu: Kisaku, Inc., 1985.

Saito, Ryuzu. *Japanese Coiffure.* Tokyo: Japan Tourist Bureau, 1939.

Sakai, Robert K., and Mitsugu Sakihara. "Okinawa." In *Kodansha Encyclopedia of Japan.* New York: Kodansha International, 1983. Vol. 6, pp. 84–91.

Sakihara, Mitsugu. "A History of Okinawa." In *Uchinanchu: A History of Okinawans in Hawaii.* Ethnic Studies Oral History Project, United Okinawan Association of Hawaii. Honolulu: University of Hawaii Press, 1981. Pp. 3–22.

Scott, A. C. *Chinese Costume in Transition.* Yokohama: General Printing Co., 1958.

Scott, E. B. *The Saga of the Sandwich Islands.* Nevada: Sierra-Tahoe Publishing Co., 1968.

Shima, Yukiko, ed. and trans. *A Step to Kimono and Kumihimo.* Los Angeles: Kyoto Kimono Academy, 1979.

Shirasu, Masako. *The Kimono and Western Clothing.* Tokyo: Fashion Group, 1970.

Takahashi, Yoji, comp. *Washi* [Japanese Paper]. Tokyo: Heibonsha, 1982. No. 40, Autumn.

Takaki, Ronald. *Pau Hana: Plantation Life and Labor in Hawaii.* Honolulu: University of Hawaii Press, 1983.

Tanaka, Toshio. *A Study of Okinawan Textiles and Fabrics.* Tokyo: Meiji Shobo, 1952.

Tarrant, Naomi. *Collecting Costume: The Care and Display of Clothes and Accessories.* London: Allen & Unwin, 1983.

Umegaki, Minoru. *A Dictionary of Loan Words.* Tokyo: Tokyo Do, 1965.

University of Hawaii, Sinclair Library. Hawaiian Pamphlet File "Fashions Hawaii."

Wagatsuma, Hiroshi, and George DeVos. "Attitudes toward Arranged Marriages in Rural Japan." In *Selected Readings on Modern Japanese Society,* ed. George K. Yamamoto and Tsuyoshi Ishida. Berkeley: McCutchan Publishing Corporation, 1971. Pp. 16–37.

Wakukawa, Ernest K. *A History of the Japanese People in Hawaii.* Honolulu: The Tōyō Shōin, 1938.

Wilcox, Turner R. *Folk and Festival Costume of the World.* New York: Charles Scribner's Sons, 1965.

Yamamoto, George K., and Tsuyoshi Ishida, eds. *Selected Readings on Modern Japanese Society.* Berkeley: McCutchan Publishing Corporation, 1971.

Yamanaka, Norio. *The Book of Kimono.* Tokyo: Kodansha International, 1982.

Yoshimoto, Kamon, ed. *Kasuri Monyō Zukan* [Kasuri Design Picture Book].
Tokyo: Fujii Sumu, 1977.
Young, Nancy Foon, and Judy N. Parrish, eds. *Montage: An Ethnic History
of Women in Hawaii.* Honolulu, College of Education, University of
Hawaii, 1977.

Interviews

Abe, Kaichi and Miki. July 9 and 10, 1984.
Adaniya, Ruth. January 13, 1988.
Akamine, Tsuruko. February 3, 1988.
Akisada, Ume. June 4, 1988; August 14, 1988.
Anzai, Rikio. August 14, 1985; February 28, 1987; March 2, 1987.
Arakaki, Masu. September 20 and 30, 1989; October 28, 1989.
Arakawa, Goro. August 3, 1979–May 15, 1990.
Arakawa, Kameko (Kay). July 7, 1979; August 2, 1979; February 8, 1983;
May 6, 1987; June 5, 1989.
Arakawa, Kazuo. August 3, 1979.
Asato, Kama. June 8, 1981; May 28, 1985.
Asato, Yoshiko. November 3, 1987.
Ashimine, Taro and Kamado. May 26, 1987.
Chinen, Kiyoko. September 15, 1988.
Chong, Douglas. November 2, 1989.
Clay, Dr. Horace. 1981–1984.
Dionisio, Juan C. August 10–12, 1982.
Endo, Tamiko. November 2, 1989; February 17 and 18, 1991.
Endo, Tsuyoshi. March 25, 1985; May 31, 1985; June 2, 1986; July 6 and 7,
1987.
Fernandez, Violet. April 6, 1980.
Fujii, Harue. Summer 1979.
Fujimoto, Mitsuo and Lillian Kikuyo. December 11, 1989.
Fujitani, Bishop Yoshiaki. 1985–1990.
Funakoshi, Gijun. August 9, 1979; July 12, 1983; August 14, 1983; October 1,
1983; December 5, 1983; December 11, 1988; April 14, 1990.
Goshi, Hisao. April 14, 1989.
Gushiken, Hanako. April 9, 1986.
Harada, Shio. April 3, 1984.
Hashisaka, Mabel. March 25, 1988; October 23, 1988.
Hazama, Etsuo and Tatsuyo. May 16, 1983; November 21, 1987.
Higa, Kame. November 7, 1979; May 15, 1990.
Higa, Kameko. November 12, 1987.
Higa, Kana. May 25, 1985; October 9, 1987; November 16, 1988; March 2,
1990.
Higa, Margaret Goya. February 8, 1991.
Higaki, Nobuichi. April 3, 1987; June 6, 1987.
Hirohata, Mikiko. July 22, 1987; October 23, 1987; March 8, 1988; October
18, 1990.
Hironaga, Henry. March 9, 1988; April 12, 1988.
Hiyane, Patsy Ochikubo. June 6, 1983.
Hokama, Katsumi. April 23, 1990.
Igarashi, Hisako. June 3, 1991.
Irie, Dennis. August 17, 1990.
Ishihara, Elsie Tazawa. January 18, 1984–April 17, 1991.
Ishihara, Kana. February 19, 1984.

Ishihara, Mitsuko. November 19, 1987.
Ishihara, Yuki. February 11, 1988.
Ishikawa, George Torataro. January 22, 1986.
Isoshima, Yoshie. January 21, 1987; November 25, 1990.
Ito, Toyoko Sugimoto. July 17, 1988; October 12, 1990.
Iwahori, Fusao. February 15, 1987; November 21, 1989.
Iwai, Harriet. January 6, 1989.
Iwamura, Eijiro. August 18, 1979.
Iwasaki, Shigeto and Yaejyu. July 12, 1990.
Johnson, Dr. Rubellite Kawena. November 15, 1979.
Kagehiro, Jean Asao. January 8, 1985.
Kaigo, Shizu. February 19, 1985; July 18 and 28, 1987; January 16, 1989.
Kameya, Mitzi. May 27, 1985; October 6, 1985.
Kamimura, Seison and Gose. August 17, 1987; August 4, 1989.
Kaneshige, Owari. February 19, 1985; January 25, 1986.
Kaneshiro, Arthur. June 12, 1985; December 4, 1990.
Kaneshiro, Kamato. November 6, 1987; March 27, 1988.
Kaneshiro, Kikue. March 18, 1990; January–May 1990.
Kaneshiro, Louise. May 27, 1985.
Kaneshiro, Seiichi. November 3, 1987.
Kaneshiro, Ushijo. May 27, 1985.
Kanetake, Irene Miyagi. September 6, 1987; February 12, 1989.
Kato, Shizuko. October 27, 1985.
Katsunuma, Dorothy Hatsue. 1987–1991.
Katsunuma, Joseph and Ruth. 1987–1991.
Katsura, Iris Ekita. October 3, 1983.
Kawabata, Kyo. April 4, 1987; May 7, 1989.
Kawabata, Tokiko. January 15, 1986; April 4, 1987.
Kawakami, Sueo. 1979–1991.
Kawamoto, Sakae. May 2, 1979; September 7, 1990.
Kawano, Yukie Okuno. June 12, 1985; July 31, 1985; December 31, 1985;
    June 3, 1990.
Kearney, Bebe Kajita. April 16, 1986.
Kibota, Margo Masuko. March 12, 1987; June 20, 1991.
Kibota, Shigeko. March 12, 1987; July 22, 1988; June 20, 1991.
Kihara, Helen. May 7, 1988.
Kikugawa, Akimi and Reiko. May 1, 1985–November 21, 1990.
Kikugawa, Ayako. May 1, 1985–November 21, 1990.
Kim, Harold. July 7, 1989.
Kimura, Soto. June 6 and 8, 1985.
Kina, Alfred. November 3, 1987; January 6, 1989; February 8, 1989.
Kiyuna, Matsu. July 6, 1979.
Kobashigawa, Carol Ishihara. February 19, 1984.
Kobayashi, Torao and Takayo. December 22, 1987; January 16, 1988.
Kochi, Nobuo. May 2, 1987; August 2, 1990.
Koga, Noriyu and Sueno. August 29, 1979; February 18, 1982; June 11,
    1984; April 9, 1988.
Kohler, Alice Young. March 27, 1985; January 28, 1991.
Koike, Chiyomi. June 7, 1981; September 14, 1981.
Komagata, Rev. Shugen. August 3, 1984–March 7, 1991.
Komuro, Rhoda. August 10, 1985.
Korn, Dr. Alfons L. January 6, 1986.
Kuba, Natsue. October 18, 1987.

Kubo, Suye. November 11, 1987.
Kubota, Gaylord. August 3, 1979–May 21, 1991.
Kubota, Sumiko. April 23, 1987; July 22, 1987; October 23, 1987; October 18, 1990.
Kumasaka, Sahichi and Kaku. July 4, 1979–May 11, 1987.
Kurashige, Niu. June 8, 1985.
Kurashima, Toraki and Yukiko Murata. May 20, 1988.
Kuwahara, Yasuyo. November 11, 1987.
Lindsey, Jack and Sarah. August 22, 1979.
Maebuchi, Hamako. November 4, 1979.
Maeda, Kiyoko. October 17, 1981–August 2, 1988.
Maeda, Sadayo. September 10, 1987; May 23, 1990.
Maeshiro Tokuzen and Sumi. October 26, 1987.
Maki, Ruth Nobuko Hishinuma. May 2, 1984; October 28, 1988.
Malterre, Ernest, Jr. September 8, 1979–November 2, 1989.
Matsunaga, Kaoru. June 23, 1986.
Matsuo, Dr. Dorothy Nekomoto. April 12, 1986.
Matsuura, Bishop Gyokuei. December 11, 1986; January 20, 1988; July 1, 1989.
McGrath, Edward. September 20, 1988.
Medeiros, Suzanne. October 16, 1979.
Migita, Hatsuko. May 12, 1988.
Minagawa, Etsuko. October 5, 1979; September 9, 1984.
Miyasato, Ushiko. November 1, 1987; March 7, 1988; May 23, 1988.
Miyashiro, Bonnie. September 6, 1987; November 11, 1990.
Morimoto, Raku. July 20, 1986; August 6, 1986; October 2, 1988.
Morita, Shizuko. August 12, 1979.
Mukai, Robert and Betty. June 12, 1985; April 21, 1988.
Muroda, Robert Shigeo and Shizume. August 6, 1984–March 19, 1989.
Nagata, Hisae. May 21, 1989.
Nagata, Teruko. November 9, 1979.
Nakagawa, Masako. March 16, 1985–May 10, 1991.
Nakaguma, Douglas Takeo. February 1, 1988; January 14, 1989.
Nakahara, Doris Tatsue Ishikawa. January 22, 1986.
Nakamasu, Kama. April 9, 1986.
Nakamura, Iku. November 3, 1987–May 10, 1990.
Nakamura, Kay Kimiko Nakasone. March 15, 1985; August 19, 1985.
Nakamura, Velma Ayako Kochi. May 2, 1987.
Nakano, Fumi Maeshiro. November 9, 1988.
Nakashima, Toyojiro. March 18, 1986.
Nakasone, Kame. March 9, 1991.
Nakasone, Ushii. March 15, 1985–August 9, 1989.
Nakayama, Otsuru. April 9, 1985.
Nishizawa, Teruo and Kiyoko. May 7, 1986.
Oato, Shizu. November 11, 1987.
Ochikubo, James and Miyako. June 3, 1983.
Ogasawara, Nancy Kimiko. May 28, 1988.
Ogata, Alma Sonoda. October 6, 1981; September 22, 1982; July 17, 1983.
Ogawa, Mieko. August 26, 1990.
Ogawa, Tatsuno. March 2, 1985–July 9, 1989.
Ohashi, Ima. January 10, 1986; June 22, 1986.
Okada, Hideo (Major). August 22, 1979.
Okada, Tadao. August 22, 1979.

Okahashi, Rev. Seiko. June 16, 1991.
Okahata, Dr. James. May 7, 1985.
Okawaki, William. April 2, 1987.
Okita, Teru. May 22, 1988.
Omine, Tsuru. November 6, 1987.
Onishi, Katsumi. April 8, 1987.
Ornellas, Barbara Shimoko Kochi. August 19, 1988.
Oshiro, Keith K. September 6, 1987.
Oshiro, Matsue. November 3, 1987.
Oshiro, Mitsuo and Sumiko Nakamura. June 26, 1989.
Oshiro, Ruth Higa. November 6, 1987–May 15, 1990.
Oshiro, Tomi. March 30, 1986; November 22, 1989.
Oya, Kumashiro. November 4, 1979; February 20, 1984.
Oyama, Kazuma. August 20, 1979; September 8, 1979; July 14, 1984.
Oyama, Tsuyoshi. December 1, 1982–January 26, 1988.
Oyama, The Reverend Yodo. 1977–1990.
Saito, Clara Satoe Ishikawa. January 22, 1986.
Saito, Nobuko. May 23, 1988.
Saito, Tei. August 1, 1979; March 10, 1980; June 9, 1983; October 3, 1985;
    May 15, 1988.
Saito, Zenbei. August 16, 1979–October 3, 1984.
Sakato, Barbara. July 16, 1986.
Sakihara, Jean. September 6, 1987; November 28, 1987.
Sakihara, Dr. Mitsugu. November 15, 1984.
Sasano, Samuel. June 8, 1987.
Sato, John and Lillian Higa. February 9, 1988.
Sato, Robert Yoichi. July 8, 1985; July 10, 1988.
Sato, Torajiro. October 6, 1983; November 1, 1984; January 20, 1988.
Sato, Yasu. March 10, 1979; July 13, 1984.
Schleif, Margaret (now Mrs. Ehlke). June 7, 1979; August 17, 1979.
Schwartz, Alice Kuroiwa. January 16, 1986.
Segawa, Katsu. March 1, 1985.
Shigemura, Grace Kiyoko. July 22, 1985; April 23, 1987; October 18, 1990.
Shikada, Kikue. April 4, 1987.
Shimabukuro, Takeo and Masae. November 3, 1987; May 25, 1988; June 7,
    1988.
Shimaoka, Umeyo. June 9, 1988.
Shimojo, Uto. September 6, 1987; March 14, 1990.
Shinno, Nobuo. January 18, 1989.
Shinozawa, Sagami. February 20, 1984; September 24, 1984; May 28, 1985.
Shirae, Kazue. June 12, 1985.
Shiroma, Chiyoko. March 8, 1989; January–May 1990.
Shiroma, Suye. November 3, 1989.
Sinoto, Kazuko. August 3, 1979; April 11, 1984.
Sugai, Komano. August 24, 1990.
Sugai, Wallace. August 24, 1990.
Sugimoto, Amy Umeko. May 2, 1982–July 16, 1988.
Suzuki, George Wasaku and Elaine Yayoe. August 6, 1979–May 15, 1991.
Suzuki, Jiro. August 10, 1986; February 17, 1987.
Suzuki, Kiyomi. October 6, 1985; July 21, 1990; August 14, 1990.
Tabusa, Masaki and Ayako. August 3 and 12, 1987.
Tachikawa, Sae. October 3, 1979; November 12, 1979.
Tagami, Bessie Endo. June 12, 1985; July 3, 1987.

Takamoto, Kimiko Kochi. August 19, 1988.
Takashima, Kay Kisoe Ishikawa. April 9, 1986.
Tamashiro, Ushi. April 22, 1985; August 27, 1985.
Tamura, Masae. July 18, 1987; January 16, 1989.
Tanaka, Katsuma. August 6, 1979; November 17, 1989.
Tanigawa, Yoshino. January 9, 1985.
Tanimoto, Matsujiro and Taniyo. April 27, 1979; July 25, 1979; August 16,
    1979; May 10, 1984; October 12, 1984; May 6, 1986.
Tanji, Misao. March 16, 1985.
Tanoura, Kay Shinsato. May 5, 1985.
Tasaka, Kenichi. June 4, 1985; October 17, 1990.
Tazawa, Haruno. August 6, 1979; November 10 and 15, 1979; January 15,
    1984; February 3, 1986; June 30, 1988; May 21, 1990.
Todani, Robert and Toshiko. March 14, 1988; May 2, 1991.
Toki, Kamezo and Taga. November 2, 1984–May 6, 1986.
Toki, Wilfred and Shige. March 1, 1985–June 18, 1990.
Tokuhama, Beatrice. November 12, 1989.
Toshima, Linda Hiroko. June 3, 1991.
Toyama, Tsuruko. July 29, 1979; September 16, 1986.
Tsukayama, Kana. February 17, 1988.
Tsunehiro, Yuri. January 13, 1988.
Umehara, Toku. 1985–1991.
Uyehara, Henry. March 17, 1988.
Uyeno, Haru. August 7, 1979; October 8, 1981; July 29, 1987.
Wakasa, Ise. April 10 and 22, 1988.
Wakukawa, Dr. Seiyei. August 17, 1980; March 23, 1985.
Watanabe, Masao (Cranky). 1980–1988.
Watanabe, Tsuruye. May 2, 1987.
Woodard, Gary. November 1 and 7, 1989.
Yahiro, Kimiko. June 23, 1986; June 3, 1987; July 5 and 16, 1987; October
    23, 1987; April 3, 1990.
Yamada, Kay. July 5, 1988.
Yamamoto, Fumiko. July 7, 1988.
Yamamoto, Tsuneichi. June 9, 1979; March 1, 1980.
Yamanaka, Sally Isae Ishimoto. March 9, 1980–May 28, 1990.
Yamasaki, Hisako. April 16, 1986.
Yamashita, Mary Shikada. April 1, 1987.
Yanagihara, Tomoyo Kimura. February 29, 1984–June 24, 1991.
Yanai, Sadato. January 21, 1980–June 10, 1990; June 24, 1991.
Yasui, Ryoto and Kimiyo. August 1, 1987–July, 14, 1989.
Yokota, Elaine Haruko Watanabe. August 6, 1979; June 8, 1984.
Yoneji, Matsue. March 3, 1988; October 15, 1990.
Yonemura, Kiyoshi. August 30, 1983; October 29, 1984.
Yorita, Eiko. September 3, 1979; January 12, 1985; May 1, 1987; June 8,
    1989; August 3, 1988.
Yoshida, Kiku. July–August 1979; March 10, 1984; July 29, 1987; August 3,
    1988; June 8, 1989.
Yoshimoto. Fumiko. November 17, 1989.
Yoshitake, Shigeyuki. September 6, 1985–May 14, 1990.

Index

About the Author

Barbara Kawakami, who began her academic career
past the age of fifty, earned her degrees, a B.S. in
Textile and Clothing and an M.A. in Asian Studies,
from the University of Hawai'i. Prior to that she was
a dressmaker-designer and homemaker. Mrs. Kawakami was born in Japan and raised on a sugarcane
plantation in Hawai'i. Her knowledge of various Japanese dialects as well as her plantation upbringing
prepared her for the many interviews of Japanese
immigrants she has conducted.

Because of her extensive knowledge about picture
brides and immigrant clothing, she is frequently
called upon to serve as a consultant. She is a member of the Japanese American National Museum
advisory council and a researcher and consultant for
Hawaii Public Television, Waipahu Cultural Garden
Park, NHK (Japan) Television, and Bishop Museum.
She has designed immigrant clothing displays at
numerous festivals and exhibits, and she lectures
widely on her areas of expertise.

CPSIA information can be obtained
at www.ICGtesting.com
Printed in the USA
FFOW03n1753290517
36118FF